Forev...

There are many ways to understand, an[...]t rid-
dle"—the question of how to prepare fi[...]ement
wherein your money will last as long as you remain alive, an [...]owable
amount of time. The best solution, now almost entirely unattainable, is to
work for and (the tricky part) collect the payout from a defined benefit pension plan.

All of the solutions currently proposed and debated, including the one
examined in this book, are workarounds. They mostly try to replicate the
security and predictability of a defined benefit plan without the plan itself.
These approaches therefore assume—unfortunately, correctly—that it is the
individual's responsibility (possibly with the employer's help) to save whatever
amount of money is needed for retirement, then to spend down that amount
so that (1) she does not run out of money before she dies and (2) her spending is not so meager, out of fear of running out of money, as to make life
miserable.

No wonder Bill Sharpe, the father of modern finance, has called retirement finance the most daunting topic he has ever worked on.

The method I favor is very simple: Save as much money as possible, then
spend it using a blend of (1) a spending rule that considers the changing
market value of an individual's portfolio of conventional investments and (2)
some kind of annuity, used for longevity insurance.[1] I prefer deferred annuities, which do not tie up much capital and are a "pure" longevity insurance
product. The not inconsiderable risk is that the insurance company that issued
the annuity will not be around to make the payments when the time comes.

To arrive at the foregoing concise formula by which one can, in the words
of Mr. Spock, "live long and prosper," I have radically oversimplified the
retirement problem:

- "As much money as possible" might not be much money. We are not all
  upper middle class or wealthier.

- People get sick, lose their jobs, become responsible for sick or aging family members, watch their industries disappear, and face other unexpected
  hardships.

- Markets go down as well as up, and sometimes they stay down for long
  periods.

---

[1]See Waring and Siegel (2015) and Totten and Siegel (2019).

- On the positive side, people also inherit money, receive big promotions and raises, sell their houses for multiples of what they paid, and otherwise experience unexpected good fortune.

- You could live a much shorter life than you expect and wish you had spent more money on enjoying yourself.

- You could live a much longer life than you expect and have large expenses toward the end. My grandfather, born during the first Grover Cleveland administration, lived until 1991—more than a century. As a young man, I had to help pay for the last few years of his life. (He attributed his longevity to not being married—widowed at a young age, he seemed to prefer his own company after that.)

In this CFA Institute Research Foundation monograph, Jacques Lussier, former chief investment officer of a Canadian asset management firm and a longtime friend of both CFA Institute and CFA Institute Research Foundation, takes a different approach to analyzing retirement problems: Monte Carlo simulation. This kind of analysis has proven useful in understanding complex situations in many fields, from aeronautical engineering to derivatives pricing, because it explicitly considers *all* the potential outcomes of an action—that is, the entire probability distribution, not just its statistical "moments" (say, mean and standard deviation).

The only hitch is that you need to have a handle on all the potential outcomes, which may or may not be normally distributed and are more likely than not to contain fat tails and black swans. Fortunately, complicated as it is, retirement planning does not come close in complexity to aeronautical engineering or the pricing of certain kinds of derivatives. Thus, Lussier's simulations are quite realistic and complete.

In addition, Monte Carlo simulation allows you to study the interactions *between* variables, such as the risk of losing your job *and* experiencing a negative market return simultaneously. It also helps you see how processes evolve over time—for example, by placing the negative market return at the beginning, in the middle, or near the end of one's career or life. These dynamics make a big difference in prosperity. For example, the stock market crash of 1987 did not affect me much because I was too young to have more than a token amount of money. If another crash were to happen soon, however, I would be in trouble. A competent advisor would thus recommend a fairly conservative investment strategy for me in my dotage.

In this substantial volume, Lussier does much more than present a framework for analyzing retirement challenges. He provides a set of solutions, called Secure Retirement, that considers the massive number of institutional features and quirks that complicate retirement planning. These include differential tax rates on different kinds of investments, the amazingly complex Social Security payout formula, the various kinds of tax-preferred and taxable accounts, the multiplicity of annuity types, and the dizzying array of life insurance products.

As a Canadian, Lussier is familiar with more than one country's retirement institutions, offering an international perspective to the book.

Finally, Lussier's work is informed by behavioral economics and finance, and he knows full well that people are not always rational—if they ever are. He weaves behavioral themes into his stories and methods, and this knowledge makes the potentially dry discipline of retirement planning come alive for the reader.

The CFA Institute Research Foundation is extremely pleased to present Jacques Lussier's *Secure Retirement: Connecting Financial Theory and Human Behavior.*

Laurence B. Siegel
Gary P. Brinson Director of Research
CFA Institute Research Foundation
August 2019

References

Totten, Thomas L., and Laurence B. Siegel. 2019. "Combining Conventional Investing with a Lifetime Income Guarantee: A Blueprint for Retirement Security." *Journal of Retirement* 6 (4): 45–59.

Waring, M. Barton, and Laurence B. Siegel. 2015. "The Only Spending Rule Article You Will Ever Need." *Financial Analysts Journal* 71 (1): 91–107. https://tandfonline.com/doi/abs/10.2469/faj.v71.n1.2

Acknowledgments

Some book projects happen because of specific circumstances. Nearly four years ago, I was approached by David Oaten, former CEO of Pacific Global Advisors, to research a more efficient design for managing 401(k) plans. Over the years, David and I discussed the financial, structural, social, informational, and behavioral challenges facing US retirees. This interaction initiated my research interest into this important topic, and without it, *Secure Retirement* would likely never have been written.

My former colleague and friend Guy Desrochers, CFA, read many evolutions of *Secure Retirement* from its very beginning. Guy helped me write at a level appropriate to the book's targeted audience: serious investors, investment professionals, and service providers. If the content of my writing was unclear to Guy, I knew I had to rethink the message and sometimes its perspective.

CFA Institute and its Research Foundation offered the perfect partners for publishing *Secure Retirement,* considering the CFA Institute mission of promoting the highest standards in ethics, education, and professional excellence as well as its Future of Finance initiative. Hence, I would like to thank Bud Haslett, CFA, Executive Director of the CFA Institute Research Foundation, and the CFA Institute Research Foundation Board of Trustees for accepting this project, as well as Laurence B. Siegel, the Gary P. Brinson Director of Research at the CFA Institute Research Foundation, for investing his time as content editor while he was completing his very own new book. I accepted nearly 100% of his recommendations.

I realize how much better a book can be once it has been reviewed by dedicated editors who not only enhance the quality and understanding of the text but also identify many inconsistencies that an author becomes blind to. I much prefer the version of *Secure Retirement* that has been improved by the work of all the editors on this project.

With *Secure Retirement,* I have now written more than 1,200 pages of published material in eight years and likely as much unpublished work. My wife Sandra has been patient with my evenings, weekends, and sometimes vacations spent researching and writing. On the plus side, because we normally prepare our dinners together, to make time for my work we have instead become frequent guests at our favorite nearby restaurants, making new friends in the process.

1. Introduction

1.1. The Context

The average individual in the United States will work approximately four decades and retire by age 63 (Wallace 2018). As of that age, the average man and woman will live another 20 and 22 years, respectively. Averages tell only part of the story, however, because approximately 28% of men and 39% of women will live past age 90.

Few challenges in life are as daunting as planning toward and through retirement, a process that can extend six decades or more from beginning to end. Preparing for retirement is about intertemporal shifting of consumption, appropriate financial planning, and managing fears and emotions. How much should I reduce my consumption preretirement to accumulate enough assets to support my postretirement consumption needs? How should my savings be allocated across different asset classes throughout my lifetime? What actions must I take to maximize the likelihood of achieving my income goal? What should I do if a financial crisis occurs?

Social Security and defined benefit (DB) pension plans were designed to answer these challenges on behalf of workers. The objective of Social Security is to alleviate old-age poverty and provide a minimum level of inflation-adjusted income in retirement. It is not, however, meant to maintain the standard of living to which many beneficiaries were accustomed while working. DB plans were usually created, in combination with Social Security, to allow workers to ensure a level of inflation-adjusted income of at least 70% of the preretirement amount, a level often recommended to maintain the standard of living achieved preretirement.

During the last three decades, however, defined contribution (DC) plans have become the dominant type of private-sector employer-sponsored plan. Whereas DB plans are designed to achieve an income goal under specific parameters, such as the number of work years and age at retirement, DC plans support the accumulation of wealth without promising an income guarantee or even an income target. In 2013, DC plans accounted for 94% of all employer-sponsored plans. Active DC participants outnumbered those in DB plans by a ratio of 5 to 1.

Despite the prevalence of DC plans, 44% of working households have no accumulated savings in a DC plan, and 39% do not even have access to such a program. The situation is worst for low-income working households, as only 25% of households in the lowest quartile of income have accumulated any assets within a DC plan, whereas 81% of households in the top quartile of income have. The discrepancy is significantly explained by plan access. Only 40% of low-income households have access to DC plans, whereas 84% of high-income households do (Government Accountability Office 2017). Another factor is ability, or perceived ability, to make contributions; the data show, obviously, that many lower-income households with access to a DC plan have not contributed to it.

The decline of DB plans has transferred much of the responsibility of retirement decision making from the employer to the worker. This is especially true post retirement because participants in DC plans will often no longer benefit from the institutional investment advice and portfolio management services provided to them through their employers' plans.

Unfortunately, most individuals are cognitively ill equipped to deal with an undertaking as complex as retirement planning. Participants in DC plans have historically proved themselves incapable of saving enough money, making appropriate investment decisions, and efficiently converting assets into income for spending when retired. Vanguard reports that the median balance of participants aged 65+ among the plans it administers, as of the end of 2016, was $60,724. This figure translates into a life annuity with an annual payout of approximately $4,000.

Vanguard also reports that participants' median contribution is currently 5% of income, although it increases to 10% when including the employer match. Even a combined contribution of 10% may be insufficient unless the participant starts contributing very early and financial markets deliver reasonable returns. Finally, participants who selected target date funds (TDFs) have achieved a greater median and average performance over the last five years than those making their own investment choices, likely because TDFs bring greater investment discipline to some investors who would otherwise act impulsively (Utkus and Young 2017).

These conditions are not entirely the participants' fault. Beyond the sheer complexity of preparing for and living through retirement, as well as the greater financial pressure on lower-income workers of achieving an appropriate savings rate, lack of access to support tools and unbiased professional advice is also a problem. Although 65% of DC plan participants have access to online advice, most participants are probably not receiving the level of comprehensive advice they need. In addition, participants do not fully understand longevity risk, which is the likelihood they will live considerably longer than average (that is, longer than their life expectancy).

Given these conditions, employer plans are adjusting to the greater uncertainty and level of personal responsibility faced by participants. New regulations introduced in the Pension Protection Act of 2006 and made effective 24 December 2007 have made it legally easier for plan sponsors to offer an investment default option, defined as a qualified default investment alternative (see Invesco 2015). Since then, the number of participants taking advantage of a professionally managed asset allocation fund (such as a TDF) has significantly expanded. As of 2016, 92% of plan sponsors offer TDFs, up from 58% in 2007. Also, 29% of total plan assets and 50% of all new contributions are allocated to TDFs, up from 7% and 12%, respectively, 10 years earlier. Nearly half of all plan sponsors offer plan features intended to fight behavioral pitfalls that ensnare participants, such as lack of planning skills or procrastination. Such features include automatic enrollment and autoescalation (i.e., precommitted savings rate increases).

According to a survey conducted by Charles Schwab (2017), however, 40% of individuals spent five hours or more planning their next vacation but only 16% spent as much time researching their 401(k) options. If we are to instill a greater sense of priority about retirement planning among future retirees, whether they have access to a DC plan or not, more must be done to communicate the relevance of this effort and explain how it can be achieved most efficiently. For example, how many households have answers to all of the following questions?

- How much income, above what Social Security will likely provide, do I need?

- What percentage of my income should I save, considering how much wealth I have already accumulated and how long I expect to work?

- What is the significance of my employer's contribution to my retirement income?

- What is the effect of retiring earlier or later than expected?

- Is the TDF strategy the most appropriate, and are all TDFs similar?

- Is my asset allocation decision independent of how long I have been saving even if my retirement horizon remains the same?

- Should I favor an indexing or active approach to investing?

- Should I consider insurance products such as life annuities, fixed annuities, or a variable annuity with a guaranteed lifetime withdrawal benefit (GLWB) rider? If no, why not? If yes, when should they be purchased and what annuity features should I incorporate or avoid?

- Should reverse mortgages be part of my toolbox?

- What would be the consequence for my retirement income if Social Security Trust Fund assets are depleted as expected in the early 2030s and US laws are not changed?

- How should I react to or prepare for a potentially severe market downturn? What are my options? Is the answer the same whether I am 20 years from retirement or 5 years post retirement?

- How do I protect myself against longevity risk or being sick? What if I live to be 100 years old?

- What frequency of monitoring is required, and in what circumstances should I adjust my retirement plan?

- What are the most common behavioral pitfalls, and what features of a plan design can better address the negative aspects of financial planning attributed to participant behavior?

- What improvements to the retirement planning process can we expect in the coming years?

The objective of *Secure Retirement* is to provide a comprehensive and documented framework for designing and implementing a retirement plan throughout the life of any participant, whether or not that participant has access to an employer-sponsored plan. It is also to advise those who have responsibilities for designing retirement products and/or structuring corporate retirement plans how they can efficiently improve the income security of future retirees.

Finally, other books, such as *From Here to Security* by Robert L. Reynolds (2017), address the public policy aspects of retirement preparedness, while *Retirement Game-Changers* by Steve Vernon (2018) discusses general retirement principles and strategies as well as lifestyle recommendations. In comparison, *Secure Retirement* provides the justifications and guidelines for designing and implementing better policies and strategies. For example, although Reynolds indicates that the three major tasks that must be completed to improve the retirement system are (1) making Social Security solvent, (2) extending workplace savings options available to all working Americans, and (3) aiming for a savings rate of 10% or more, the specific details about how we can and should more efficiently implement private-sector solutions are important.

1.2. The Book Structure

The book is divided into eight chapters in addition to this one. Chapter 2 illustrates the relationship between savings, saving horizon, investment returns, retirement timing, and longevity, assuming certainty on all variables. Using a simplifying certainty assumption, although unrealistic, illustrates the relevance of the most significant aspects of retirement planning.

Starting with Chapter 3, the certainty assumption is gradually removed to illustrate the interaction between investment return uncertainty and periodic savings during the accumulation process and the implications of this interaction for investment policy. It also reviews the literature on time diversification—whether equity is riskier or less risky in the long term—and the consequences of integrating human capital to determine the allocation to risky assets. Finally, it discusses and tests allocation methodologies that allow for a more efficient risk management of financial assets.

In contrast, Chapter 4 evaluates the implications for investment policy resulting from the interaction between investment return uncertainty, periodic withdrawals, and longevity. It discusses the potential benefits of annuities and how to address the longevity uncertainty. Finally, it discusses the effect of Social Security on the overall investment policy.

Chapter 5 integrates our understanding of the accumulation and decumulation processes and identifies factors that should affect the transition from accumulation to decumulation. To that end, Chapter 5 reviews the evidence regarding mean reversion in asset returns—the idea that low financial returns may be followed by a recovery and vice versa—and the recognition that "optimal" portfolios for long-term investors, who value wealth for the standard of living it affords them, can differ from those of short-term investors (see Campbell and Viceira 2002). It also discusses the usefulness of inflation-linked bonds and the effect of the real rate of return on allocation choices.

Chapter 6 covers the process of integrating the accumulation, decumulation, and transition phases. It discusses the approaches and methods that could be used to solve this challenge, the design of objective functions (i.e., measures of the level of satisfaction investors derive from consumption and wealth), and calibration of the parameters of such functions. It also presents a literature review of empirical attempts at calibrating portfolio risk and withdrawal rates in retirement. It presents the results of several simulations designed to evaluate the effect of incorporating annuities, timing Social Security, and dynamically adjusting the savings rate, the retirement date, and the level of retirement income according to portfolio performance. It also evaluates whether these adjustments contribute to a greater level of lifetime utility.

5

Chapter 7 accounts for specific complexities and options available to retirees. The chapter explains the value of appropriately allocating savings across 401(k) plans, IRAs, and Roth IRAs, the role of life insurance, the choice between indexing and active management, the level of income required in retirement, and whether reverse mortgages and variable annuities should be considered. It also evaluates the adjustments that must be made in the context of a household and the effect of adjusting life expectancy to individuals' socioeconomic status.

Chapter 8 presents an integrated retirement-planning framework that incorporates most of the components explored in this book. It then presents a comprehensive case study illustrating the power and efficiency of the principles discussed. Beyond evaluating the savings effort required to achieve a specific income goal and the decisions that must be made as individuals progress toward and through retirement, it describes how the proposed retirement-planning design can minimize and help manage the traditional behavioral pitfalls of investors.

As the integrated framework was being designed, it was applied in the context of the US and Canadian retirement systems. The comparison is worthwhile from a policy viewpoint. The Canadian approach to corporate retirement plans, traditional IRAs (called RRSPs in Canada), and Roth IRAs (called TFSAs in Canada) is more coherent, integrated, and efficient. Therefore, the situation of "John," our prototype investor, will also be analyzed under the counterfactual assumption that the United States implements the same tax-deferred and tax-exempt retirement policies as exist in Canada.

Chapter 9 concludes *Secure Retirement*. It covers the expected evolution of retirement planning and identifies further enhancements that can be expected in years to come. It also discusses public policy changes that could benefit investors.

1.3. Conclusion

What is the purpose of the asset management industry beyond allowing for greater efficiency of capital allocation? Some fortunate individuals seek wealth accumulation beyond what is needed for maintaining their lifestyle during the later stage of their lives. For the great majority of individuals, however, it is about financing a home, funding the education of their children, achieving a comfortable and enjoyable life during the last decades of their lives, and perhaps also leave something behind for loved ones or for a cause that is important to them. These are the investment goals that matter. In these objectives, on many levels, the industry has failed for a large portion of the general population.

We cannot overstate the importance of retirement planning. We have all heard of horrible situations of individuals facing hardships as they reached what we consider a normal retirement age. These include individuals such as Deborah, a former schoolteacher, who spent her entire 401(k) balance in four years; or Tom and Judith, who significantly underestimated their longevity—they lived to be 90 and 96 years old, respectively—and Barbara, suffering from Alzheimer's disease, who gave most of her savings to organizations she thought were legitimate charities but were not. Finally, there is the case of Bernard, who had accumulated $4 million in company stock and had no other savings but would not follow his adviser's recommendation to sell at least 50% of his holding to reinvest in a diversified portfolio because selling the company stock would trigger a significant taxable capital gain. The stock later declined abruptly by 96%.

Improving the retirement system for all has important social benefits. We live in an era where technology contributes to income and wealth disparities in the developed world. We must use that technology, and its benefits and processes, to efficiently deliver retirement solutions, implement our greater understanding of sources of risk and return achieved in recent decades, and push for closer alignment of interests between the industry and investors. We must do so to avoid maintaining an environment that further increases economic disparities among retirees as well as younger people.

Until recently, the advisory industry has focused largely on wealthy individuals. Less wealthy individuals have not benefited from the same quality of advice and investment tools, or from lower fees, although the situation has improved with the advent of exchange-traded funds (ETFs) and robo advisory tools. Nevertheless, greater efforts are required. For example, although models that incorporate human capital—that is, our ability to earn income in the future—typically lead to a greater willingness to take financial risk at any level of risk aversion, 20% of typical households at the 80th percentile of wealth have no public equity (Campbell 2017). Furthermore, many households have large holdings of their employer's stock, leading to a concentration of labor income risk and portfolio risk (Mitchell and Utkus 2005).

Beyond this aspect is also the quality-of-advice issue. Hershey and Walsh (2000) report that students with only six hours of training performed better than accountants with experience in providing financial advice. Asher, Butt, Kayande, and Khemka (2015) mention several studies that report significant variations in financial advice given by US website calculators. My own attempts at validating the retirement income estimates provided by the web calculator of a large financial institution also failed because its implicit assumptions are not fully disclosed. Finally, other research finds that financial advisers fail to correct investors' misconceptions. Instead, their portfolio recommendations are often aligned with their own financial interests (Mullainathan, Noeth, and Schoar 2012). The need remains for greater education and for financial tools whose investment principles are transparent.

Another consideration is also of utmost importance. Research shows that our ability to benefit from learned skills and knowledge declines in our 60s, while our ability to solve new problems starts declining even before, in our 20s. When asked the question "If five people all have the winning number in the lottery and the prize is $2 million, how much will each of them get?" slightly more than 50% of individuals in their 50s had the right answer but fewer than 10% of individuals in their 90s did (Agarwal, Driscoll, Gabaix, and Laibson 2009). The level of cognitive impairment, even excluding dementia, reaches nearly 30% for individuals in their 80s and 40% for those in their 90s. Cognitive changes explain why basic financial literacy skills decline, on average, in our 60s, and this process worsens gradually in our 70s, 80s, and 90s. As we age, we are less likely to make rational and informed decisions and, unfortunately, are more prone to be taken advantage of. At risk especially are those individuals in their 70s and 80s who have become financially responsible for their household for the first time after the death of a loved one (Belbase and Sanzenbacher 2017).

Finally, we must recognize one important fact: Young people are often unconcerned with retirement planning, but when they are older it may be too late to implement a successful strategy. So that preparing for retirement is rarely too late, we must offer adequate and efficient default retirement solutions for the workplace and create a savings and investment culture among those who lack access or no longer have access to such a plan. We must also raise the importance of protecting individuals who are cognitively and emotionally at risk. The purpose of *Secure Retirement* is to raise awareness of the importance of early retirement planning and provide the knowledge, tools, framework, and mentoring required to make a secure retirement feasible for most of us. As Robert Merton (2017) said in a 2017 interview: "The retirement problem is a global problem. The good news is, finance science can be used to solve it. Design things on finance principles, rather than institutionally.... If you design on financial principles, it will work everywhere in the world." Designing retirement solutions using finance principles is the goal of *Secure Retirement*.

2. In a Certain World, Retirement Planning Is Simple

The absence of uncertainty makes retirement planning easy. The solution is straightforward if you know when a participant will start saving, what portion of his income he will save, how his income will grow, what level of real returns financial markets will deliver on average, what the patterns of those returns will be, when the participant will retire, how healthy he will be, and how long he and his dependent will live. Otherwise, retirement planning may seem like a daunting task.

Although unrealistic, presenting and analyzing simple scenarios in which all the parameters are known and financial markets are frictionless helps to communicate retirement planning challenges. These scenarios allow one to isolate the relevant retirement parameters and assess their significance. In later chapters, we will peel away the certainty assumption one parameter at a time to evaluate the potential financial effect of each source of uncertainty and how the uncertainty can be addressed. This process, once completed, reveals the complexity of retirement planning in the real world and shows that complex solutions are not necessarily required to address this complex problem. Chapter 2 remains unconcerned with the appropriate level of retirement income target. That topic will come later.

2.1. The Case of John

John is 30 years old, single, and without savings. He will retire at age 65 and will live until he is 85. John earns $60,000 per year, and his income will increase annually in line with the inflation rate of 2%. John will save 10% of his gross income annually in a retirement program and allocates to his investment portfolio monthly.[2] Once retired, he will receive a monthly retirement payout, inflation adjusted yearly, that will drain all his wealth by the time he is 85.[3] The annualized return on investment is 5.4% over this 55-year span.[4] He pays

---

[2]An IRA account allows for the tax deductibility of annual contributions and for gains in the account to accumulate tax free whatever the sources of these gains (interest, dividends, or capital gains). Withdrawals will be taxed when they occur, however. For now, we ignore these aspects.

[3]Planning for an expected lifespan of 20 years as of the age of 65 is likely too short, but this assumption is revised in Chapter 4.

[4]The return is based on a 60/40 portfolio of equity and fixed income in which annualized returns compounded monthly are, respectively, 7% and 3% on each asset class, received with certainty. The effective annualized return on the portfolio is precisely 5.383%.

Figure 2.1. Evolution of Total Wealth, Cumulative Savings, and Withdrawals

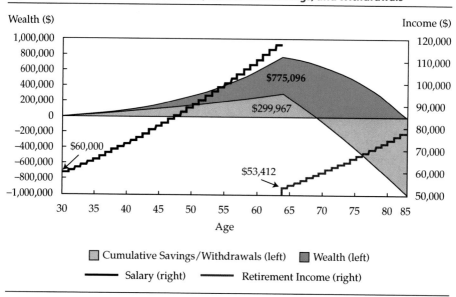

no advisory or investment management fees. John has no other expected source of retirement income. Therefore, we initially ignore the effects of other potential sources of income such as Social Security. **Figure 2.1** illustrates the dynamic of John's situation.

Under the proposed scenario, John's salary starts at $60,000, indicated by the black line on the right axis. By the time he retires, his salary will have risen to $117,641. Assuming a savings rate of 10% and an annualized ROI of 5.4%, he will have accumulated $775,096 by age 65, indicated by the blue zone using the left axis. Assuming again that the ROI remains at 5.4% and that John lives to age 85, he will be able to afford an initial annual retirement income of $53,412, indicated by the red line using the right axis. This income will rise by 2% per year and is enough to maintain approximately 44.5% of the inflation-adjusted income John was earning before retirement.[5] This example illustrates that a sustained saving effort and a high savings rate are required to achieve a significant retirement income even when there is no uncertainty.

Figure 2.1 illustrates another interesting aspect. What if John's savings had not been invested and were instead accumulated as cash, implying a 0%

---

[5] 44.5% = $53,412/[$117,641 × (1 + 2%)]. The salary earned pre retirement is adjusted by 2% to allow the retirement income earned in the first year post retirement to be compared on a purchasing power basis with the salary income earned in the previous year. Also, because John was saving 10% a year, we could also say that John will be able to generate 49.5% of his previous income net of savings.

return? In this case, John would have accumulated only $299,967—shown as the yellow zone using the left axis—at age 65. In other words, the $475,129 difference between the blue and yellow zones is the investment income generated by dividends, interest, and capital gains over 35 years, above the periodic savings contributed by John. This difference grows at an increasing rate with the passage of time, illustrating the effect of return compounding.[6] We refer to the savings period between age 30 and the retirement age as the *accumulation period*.

It is just as important, however, to generate investment returns while in retirement. For example, assuming a ROI of zero while in retirement as well, John would have a cash deficit of $997,804 by the time of his death. In other words, $997,804 is the amount of investment income generated by investing John's savings at 5.4% per year, compounded over a period of 55 years. The $299,967 of John's savings generated more than three times as much in investment income over his lifetime. We refer to the retirement period between the age of retirement and the age of death as the *decumulation period*.

This analysis raises important questions. What happens if John starts saving later, earns a lower ROI, retires earlier or later, or lives longer? The previous scenario will serve as our reference benchmark.

2.2. Impact of a Lower ROI

Assume the ROI is 4.2% instead of 5.4%. This difference could be explained by a more conservative portfolio,[7] or it could result from higher investment management and advisory fees. (At this point in the example, market returns are known with certainty and so are not a possible cause of the lower return.) Whatever the cause of the lower ROI, the financial effect on John's wealth in the absence of uncertainty would essentially be the same. **Table 2.1** presents the impact of a lower ROI on either the ratio of retirement income that can be sustained, assuming John wants to generate a retirement income until age 85,

---

[6]Return compounding refers to the fact that investment income grows exponentially with the passage of time if it is reinvested. For example, $1,000 invested for one year at 5.4% will generate an investment income of $54. If the investment income of $54 is reinvested along with the $1,000 of initial capital, $1,054 invested for one year at 5.4% will now generate an investment income of $56.92 during the second year. If the initial capital remained invested for 25 years, the capital amount would reach $3,724.05. Finally, the income generated during the 25th year would be $190.80, more than three times the income amount generated in the first year. The impact of return compounding increases exponentially with time. It also increases exponentially with the level of return.

[7]For example, 4.2% is the return that would be achieved on a 30/70 portfolio of equity and fixed income.

Table 2.1.   Impact of a Lower ROI

	Base Scenario	Lower ROI
Age at start of savings	30	30
Age at retirement	65	65
Age at death	85	85
Savings rate	10%	10%
ROI	5.4%	4.2%
Wealth at retirement	$775,096	$615,511
Wealth attributed to savings	$299,967	$299,967
Wealth at retirement attributed to investment income	$475,129	$315,545
Ratio of retirement income to work income	44.5%	44.5%
Sustainability age	85Y	79Y + 8M
Ratio of retirement income to work income		35.4%
Sustainability age		85Y

or on the duration of the targeted income, assuming John wants to maintain a ratio of retirement income equal to 44.5% of his salary income.[8]

The effect of lower returns is significant. Reducing the ROI from 5.4% to 4.2% reduces wealth as of retirement by 20.6%, from $775,096 to $615,511. The level of John's wealth attributed to his savings has not changed ($299,967). The investment income, however, decreases by 33.6%, from $475,129 to $315,545. Assuming John intends to maintain the same ratio of retirement income as in the base scenario (44.5%), he will be able to sustain this level of income only until age 79 years and 8 months. During the following month, he will have fully exhausted his wealth. If John's objective is to maintain a retirement income until age 85, the annual income will have to be reduced by 20.4%, from a ratio of 44.5% to only 35.4%. Returns do matter.

2.3.   Impact of Procrastination

Let's assume John starts saving at age 35 or 40 instead of 30. If we assume that John intends to maintain the same replacement ratio (i.e., the ratio of retirement income to end-of-career working income) as in the base scenario, how long can that ratio be fully maintained? Starting to save five years later

---

[8]Numbers in red in Tables 2.1–2.5 indicate the values that differ from the base scenario.

(at age 35) would make it impossible to pay the full retirement income beyond age 79 years and 3 months. The horizon is further reduced to age 75 years and 2 months if John starts saving at age 40.

We may also want to consider by how much the ratio of retirement income would have to decline to maintain a level inflation-adjusted income until age 85. If saving begins at age 35, the retirement income would be reduced to 34.7% of work income. And, it would be only 26.3% if saving starts at age 40. This result is simply proportional to the level of final wealth reached at retirement in the three scenarios. Both scenarios are illustrated in **Table 2.2**.

Finally, how much must John save if he intends to keep the *sustainability age*—that is, the age at which he exhausts his wealth—at 85 while maintaining the same income ratio as in the initial scenario (not illustrated)? The longer John waits, the greater the effect on the required savings rate. Waiting five years increases the required savings rate by 28%, from 10.0% to 12.8%. Waiting 10 years requires him to increase the savings rate by 69%, from 10.0% to 16.9%. The effect of delaying saving on the required savings rate is exponential.

The decline in either the level of retirement income or the sustainability age as a result of delaying the start of saving is attributable to two factors: (1)

Table 2.2. Impact of Changing the Savings Period

	Base Scenario	Savings Starts 5 Years Later	Savings Starts 10 Years Later
Age at start of savings	30	35	40
Age at retirement	65	65	65
Age at death	85	85	85
Savings rate	10%	10%	10%
ROI	5.4%	5.4%	5.4%
Wealth at retirement	$775,096	$603,717	$458,137
Wealth attributed to savings	$299,967	$268,743	$234,269
Wealth at retirement attributed to investment income	$475,129	$334,794	$223,869
Ratio of retirement income to work income	44.5%	44.5%	44.5%
Sustainability age	85Y	79Y + 3M	75Y + 2M
Ratio of retirement income to work income		34.7%	26.3%
Sustainability age		85Y	85Y

the reduction in the amount of savings committed to the retirement effort and (2) the loss of investment income. The latter is significantly more important than the former because of the effect of return compounding. For example, under the base scenario, John contributed $299,967 in savings over 35 years. Assuming John started saving at age 40, the total amount of savings contribution is reduced to $234,269, a decline of $65,698. Yet, as Table 2.2 illustrates, the decline in wealth as of retirement is $316,959, from $775,096 to $458,137. Much of the decline results from the loss of investment income of $251,260. The effect on investment income is substantial because it applies to savings that did not occur from ages 30 to 40—had savings occurred, they would have been invested for 10 additional years. We cannot overstate the importance of starting to save early when considering the effect of return compounding.

2.4. Impact of Retiring Later or Sooner

Modifying the retirement age affects two parameters: the lengths of the accumulation and decumulation periods. For example, retiring two years earlier reduces the accumulation period by two years and presumably increases the decumulation period by two years. Assuming the decision to retire earlier, at age 63, or later, at age 67, does not change John's expected longevity (age 85), **Table 2.3** indicates the effects of this decision on the retirement income ratio.

Table 2.3. Impact of Changing the Retirement Age

	Base Scenario	Retiring Sooner	Retiring Later
Age at start of savings	30	30	30
Age at retirement	65	63	67
Age at death	85	85	85
Savings rate	10%	10%	10%
ROI	5.4%	5.4%	5.4%
Wealth at retirement	$775,096	$675,867	$886,285
Wealth attributed to savings	$299,967	$276,669	$324,206
Wealth at retirement attributed to investment income	$475,129	$399,198	$562,079
Ratio of retirement income to work income	44.5%	44.5%	44.5%
Sustainability age	85Y	79Y + 6M	91Y + 3M
Ratio of retirement income to work income		37.8%	52.8%
Sustainability age		85Y	85Y

Assuming John retires at age 63, the ratio of retirement income declines from 44.5% to 37.8%, which translates into a 15.1% reduction in income. In comparison, postponing retirement to age 67 increases the ratio to 52.8%, an 18.7% rise in income. Similarly, the sustainability age is significantly affected by early or late retirement. Assuming the retiree seeks to maintain the same ratio of retirement income to work income, the period of sustainable retirement income is either reduced by 5.5 years (for earlier retirement) or increased by 6.25 years (for later retirement).

As in the previous example, these results are attributable less to the effect of reducing or increasing savings contributions by two years than to the effect of return compounding on investment income. Changing the retirement age, when it is possible, can substantially affect a retiree's well-being. It may be a last-resort option when total wealth has not reached the expected level.

2.5. Impact of Longevity

Longevity is a significant issue and a concern when planning for retirement. Under the base scenario, if John were to live beyond age 85, he would have no more income. Assuming John wants his portfolio to sustain a retirement income up to age 90 or 95, the ratio of retirement income would have to decline from 44.5% to 38.2% (for age 90), an income reduction of 14.5%; or to 34.2% (for age 95), an income reduction of 23.5%. **Table 2.4** shows the effect of living to the ages of 90 and 95 in John's case.

Table 2.4.   Impact of Changing the Longevity Assumption

	Base Scenario	Living to 90	Living to 95
Age at start of savings	30	30	30
Age at retirement	65	65	65
Age at death	85	90	95
Savings rate	10%	10%	10%
ROI	5.4%	5.4%	5.4%
Wealth at retirement	$775,096	$775,096	$775,096
Wealth attributed to savings	$299,967	$299,691	$299,691
Wealth at retirement attributed to investment income	$475,129	$475,129	$475,129
Ratio of retirement income to work income	44.5%	38.2%	34.2%
Sustainability age	85Y	90Y	95Y

2.6.   Impact of Making All the Wrong Choices

The previous examples demonstrate separately the effects of investing more conservatively or of paying higher fees, of procrastinating too long before implementing a savings plan, and of retiring early and living longer than expected. What if John makes *all* the wrong choices? He starts saving at age 40, invests too conservatively or pays higher fees without generating a higher gross return, retires at age 63, and underestimates his longevity, living to age 95. The savings rate remains at 10%. **Table 2.5** compares John's wrong choices with the base scenario.

In this case, John's ratio of retirement income would be an inadequate 14.9%, or 71.4% less than assumed under the base scenario. He contributes 29.7% less in savings than under the base scenario, but more importantly, he generates 73.3% less in investment income. Likely John would be unable to retire when planned. Fortunately, the assumption of no public support (such as Social Security) is unrealistic!

Table 2.5.   Impact of Making All the Wrong Choices

	Base Scenario	Making All the Wrong Choices
Age at start of savings	30	40
Age at retirement	65	63
Age at death	85	95
Savings rate	10%	10%
ROI	5.4%	4.2%
Wealth at retirement	$775,096	$337,935
Wealth attributed to savings	$299,967	$210,971
Wealth at retirement attributed to investment income	$475,129	$126,964
Ratio of retirement income to work income	44.5%	44.5%
Sustainability age	85Y	70Y + 2M
Ratio of retirement income to work income		14.9%
Sustainability age		95Y

2.7. Conclusion

In principle, the dimensions of retirement planning are simple. They include

- how long we save,

- how much we save,

- how much investment income we generate on our portfolio,

- when we retire,

- how much income we seek while in retirement, and

- how long we live.

Most investors significantly underestimate the effort required to achieve a comfortable retirement. Although we could easily evaluate what is required to achieve a target level of income at retirement when all parameters are known, reality is somewhat more complex. Even if we have some control over when to start saving, our ability to save substantially for retirement is influenced by many considerations, such as the purchase of a home, the cost of raising children, and unexpected career developments. We have even less control over investment return patterns, although we do have control over how we invest. We also have much less control over our longevity, although it can be influenced by lifestyle choices. Calibrating a retirement effort in the context of uncertain returns is a significant challenge even for experts.

Many other considerations have not been integrated in our analytical framework. For example, we must define an objective function: What specific life goals are we trying to optimize, and what risks and other constraints are relevant? For most investors, the goal is achieving an adequate standard of living, or income, during retirement and minimizing the likelihood of not achieving this goal. Therefore, the retirement-planning challenge does not end with retirement. Nevertheless, if we are to develop a full model of accumulation and decumulation, we must first narrow our focus and better understand the parameters that contribute to maximizing risk-adjusted wealth as of retirement. Chapter 3 addresses investment return uncertainty in the context of accumulation.

3. Understanding the Accumulation Period

The effects of investment return uncertainty are often discussed in the context of static wealth, without considering contributions or withdrawals. Assuming an initial savings amount of, say, $20,000 and no further savings contribution, we could estimate the distribution of final wealth that can be expected 10 years from now, given a specific asset allocation policy. The effect of return uncertainty on the evolution of wealth, however, can be very different in the context of accumulation and decumulation. For example, we could also estimate the distribution of wealth that can be expected 10 years from now assuming 10 consecutive annual savings contributions, starting at $2,000, and increasing annually by the expected rate of investment return.[9] How different would the distribution of expected wealth be in each scenario after 10 years? Does the accumulation process influence the "optimal" asset allocation decision? Is there a consensus on this issue among industry and academic experts?

Four investment-specific factors significantly affect the financial situation of individuals as they accumulate wealth toward retirement, namely,

- average level of real returns (i.e., returns net of inflation) that financial assets such as equity and fixed income have delivered during the accumulation period;

- pattern of returns (i.e., their volatility and sequence);

- investment policy, specifically how aggressive or conservative the allocation to financial assets is during the accumulation period, as well as how the level of investment aggressiveness changes over time; and

- attractiveness of financial conditions as the individual nears retirement, such as the real bond yield (i.e., yield net of inflation), because these factors will affect what happens after retirement.

All things being equal, higher real investment returns are preferable to lower real returns. For example, the annualized return of a portfolio invested 60% in US equity and 40% in fixed income between 31 August 1982 and 31 August 2017 was 10.4%. The average inflation rate was 2.8%, implying a real return of 7.6%. This return is significantly higher than the 3.4% annual real return that we assumed on a 60/40 portfolio in Chapter 2, consisting of

---

[9]In both cases, the present value of savings contributions would be $20,000.

a 5.4% gross return on the portfolio minus a 2% inflation rate. Furthermore, the annualized real return of 7.6% was not achieved in a stable fashion.

Figure 3.1 illustrates the "rolling" three-year annualized real return on a 60/40 portfolio between 31 August 1985 and 31 August 2017 (i.e., with the first three-year period running from 31 August 1982 to 31 August 1985, and so on). The average annualized real return in the first half of the period was 11.1%, whereas it was only 3.5% in the second half when the markets experienced two significant equity drawdowns: the bursting of the technology bubble in 2000–2002 and the liquidity crisis of 2007–2009. Furthermore, the yield on 10-year T-bonds was 12.81% in August 1982, with 12-month inflation running at approximately 5.9% at the time, whereas the yield was only 2.12% in August 2017 with 12-month inflation running at 1.7%. Clearly, the much lower level of real bond yields in August 2017 made retirement planning more challenging. For example, an investor wanting to acquire annuities as part of her retirement solution would receive less favorable terms in a low bond yield environment.

Investors have no control over the level of real return that financial markets deliver during their lifetime. Nor do they control the pattern of returns during the accumulation and decumulation periods or the real bond yield that will prevail when they retire. They do control their investment policy, however. A better understanding of how portfolio wealth is affected by the patterns of financial asset returns at different investment horizons can influence the recommended allocation policy between low-risk and risky assets. Furthermore, the level of the real bond yield observed as an investor

Figure 3.1. Evolution of Three-Year Real Annualized Compounded Return (60/40 Portfolio)

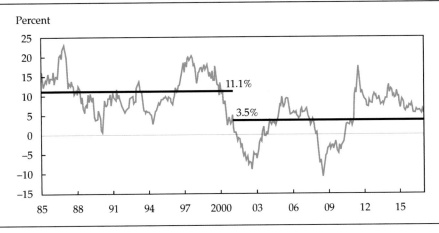

approaches retirement should affect how the investor prepares for his decumulation period.[10] Chapter 3 addresses the first issue. Chapter 5 addresses the second.

3.1. How the Pattern of Returns Influences Retirement Wealth

We can learn little by comparing scenarios of significantly different projected annualized portfolio returns. We can learn much, however, from comparing scenarios that share an identical annualized return but have widely different return *patterns*. To understand the significance of return patterns, we consider three patterns over a period of 35 years, all of which have an average annualized return of 5.4%, and apply these returns to John's situation:

- Scenario 1 (stable): A stable monthly return of 5.4% annualized—the same as in Chapter 2. A stable monthly return is unrealistic but allows for a comparison with the other two patterns.

- Scenario 2 (modified actual): The monthly returns actually observed between September 1982 and August 2017 adjusted using a scalar (a uniform amount added or subtracted—in this case, subtracted—each month) such that the yearly average compounded return is 5.4%.[11] This adjustment allows us to maintain the pattern of relative returns observed over this period while allowing for a fairer comparison with Scenario 1.

- Scenario 3 (time inverted): Inverting the returns observed in Scenario 2. In this scenario, the return observed in August 2017 is applied to September 1982, and so on.

Figure 3.2 illustrates the evolution of the market value of a single investment of $1,000 made at the beginning of the 35-year period, assuming each of the three return scenarios.

Unsurprisingly, all scenarios lead to a final wealth of $6,267. When there are no intermediate savings contributions, the final wealth is unaffected by the pattern of returns if all scenarios have the same annualized return over the full period. The cumulative wealth, however, varies greatly at different times. After half the time has elapsed, the total wealth ranges from a low of $1,178 to a high of $5,317—a difference of 351%! We can conclude from this figure that the modified actual scenario generated annualized returns greater

---

[10]For example, the real bond yield as of retirement would significantly affect the attractiveness of lifetime annuities.

[11]In other words, the average yearly compounded return of 10.4% observed for this period was adjusted down to 5.4% while maintaining the same relative pattern of returns.

Figure 3.2. Evolution of the Market Value of $1,000 over 35 Years (60/40 Portfolios) Assuming Three Return Scenarios

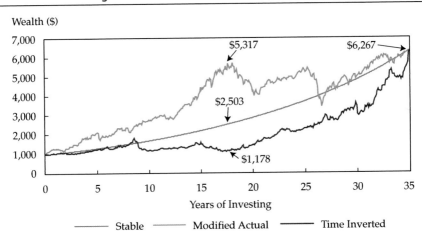

than 5.4% in the first half and lower in the second half, whereas the time-inverted scenario had, by design, a reverse pattern. Wealth under the modified actual scenario was significantly affected downward in the second half by the two equity corrections. The time-inverted scenario was affected by the two equity corrections in the first half but then benefited from strong returns in the second half.

We return to John, who periodically saves 10% of his income. **Figure 3.3** illustrates what happens to his cumulative wealth assuming periodic monthly savings contributions and the three previous return scenarios. Although all three scenarios have an annual return of 5.4% over the full period, they lead to widely different cumulative wealth.

The stable scenario leads to the same retirement wealth as that reported in Chapter 2 ($775,096). The modified actual scenario, however, which includes two equity corrections in the later years, ended with a retirement wealth of only $552,721. The time-inverted scenario, which absorbed these two equity corrections in the earlier years, ended with a retirement wealth of $1,072,021. After half the savings period had elapsed—at age 47 years and 6 months—the accumulated wealth was, respectively, $116,455, $197,880, and $281,148 for the three scenarios. The modified actual scenario had the best performance.

The figure also shows, on the right axis, how the annualized average realized return evolved as years passed for both the modified actual and

Figure 3.3. Evolution of Wealth and of the Average Yearly Compounded Return (60/40 Portfolio)

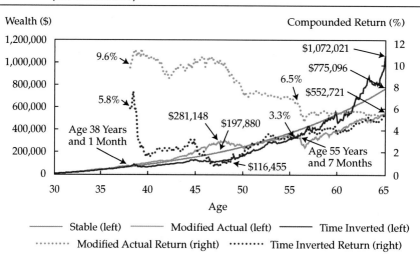

time-inverted scenarios.[12] This information is not presented for the stable scenario because the answer is 5.4% at every point in time. As per our assumption, all three scenarios delivered the same 5.4% compound return over the 35 years. For the modified actual and time-inverted scenarios, however, the pattern of returns differs in the intervening years, leading to interesting observations.

For example, when the investor is 38 years and 1 month old, all three scenarios lead to very similar wealth, although the annualized returns as of that age are 5.4% for the stable scenario and, respectively, 5.8% and 9.6% for the modified actual and time-inverted scenarios. Furthermore, when he is 55 years and 7 months old, both the modified actual and time-inverted scenarios lead to a similar level of wealth although the average yearly compounded returns are, respectively, 3.3% and 6.5% at that moment. Also when the investor is that age, the stable scenario leads to higher wealth than the modified actual scenario despite having a lower average yearly compounded return (5.4%).

Clearly, the interaction between the saving patterns and the way portfolio returns materialize over time matters during the accumulation period. But

---

[12]The figure shows this information starting only after several years to avoid the huge fluctuations that can be observed when calculating average early compounded returns over short periods of time. For example, a return generated in the first month of either +5% or −5% would imply annualized compounded returns of, respectively, +79.6% and −46.0%.

does the significance of this interaction differ between the earlier and later parts of the accumulation period? If yes, why and how should this understanding affect the investment policy and the evolution of risk taking during the accumulation period?

3.2. Industry Approach to Handling Market Risk and Fear over Time

In the last decade, target date funds (TDFs) have become a preferred retirement investment product. These funds are designed to provide investors with well-diversified portfolios whose allocation to riskier assets within the fund—usually equities—decreases automatically over time as investors near retirement. Some TDF products also continue to manage investors' assets beyond the retirement phase. The asset allocation's evolution over time is often called a *glide path*. **Figure 3.4** presents the most and least aggressive glide paths of nine TDF fund families surveyed.[13]

Most glide paths are similar in structure. They apply a high equity allocation—usually 90% or more—until approximately 20 to 25 years from retirement, then go through a transition period in which the equity allocation decreases significantly over the following two decades, and finally maintain a much lower equity allocation during retirement. The two examples show

Figure 3.4. Examples of Two Glide Paths

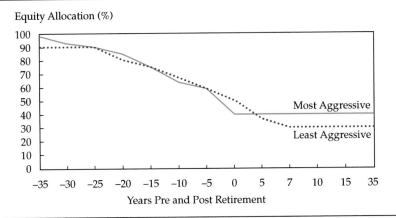

[13]Most and least aggressive glide paths have been defined for now as those with the highest and lowest average yearly equity allocation between year −35 pre retirement and +35 post retirement. Although not necessarily the most appropriate definition, these parameters do provide some perspective.

a stable equity allocation either after retirement or starting seven years post retirement. Some glide paths continue to adjust the equity allocation downward even 30 years post retirement, however. Finally, although we referred to these two glide paths as among the most and least aggressive ones, the difference in average yearly equity allocation over the 70-year period is only 4.3%.

Why would it be better to allocate more to riskier assets such as stocks when we're younger than when we're older? An often-used reason is that stocks are believed to be safer over long horizons than over short horizons. Disappointing annual performance for the stock market tends to be followed by better performance, which makes longer-horizon returns appear less volatile, at least on an annualized basis. An older investor closer to retirement may not have the luxury of waiting for a plummeting market to bounce back and should allocate less to stocks.[14]

Some advisers believe, however, that the concept of downward-sloping glide paths, as they are usually structured, is flawed. Using a Monte Carlo simulation, Esch and Michaud (2014) evaluated 101 glide path patterns over an accumulation period of 40 years with varying degrees of declining and increasing equity allocation. They also considered a balanced portfolio, maintaining a constant 40/60 equity/fixed-income allocation.

The authors generated thousands of equity and fixed-income return scenarios, allowing them to evaluate the ending wealth of all 101 glide paths for each scenario. All glide paths were calibrated to have the same volatility of terminal wealth to make them risk comparable. At one extreme, a glide path started with an equity allocation of 98.04% and ended with an allocation of 0%; at the other extreme, a glide path started with an equity allocation of 0% and ended with an equity allocation of 59.48%.[15] Esch and Michaud (2014) come to two conclusions:

- No glide path is clearly superior. Although the highest average terminal value was obtained by the glide path starting with an equity allocation of 53.24% and ending with an equity allocation of 32.38%, the range of average terminal values across all glide paths was small.

- The best glide path clearly depends on the pattern or timing of returns, so there is no single solution that applies to all return patterns. For example, the optimal glide path for an investor retiring in early 2000 after a strong

---

[14]This view has been challenged by several academicians, and their arguments appear later in this chapter.
[15]The upward- and downward-sloping glide paths that lead to the same volatility of end wealth are not mirror images of each other, nor are they symmetric, because the level of wealth is low when savings are initiated but much larger as retirement approaches.

performance of equity and fixed income over the previous two decades, with interest rates remaining relatively high at the end, would clearly be different from that of the same investor retiring in early 2009 after an equity market meltdown and with low interest rates.

Overall, Esch and Michaud (2014) conclude that a predetermined schedule of asset allocation that ignores information updates is unlikely to be the best way to optimize retirement wealth.[16] Unfortunately, we cannot easily forecast what specific pattern of returns will prevail in the future. A process that would integrate information updates implies a dynamic allocation, which is more challenging to explain to plan participants and also more difficult to implement. For example, the equity allocation could be determined by using information about the relative importance of human capital wealth and portfolio wealth and tracking their evolution over time, by forecasting equity volatility, by using an option-like approach such as constant portfolio protection insurance (CPPI), or by using other methods. It could also be based on a combination of processes. Several dynamic allocation processes are discussed in this and other chapters. Moreover, this chapter also illustrates the rational policies that should be implemented even when using a predetermined schedule of asset allocation.

Some authors have even more definite opinions about the industry approach that favors downward-sloping glide paths. Arnott, Sherrerd, and Wu (2013) believe that the basic principle of a glide path with a declining equity allocation is flawed. Most importantly, they argue that a lower equity allocation as an investor approaches retirement is not optimal because the allocation to risky assets is high when wealth is low (at the beginning of the accumulation period) and low when wealth is high (at the end of the accumulation period).[17]

Using historical returns over 141 years from 1871 to 2011, Arnott et al. evaluated the level of wealth accumulated over all possible horizons of 41 years. They concluded that a static allocation such as 50/50 equity/fixed income performs better and has no more downside risk than a declining

[16]Although interesting, the authors' approach would have been more valuable had the problem been defined in terms of maintaining the same volatility of future consumption. For example, for a given glide path, two return scenarios could lead to the same wealth but end with very different real-rate environments, implying that the wealth accumulated in each path may not buy the same amount of annual consumption in retirement. For example, rising real rates at the end of the accumulation period would lead to lower fixed-income returns but to more attractive real retirement/annuity income.

[17]This argument was initially made by Shiller (2005). However, Shiller mentions that the justification for such a view assumes persistent correlation between labor income and equity returns.

allocation of 80 toward 20 so that the average is 50/50 over time.[18] A rising allocation of 20 toward 80 performs even better and still does not have more downside risk, although that result may be time dependent.

Estrada (2013) made a similar argument in a global context looking at numerous mirror strategies such as 70/30 and 30/70. Arnott and Estrada explain that even if a rising allocation can lead to larger losses at the very end of the accumulation period, these potential losses would have been more than offset by stronger gains earlier in the period.[19] Overall, Estrada concludes that contrarian or balanced equity strategies provide investors with higher mean and median terminal wealth than traditional life-cycle strategies that have a declining equity allocation. Although he recognizes that strategies with a high equity allocation close to retirement expose investors to greater downside risk, he points out that the potential for bad luck should be more than offset by greater capital accumulation over a working lifetime. For example, Estrada indicates that looking at the worst decile of terminal wealth, the downside potential of rising glide paths is no more than that of declining glide paths, whereas the upside potential is much greater.

Estrada's view may be difficult to reconcile with the justifications laid out earlier (i.e., that stocks may be safer over long horizons and that younger investors' future income is akin to an implicit bond allocation). Again, if stocks are safer in the long run, a long-horizon investor should allocate more to stocks early in the accumulation phase and less to a risk-free asset like cash or a short-term government bond, supporting the argument for declining glide paths. This conundrum exists simply because both Arnott and Estrada's conclusions are flawed for structural and behavioral reasons, which we explore in the following sections.

3.3. Structural and Behavioral Arguments against Rising Glide Paths

To understand the wealth dynamics of glide paths, let's analyze four glide paths using the structure of John's saving inflows over an accumulation period of 35 years:

---

[18]Many studies form their conclusions using historical return data and rolling periods. Even 141 years does not provide many path experiences when the investment horizon is 41 years. Rolling periods use the same return data several times, and some data will obviously be used more often. For example, the first and last years are used only once, whereas observations in the middle of the dataset will be used 41 times. A well-designed Monte Carlo simulation would provide more-effective conclusions.

[19]Other authors have supported rising glide paths in retirement, including Kitces and Pfau (2014).

- a static equity allocation of 60% (60–60),

- an equity allocation declining from 80% to 40% (80–40),

- an equity allocation rising from 40% to 80% (40–80), and

- a more traditional glide path structure maintaining a 90% equity allocation for the first 15 years, declining gradually to 50% over a period of 10 years, and remaining at 50% until retirement (90–50).

Figure 3.5 illustrates these glide paths. The average yearly equity percentage allocation of the first three glide paths during the entire accumulation period is 60%.[20] The average allocation for the fourth glide path, however, is 72.9% because the allocation to equity remains higher than that of any other glide paths for the first 21 years. The question is, is that glide path really riskier than the others?

Before addressing this question, **Figure 3.6** illustrates the wealth accumulated according to each glide path, assuming for now the same stable returns as in Chapter 2. The traditional glide path accumulates wealth at a faster pace than any of the other three, but the 40–80 glide path achieves a similar wealth level as of the retirement date. The 80–40 allocation results in the lowest accumulated level of wealth. Are any of these results surprising?

To answer this question, we first must realize that each glide path's average equity percentage allocation can be very different from the average equity

Figure 3.5. Initial–Final Equity Allocation of Four Glide Paths

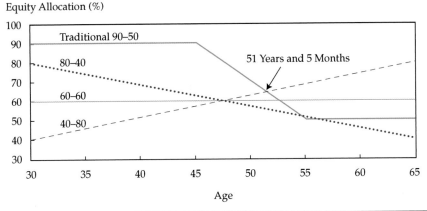

[20]The average allocation to equity is 60% if we use beginning-of-the-month allocations (after a monthly rebalancing). If we were to use end-of-the-month allocations, it would be slightly higher because the return on equity is greater than the return on bonds.

**Figure 3.6.   Cumulative Wealth According to Four Glide Paths
(Initial–Final Equity Allocation)**

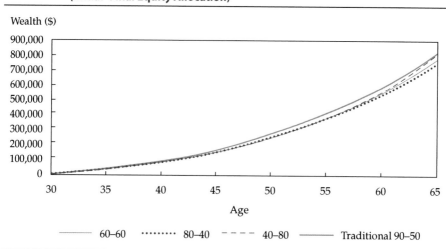

dollar allocation of each corresponding portfolio because the investment portfolio size is expected to grow over time, not only from returns but also from periodic savings contributions. For each glide path, **Table 3.1** presents the final wealth, the average percentage equity allocation, and the average dollar equity allocation.[21]

The argument that traditional glide paths are flawed because they apply higher equity allocation when wealth is smaller ignores the power of return compounding and the evolution of the portfolio's risk structure. First, the 40–80 glide path is more profitable than the 80–40, but the exposure to equity

Table 3.1.   Impact of Glide Path Structure on Final Wealth

Glide Paths (Initial–Final Equity Allocation)	Final Wealth at 65 (Savings Starting at Age 30)	Average Equity Percentage Allocation	Average Equity Dollar Allocation
60–60	$775,096	60.0%	60.0%
80–40	742,479	60.0	50.8
40–80	809,448	60.0	69.6
Traditional (90–50)	809,929	72.9	59.1

---

[21]The structure and timeline of the 90–50 glide path was chosen deliberately because it leads to approximately the same average equity dollar allocation as a 60–60 glide path. In this chapter, we alternate between 90–50 and 90–60 glide paths. Proper calibration will not be completed until Chapter 6.

Figure 3.7. Initial–Final Equity Dollar Allocation of Four Glide Paths

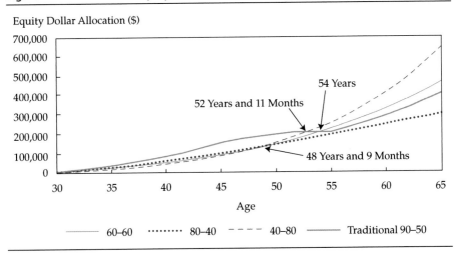

in dollar terms is far higher on average. In other words, a 40–80 glide path is not the mirror image of an 80–40 glide path in terms of risk. Similarly, the average equity percentage allocation of the traditional glide path is far higher than that of the 40–80 glide path, but its average equity dollar allocation is far less, and significantly so in the last decade of savings. Still, both glide paths lead to a similar end wealth.

Figure 3.7 presents the equity dollar allocation of all four strategies over time. When the investor is 48 years and 9 months old, all glide paths except the traditional one have essentially the same equity dollar allocation. The divergence across glide paths really shows in the last decade or so. The traditional glide path has a higher equity dollar allocation early in the first two decades, but the exposure becomes less aggressive than the 40–80 glide path after age 52 years and 11 months or the 60–60 glide path at age 54.

The left segment of **Table 3.2** explains the dynamic of compounded returns for the two most profitable glide paths, the traditional and the 40–80.

Table 3.2. Evolution Wealth for 40–80 and Traditional (90–50) Glide Paths under Modified Assumptions

Glide Paths (Initial–Final Allocation)	Wealth at 51 Years and 5 Months	Wealth at 65 if 40–80	Wealth at 65 if Traditional (90–50)
40–80	$277,647	$809,448	$736,241
Traditional (90–50)	315,506	891,276	809,929
Spread	37,859	81,828	73,688

First, the traditional glide path has a higher equity *percentage* allocation until John is age 51 years and 5 months, as well as a greater equity *dollar* allocation until the participant is 52 years and 11 months old (see Figures 3.5 and 3.7). The traditional glide path accumulated 13.6% more wealth, or $37,492, as of age 51 years and 5 months, but the 40–80 glide path makes up for most of the lost wealth through a more aggressive equity allocation afterward.

Table 3.2 also shows what the accumulated wealth would be if each glide path switched to the allocation of the other one starting at age 51 years and 5 months. For example, if the traditional glide path switched to the 40–80 allocation at that time, the final wealth would be $891,276. In the case of the 40–80 glide path, it would be only $736,241. In other words, because the 40–80 glide path accumulated $37,859 less wealth as of age 51 years and 5 months, it must take substantially more risk than the traditional glide path to generate an extra $73,688 afterward ($809,929 versus $736,241).

Even though our analyses do not yet incorporate return uncertainty, several conclusions can reasonably be reached:

- The first question to ask is not whether a rising glide path is preferable to a declining glide path but whether it is efficient to maintain a higher level of portfolio risk in the initial savings years and for how long. As Figure 3.7 and Table 3.2 illustrate, if we can make a strong argument that risk can be sustained in the initial years (a topic for the next section), investors should not abandon the excess wealth that can be generated early on and still benefit from return compounding, no matter what portfolio allocation is recommended later.

- From a behavioral point of view, investors should also prefer the traditional glide path to the 40–80 glide path. The 40–80 glide path achieves a level of wealth like that of the traditional glide path at retirement but exposes participants to far greater risk as retirement nears through a larger average equity dollar exposure.

Participants exposed to the rising equity glide path may have concerns over the level of equity exposure in the final accumulation years and will be significantly hurt financially if a substantial market decline occurs. Any market downturn will significantly increase most investors' anxiety level. Telling investors who are currently 35 years from retirement not to worry about taking increasing risk over time (using a rising equity glide path) instead of taking decreasing risk (using a declining equity glide path) because they are likely to reach a similar and possibly greater level of wealth at retirement may provide some reassurance, but it will not help manage the fears and emotions of investors who are just a few years from their expected retirement. As participants approach retirement and have better information about their prospective wealth, they build expectations about their lifestyle during retirement and develop a greater sensitivity to financial risk.

- Having a portfolio that becomes gradually more conservative for a period that could last several decades can significantly affect retirement income. If downside risk could be reduced, most individuals would consider taking more risk during the decumulation period. Therefore, designing a retirement plan that allows one the confidence to target greater expected returns without creating excessive fear is essential. This aspect is a central consideration in *Secure Retirement*.

3.4. Is Equity Truly Less Risky in the Long Run?

As specified previously, the principle of a declining glide path is often supported by the argument that stocks are less risky in the long run. But are they? According to Jeremy Siegel (1994, p. 94):

> Stocks are unquestionably riskier than bonds or bills in the short run. In every five-year period since 1802, however, the worst performance in stocks, at –11 percent per year, has been only slightly worse than the worst performance in bonds or bills. For 20-year holding periods, stocks have never fallen behind inflation, while bonds and bills have fallen 3 percent per year behind the rate of inflation over this time period. …The fact that stocks, in contrast to bonds or bills, have never offered investors a negative real holding period return yield over periods of 17 years or more is extremely significant. Although it might appear to be riskier to hold stocks than bonds, precisely the opposite is true: the safest long-term investment for the preservation of purchasing power has clearly been stocks, not bonds.

Stating that stocks are safer in the long run than in the short run, however, implies that we believe, among other implicit assumptions, that stock returns are mean reverting. In other words, what goes up must come down and vice versa, making equity more attractive when performance has been weak and less attractive when it has been strong. This is the reasoning behind the concept of time diversification—the conjecture that equity is less risky over long investment horizons.

The idea of time diversification has come under scrutiny again in recent years because of the growing emphasis on target date strategies recommending a higher equity allocation initially that then declines toward and through retirement. And although Siegel concluded that equity risk declines in the long run, there are other opinions.

Let us start with the assumption that equity returns do not necessarily mean revert. If we assume returns in equity markets are *independent and identically distributed* (i.i.d.), implying that returns are drawn from a distribution having a stable mean and variance and are without autocorrelation at any lag, it can be shown that the variance of returns over K periods is simply K multiplied by the variance of a single period (σ^2):[22]

$$\sigma_K^2 = K \times \sigma^2 \text{ and } \sigma_K = \sqrt{K} \times \sigma.$$

Hence, under i.i.d., variance is proportional to the time horizon (K). In plain language, the same level of risk is maintained over longer horizons; there is no time diversification. If returns did mean revert, however, equity variance at a longer horizon would be less than proportional to K. This dynamic would make equity more attractive to long-term investors and encourage those investors to increase their equity investments following a market downturn or decrease during an upturn (Gropp 2004). The effect of mean reversion is discussed later in this chapter, but the evidence on mean reversion is discussed in Chapter 5.

Proponents of time diversification believe that the probability of expected losses declines as the horizon increases. This logic is used to justify a higher allocation to equity for long-term investors. Several counterarguments have been made, however:

- Statman (2017) and Samuelson (1994) believe this decrease results from a framing error. Although they agree that the probability of losses may decline as the horizon increases, it could be shown that the size of losses, should they occur, could increase. As Samuelson (1994, p. 17) wrote, "When a 35-year old lost 82% of his pension portfolio between 1929 and 1932, do you think it was foreordained in heaven that it would come back and fructify to +400% by his retirement at 65?" Both Samuelson (1969) and Merton (1969) conclude that in the absence of human capital, individuals should maintain constant portfolio weights, in line with their risk aversion, throughout their lifetime.

- Pastor and Stambaugh (2011) go even further and explain that stocks may be riskier in the long run even in the presence of mean reversion

---

[22]Given that periodic returns (μ) are annualized linearly and the standard deviation is a function of the square root of time, it also means that the Sharpe ratio of any investment appears more favorable if a longer time interval is used. Therefore, Sharpe ratios of different investments must be compared using similar time intervals, and a higher Sharpe at a longer time interval does not necessarily indicate time diversification.

of returns. In their opinion, mean reversion is only one of four components of portfolio return variance, the others being i.i.d. uncertainty, uncertainty about current and future expected returns, and *estimation risk*—that is, the possibility that your estimate of the mean or standard deviation of a distribution is incorrect. According to Pastor, the conventional wisdom that equity investors face less volatility in the long run is based on historical measures of volatility that are calculated using known (i.e., historical) mean returns. Allocation decisions must be based on forward-looking measures of volatility and future mean returns, which can change drastically. Annualized total equity returns may have been 9.93% from 1926 to 2017, but future mean returns can be estimated only indirectly; that is, they are not obtained from market data such as a bond yield. This uncertainty compounds over time and may have a greater effect than the benefits of mean reversion.

- Bodie (1995) uses option pricing theory to explain that stocks are riskier in the long run. Like Samuelson, he indicates that the probability of a shortfall is a flawed measure of risk because it ignores the size of a potential shortfall. He states: "Taking as the measure of the riskiness of an investment the cost of insuring it against earning less than the risk-free rate of return over the investor's time horizon, I show that the riskiness of stocks increases rather than decreases with the length of that horizon. These results hold both under the assumption of a 'random-walk' process for stock returns and for the kinds of 'mean-reverting' processes that have been reported in the economics and finance literature" (Bodie 1995, p. 18).

- Finally, Kritzman and Rich (2002) and Trainor (2005) make a different type of argument. They point out that within-horizon risk is far greater than end-of-horizon risk and that the former tends to increase as the horizon lengthens whereas the latter decreases. In other words, the likelihood of a 25% cumulative loss after investing in equity for five years (i.e., an ending value less than or equal to 75 cents per dollar originally invested) is far lower than the likelihood of having sustained at some point in time a 25% loss during those five years. For example, Trainor estimates the risk of a 10% or 25% equity loss as of the end of the five-year period as being, respectively, 10.7% or 4.5% when the horizon is five years, whereas the within-horizon probabilities are, respectively, 56.5% and 19.5%. Although this fact does not change the end-of-horizon probability, it can influence investor behavior and risk aversion. Trainor explains that the path of wealth and cumulative returns affects the likelihood of a strategy's success or failure. Therefore, individuals facing a significant return shock (such as 2008) may have abandoned their strategy before they could benefit from the market reversal that occurred.

This literature does not support the principle of a riskier allocation to stocks when the investment horizon is long. Risk tolerance, not investment horizon, would be the primary determinant of equity allocation, although Pastor and Stambaugh (2011) concede that the conventional wisdom that equity is less risky in the long run could be used to convince investors to adopt higher equity allocations even if the reasoning proves faulty. Similarly, Statman (2017) believes that the concept of time diversification is flawed but also that it helps manage investors' fears. In other words, an unwarranted belief in time diversification may increase our risk tolerance. Fortunately, there are better arguments that still support the principle of a declining glide path.

3.5. Justifications for a Declining Glide Path

We have already made a behavioral argument in favor of declining glide paths. Whether or not we believe that a declining glide path is justified from a risk and utility point of view, we understand that investors fear uncertainty more intensely as they approach retirement. Nonetheless, at least three potential structural reasons argue in favor of declining glide path.

The first justification comes from Nobel Prize–winning economist Robert Merton (1969). The argument goes as follows: Say you determine that the optimal mix of stocks and bonds is 60/40. Although your financial portfolio typically consists of stocks and bonds, you have another portfolio to manage. Your "life" portfolio contains a different important asset: human capital. Human capital is the present, capitalized value of your future labor income, some of which you will presumably save and invest. When you are young and beginning your career, your stream of future savings looks like a bond: You will receive regular "coupons" (paychecks) in the future, and you will save part of your income every year until retirement. For example, we assumed in Chapter 2 that every year John saves 10% of his $60,000 income.

Therefore, it is appropriate to include human capital within the total "life" portfolio of assets. As such, the exposure to risky assets such as equity (E) should be compared with one's total "life wealth," which is also composed of bonds (B) and human capital (HC), and should be calculated as

$$\frac{S}{S + B + HC_S},$$

Eq. 3.1

where HC_S is defined as the present value of the part of your future income that is saved, $S + B$ your "savings" portfolio, and $S + B + HC_S$ your "life" portfolio. Hence, your stream of savings acts as an implicit bond allocation, assuming your HC is not too risky. Therefore, if you aim at having a 60/40 "life" portfolio and have accumulated only a small amount of financial wealth through your past savings, but the present value of your future savings is significant, your allocation within the "savings" portfolio should be tilted toward more stocks—for example, 90/10. As you age, the present value of your future savings from labor income becomes a smaller part of your "life" portfolio. Therefore, you will need to hold more bonds in your "savings" portfolio to attain your desired 60/40 allocation.

Hence, the principle of a declining equity allocation to riskier assets in proposed industry glide paths can also be justified by the argument that as investors approach retirement, the present value of their human capital declines because there are fewer remaining years of work and savings, whereas the dependence on the financial capital accumulated in the past increases. In other words, for a given level of risk aversion, it is important to properly recognize all sources of wealth and their associated risks when stating the investor's retirement challenge.

The second structural justification in favor of declining glide paths is derived from the work of Trainor (2005) and involves the human capital component. As previously stated, Kritzman and Rich (2002) and Trainor looked at the within-horizon risk of investing. In addition, Trainor looked at the within-horizon risk in the context of a dollar cost averaging (DCA) strategy. As an example of a DCA strategy, assume a given amount of initial capital and a 36-month horizon. In the first month, 1/36 of wealth is invested in equity and the balance in a risk-free asset. In the second month, 1/35 of the amount invested in the risk-free asset is converted to equity, and so on, until all available capital has been invested in equity. **Table 3.3** presents a comparison of a fully invested strategy with a DCA strategy implemented over a period of 3 years, assuming a 20-year horizon and an initial capital of $100,000. In other words, the only purpose of the DCA strategy is to smooth the cost of building the full equity exposure in the initial 3 years of the full 20-year horizon. According to Trainor, using a DCA approach reduces expected wealth but also significantly reduces the within-horizon probability of large expected losses. Although this study does not directly address the issue of a declining glide path, an interesting parallel can be made.

DCA is somewhat similar to an accumulation process in the context of human capital. Consider an investor in the initial stage of accumulation, assuming a horizon of 35 years. This investor has an initial wealth consisting

Table 3.3. Probability of End-of-Horizon and Within-Horizon Losses Assuming a 20-Year Horizon: Fully Invested vs. DCA Equity Strategy

	Fully Invested	Dollar Averaging, 36 Months
	End-of-Horizon	End-of-Horizon
Mean final wealth (initial wealth of $100,000)	$672,750	$620,638
Loss of 10% or more at end of period	1.8%	1.8%
Loss of 10% or more within horizon	59.70%	42.90%
Loss of 25% or more at end of period	1.0%	0.9%
Loss of 25% or more within horizon	24.40%	16.30%

Source: Kritzman and Rich (2002).

entirely of human capital. Assuming she is a tenured professor, her human capital is almost a risk-free asset. In the first year, the investor extracts 1/35 of her human capital, which she invests in a 60/40 portfolio. She now has a balance of 34 years' worth of human capital. In the second year, she extracts 1/34 of her remaining human capital, and so on. The real return on the portfolio of liquid assets—equity and bonds—is uncertain, but the return on human capital may be more stable because it is likely related to wage inflation. Moreover, the increase in efficiency of the savings process stemming from the implicit averaging is likely greater in the beginning of accumulation, when the ratio of liquid assets to human capital is low, than in the end of accumulation, when the ratio is high. The reason is that it is difficult to benefit from DCA when you are already very capital rich in relation to your periodic savings.

This logic leads us to have a greater allocation to equity in the liquid asset portfolio at the beginning and a lower allocation as the end horizon nears. In other words, the accumulation process itself may smooth the risk of wealth accumulation even if financial market returns are not mean reverting.

To support this view, we first completed several simulations using 10,000 scenarios (not illustrated). One set of simulations compared the compounded yearly market returns (time-weighted return) with the internal rate of return (IRR) of the accumulation strategy. In other words, in the first case, we are looking at the annualized return irrespective of the savings contributed each year; in the second case, we are looking at the IRR that equates the periodic savings contributions with the final amount of wealth. Results indicate that in approximately 70% of all scenarios, the IRR is greater than the time-weighted return. This first set of simulations supports the argument that the accumulation process itself smooths financial returns.

In addition, an even more interesting test can be made. If a smoothing process occurs in accumulation, even in the context of i.i.d. returns, and if this process is less efficient as the level of human capital declines, it may be profitable to initiate the accumulation savings effort with a higher equity allocation and end the savings effort with a lower equity allocation. Therefore, a second set of Monte Carlo simulations compared the IRRs of a 60/40 fixed allocation with the IRRs of a glide path starting with a 90/10 allocation and gradually transitioning to 60/40 between years +20 and +30. In this case, the IRRs resulting from the declining glide path were greater in more than 94% of all scenarios. Had the transition occurred five years earlier, the percentage would be approximately 96%. More precise and informative simulations appear toward the end of this chapter.

The third structural justification in favor of declining glide paths is the possibility that returns on risky assets mean revert. Although the evidence on mean reversion is mixed, as discussed in Chapter 5, we can address the potential benefits of mean reversion if it exists. Let's consider the example in **Table 3.4**. An investor can either commit an initial contribution of $3,000 (Pattern 1) to her savings plans or make three successive contributions of, respectively, $1,000.00, $1,054.00, and $1,110.92 (Pattern 2). In both cases, the investor made savings contributions with a present value of $3,000, assuming a discount rate equal to the expected compound annual return of 5.4%. However, under Pattern 1 no human capital is left after the first contribution has been made, whereas Pattern 2 incorporates an initial amount of wealth and future savings from human capital in the following two periods.

The two cash flow patterns are subjected to five different return scenarios that all lead to an annualized compounded return of 5.4%: a stable or constant

Table 3.4. Impact of Savings and Return Patterns on Final Wealth

Return Scenarios	Returns Year 1	Returns Year 2	Returns Year 3	Average Annualized	Final Wealth Pattern 1	Δ Final Wealth Pattern 2
1	5.40%	5.40%	5.40%	5.40%	$3,512.72	$0.00
2a	−14.60	30.08	5.40	5.40	3,512.72	274.22
2b	−14.60	17.09	17.09	5.40	3,512.72	404.12
3a	25.40	−11.41	5.40	5.40	3,512.72	(186.75)
3b	25.40	−3.37	−3.37	5.40	3,512.72	(284.17)

Note: Pattern 1: single contribution of $3,000; Pattern 2: successive contributions of $1,000.00, $1,054.00, and $1,110.92, respectively.

return scenario (Scenario 1); a scenario with an initial return shock of –20% against the expected return, assuming a recovery over one or two years (Scenarios 2a and 2b,); and a scenario with a positive return shock of +20% reversed over one or two years (Scenarios 3a and 3b). The last two columns express, respectively, the final wealth assuming the first cash flow pattern and the difference in wealth between the first and second cash flow patterns. We can conclude the following from Table 3.4:

- When dealing with a single initial savings amount, the pattern of return is irrelevant. All that matters is the annualized return.

- A scenario incorporating a negative return shock leads to a greater final wealth level than a no-shock scenario in a context of accumulation. The effect is more significant if the return recovery is stretched over a longer period.

- A scenario incorporating a positive return shock leads to a smaller final wealth level than a no-shock scenario in a context of accumulation, although the decrease is not as significant as the wealth increase observed in the case of negative return shock.

The example also illustrates the idea that if low returns are followed by high returns and vice versa, the equity returns may be less volatile in the long run than in the short run. Although we do not illustrate this dynamic, we can conclude that these effects would be amplified with the size of the shock and with the level of risk in the portfolio.

3.5.1. Understanding the Impact of Return Shocks from Early Accumulation to Retirement. The example in Table 3.4 applies to an individual who is just starting to accumulate wealth. What happens if we consider a downward-sloping glide path and assume negative return shocks occur at different times over a savings period that extends several decades? Several analyses are presented. The first analysis looks at the effect of a negative return shock occurring at any point in time in the context of the traditional glide path. This analysis assumes a stable equity allocation of 90% in the first 15 years, a declining allocation toward 50% over the following 10 years, and a stable allocation at 50% thereafter. The savings contributions increase by 2% each year. Four scenarios of recovery after a return shock are assumed: The market recovers over one, three, or five years, or it does not recover at all. Although the portfolio is composed of equity and fixed income, the return shocks and their recoveries occur only within the equity segment. (A combined equity and bond shock is discussed later.) We assume an equity shock of −32.5%.[23] The objective is to evaluate the excess wealth gains result-ing from a shock against a no-shock scenario.

Figure 3.8 presents the level of excess wealth resulting from the equity shock. The results are not entirely intuitive and require more explanation. The figure identifies three distinct periods: initial accumulation at a high equity level, transition, and final accumulation at a lower equity level.

Initial Accumulation: As expected from the example in Table 3.4, a nega-tive equity shock benefits the portfolio, and a longer recovery is even more beneficial. The excess wealth gains decline rapidly, however, as we overlap the period where the glide path transitions from a 90% equity allocation toward a lower allocation, especially if the recovery period is long.

Transition: The wealth gains under the three- and five-year recovery sce-narios decline significantly at the end of the initial accumulation period and in the five-year recovery scenario become even slightly negative in the transi-tion period before bouncing back toward the end. The explanation is simply that if a return shock occurs early in the transition, the portfolio wealth may not fully recover from this shock because the allocation to equity is being gradually reduced. If the shock occurs late in the transition, this effect is diminished because much of the reduction to the equity allocation has already

Figure 3.8. Excess Portfolio Wealth (%) According to Timing of Equity Shock (−32.5%) and Length of Recovery for the 90–50 Glide Path

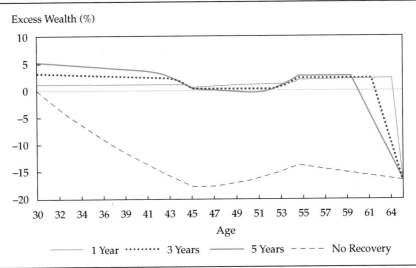

[23]This shock corresponds to a loss of value of approximately 20% in the context of a 60/40 allocation.

been completed by the time the shock occurs. Intuitively, we could conclude that the faster the transition toward a lower equity allocation, the greater the negative effect on excess wealth—and the converse also applies. It may also indicate that the occurrence of a shock should affect the planned asset allocation adjustments, especially if we believe in mean reversion.

Final Accumulation: The pattern of excess wealth in the third period is puzzling. First, we should ignore for now the decline in excess wealth that occurs at the very end. This decline occurs because we end our analysis as of the retirement date and there is insufficient time to recover from the negative return shock. This aspect will be addressed as we incorporate the transition to the decumulation period. At the beginning of this period, however, we no longer observe a decline of excess wealth as we near retirement. Why does the negative shock have such a significantly positive effect even though the allocation to equity is much smaller than in the initial accumulation phase?

The reason is the diversification bonus resulting from portfolio rebalancing between equity and bonds.[24] This effect is always present but becomes more significant as the allocation between equity and fixed income equalizes. To understand the diversification bonus, consider the examples in **Table 3.5** across two scenarios of asset allocation: 90/10, as in the initial accumulation period of our previous example, and 50/50, as in the final accumulation period. We ignore the transition period and the periodic savings contributions because periodic savings would complicate the interpretation of the data without adding further substance to the explanation. Thus we assume an initial wealth amount only. The expected compound annual returns of equity and fixed income are, respectively, 7% and 3%, implying average monthly compounded returns of 0.57% and 0.25%. The examples assume a 61-month horizon, consisting of an initial 1-month return shock followed by a 60-month recovery.

The first two lines of the table present different return scenarios for equity, bonds, and the two portfolios, separately for the first month and for all remaining months. The left section assumes stable returns, and the middle section assumes an equity-only shock of −32.50%. In all cases, the annualized compounded returns of equity and bonds are set to remain, respectively, at 7% and 3%. We ignore the third section for now.

The third and fourth lines illustrate the arithmetic average returns and compounded returns over 61 months for the stock, bond, 90/10, and 50/50 portfolios. As is well known, the only circumstance in which the average return and the compounded return are identical is when there is no volatility

---

[24]The issue of the diversification bonus is covered in Chapter 4 of Lussier (2013).

Table 3.5. Impact of Equity and Bonds Shocks with Recovery on Annualized Portfolio Returns

3. Understanding the Accumulation Period

Returns	No Shock				Asset and Portfolio Return Equity Shock				Required Portfolio Recovery Return	
			Equity Allocation				Equity Allocation		Equity Allocation	
	Equity	Bond	90%	50%	Equity	Bond	90%	50%	90%	50%
Month 1 (Shock)	0.57%	0.25%	0.53%	0.41%	−32.50%	0.25%	−29.23%	−16.13%	−29.23%	−16.13%
Months 2–61 (Recovery)	0.57	0.25	0.53	0.41	1.24	0.25	1.14	0.74	1.12	0.71
Average	0.57	0.25	0.53	0.41	0.68	0.25	0.64	0.46	0.63	0.43
Compounded	0.57	0.25	0.53	0.41	0.57	0.25	0.55	0.44	0.53	0.41
Annualized	7.00	3.00	6.59	4.98	7.00	3.00	6.76	5.40	6.59	4.98
Spread					0.00	0.00	0.17	0.42	0.00	0.00

Returns	Asset and Portfolio Return Equity and Bond Shock				Required Portfolio Recovery Return	
			Equity Allocation		Equity Allocation	
	Equity	Bond	90%	50%	90%	50%
Month 1 (Shock)	−32.50%	10.00%	−28.25%	−11.25%	−28.25%	−11.25%
Months 2–61 (Recovery)	1.24	0.09	1.12	0.66	1.10	0.61
Average	0.68	0.25	0.64	0.47	0.62	0.42
Compounded	0.57	0.25	0.55	0.46	0.53	0.41
Annualized	7.00	3.00	6.86	5.61	6.59	4.98
Spread	0.00	0.00	0.26	0.63	0.00	0.00

© 2019 CFA Institute Research Foundation. All rights reserved.

41

of returns, as in the no-shock scenario.[25] In this case, the annualized compounded returns of the no-shock 90/10 and 50/50 portfolios are 6.59% and 4.98%, respectively.

If we assume an equity shock, although the monthly compounded equity return remains at 0.57%, the average return is now 0.68%, or 0.11% above the no-shock scenario. This result is to be expected: If the compounded return is the same as it is without the shock, the average return will be higher if there is volatility. If we now build portfolios from the series of returns that incorporate the equity shock, the compound annual returns of the 90/10 and 50/50 portfolios will rise to 6.76% and 5.40%, increasing by 0.17% and 0.42%, respectively, even though the compound annual returns of equity and bonds are the same as before. This increase occurs for three reasons:

- The average equity return is larger than in the no-shock scenario (this is attributed to the return volatility).

- There is a correlation of zero between the equity shock and the bond return; that is, the bond return is unaffected by the equity shock, implying a powerful diversification effect.

- The portfolio is implicitly rebalanced every month, thereby allowing the investor to capture the benefit of diversification between equity and fixed income.[26]

The effect is more powerful for the 50/50 portfolio than for the 90/10 portfolio because a more balanced risk exposure across asset classes is required to achieve a diversification bonus. It is the unavoidable consequence of combining imperfectly correlated assets. Diversification benefits come in the form not only of reduced risk but also of increased compound annual returns.

The top-right part of Table 3.5 illustrates that in the presence of a diversification bonus, we do not even need a full recovery following a negative return shock to achieve the same compound return on the portfolio. Compound annual equity returns of 6.81% and 6.15% (not shown explicitly), respectively, are enough to achieve this goal for the 90/10 and 50/50 allocations. The 50/50 allocation requires a lower compound annual equity return because the diversification bonus has a larger effect on a more balanced portfolio allocation.

---

[25]The relationship between average return and compounded return is Compounded return = [Average return] − [Impact of volatility]. In the case of a normal distribution, it is approximated by Compounded return ≈ [Average return] − [$1/2\ \sigma^2$].

[26]Although a monthly rebalancing may not be possible, any systematic rebalancing mechanism will trigger a diversification bonus. For a discussion on the subject, consult *Successful Investing Is a Process* (Lussier 2013).

The diversification bonus could be even more powerful a lower correlation (even negative) between equity and fix bottom part of Table 3.5 indicates what would happen if t.. were accompanied by a positive bond shock—declining bond yields and rising bond prices—and a complete recovery ensued. In this case, the effect on both portfolios' compounded returns is even greater because we now assume a negative correlation between equity and fixed income. We can conclude from these examples that a positive correlation reduces some of the benefits of the diversification bonus.[27] If the correlation is +1.0 (equities and bonds move exactly together), there is no diversification bonus at all.

Figure 3.9 illustrates how the excess compounded return attributed to a return shock relates to the equity allocation and the size of the shock. Three observations appear relevant:

- The excess return is larger for a more balanced allocation. In fact, it appears that the equity allocation that maximizes this effect is slightly greater than 50%.

- The excess performance increases in a nonlinear way with the size of the shock. Twice the shock generates more than twice the excess return.

- Although there is a specific equity allocation that maximizes the diversification bonus, there is a zone where the bonus remains close to the maximum. For example, any equity allocation between approximately 42.5% and 65.0% leads to an excess compound annual return that is within 5% of the maximum. This finding provides much flexibility for calibrating a glide path.[28]

---

[27]An example of market circumstances that could lead to a positive correlation would be an equity and bond shock caused by an inflation surprise.

[28]To better understand why the excess return behaves in this way, we derived an equation expressing the excess return as a function of the equity allocation, the expected return on equity and bonds, the size of shocks, and the recovery time. We concluded the following:

- The equity allocation that maximizes the excess return is not very sensitive to the length of the recovery period, although it nears 50% as the recovery period shortens.

- What explains that the equity allocation maximizing the excess return is greater than 50% is simply that the allocation is slightly tilted toward the asset that generates the greatest relative shocks and benefits from the strongest relative recovery, which is equity in our example.

- The excess return of a shock over a specific period is not extremely sensitive to recovery duration. For example, if we consider an equity shock of −32.5% and a bond shock of +10% in the initial month, as well as a period of 61 months for the analysis but a recovery that can last either 24 months or 60 months within that period, the excess returns are, respectively, 65 and 63 bps, as shown in Table 3.5.

Figure 3.9. Excess Return Attributed to Specific Return Shocks Followed by a Recovery

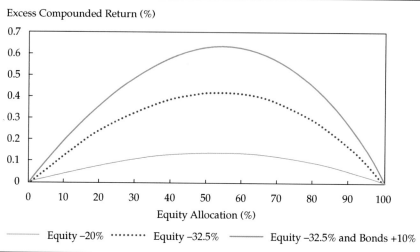

The diversification bonus explains why the excess wealth attributed to a shock in Figure 3.8 was greater than expected in the later stage of accumulation. In the earlier stage, the accumulation process benefits more from a return shock because portfolio wealth is smaller relative to the future savings contributions, but the diversification bonus contributes less to this wealth because the equity allocation is dominant. In the latter stage of accumulation, the accumulation process benefits less from a shock, but the effect of the diversification bonus is greater.

3.5.2. Comparing a Balanced Portfolio and a Glide Path: The Case of John.
The discussion so far supports the principle of declining glide paths. A higher level of risk in the initial accumulation period is warranted in the presence of significant human capital, and even more so if financial market returns are mean reverting. The transition period from working to retirement requires careful calibration. A speedy transition may lead to a loss of wealth if a return shock occurs. Finally, although a lower allocation to equity leads to a lower expected return during the final accumulation period, the decline is partially muted by the diversification bonus. Diversification and rebalancing reduce the implicit cost of a more conservative allocation. It would make sense to use this benefit when wealth and financial risk are greater and when the effects of the accumulation process are less significant, close to retirement. Furthermore, the higher allocation to fixed income during the end of the

accumulation period provides a more effective interest rate hedge for investors wanting to acquire annuities in decumulation.

How would these different considerations play out if we applied the modified actual and time-inverted return scenarios and the stable return scenario to the traditional glide path for John? How would the wealth level at the midpoint (age 47.5) and at retirement (age 65) differ from what would have been achieved assuming a stable 60/40 allocation? **Table 3.6** summarizes this information.

Three observations can be made:

- Consistent with the results presented in Table 3.1, the traditional glide path outperforms the 60/40 balanced portfolio, assuming stable equity and fixed-income returns.

- Assuming a modified actual scenario, the traditional glide path ends with nearly 12.1% more wealth because it benefited from early strong returns on a higher equity allocation.

- Assuming a time-inverted scenario, the traditional glide path ends with only 2% less wealth even though it had a larger allocation to equity early on when the two equity shocks occurred. Its final wealth is less only because at the very end of the accumulation process—specifically, in the last three months—the equity returns were very strong when the equity allocation was 50% instead of 60%.

Overall, the traditional glide path performs relatively well against the 60/40 balanced portfolio in all three circumstances. Again, this result supports the argument that taking significant risk early in the accumulation process makes sense because the process itself smooths the effect of poor performance on wealth. The transition to a lower equity allocation allows one to lower the financial risk close to retirement and increases the efficiency of diversification.

Table 3.6. Wealth at Ages 47.5 and 65 Assuming a Stable Equity Allocation (60–60) and a Traditional Glide Path (90–50)

	Age 47.5		Age 65	
Glide Paths	60–60	90–50	60–60	90–50
Stable returns	$197,880	$220,032	$775,096	$809,929
Forward corrected	281,148	368,378	552,721	619,619
Backward corrected	116,455	103,464	1,072,021	1,053,488

3.6. Estimation and Further Understanding of Risk in the Context of Accumulation

Until now, we have made our arguments for a declining glide path mostly by using scenario analyses, some Monte Carlo simulations, and sound financial and behavioral principles. We now validate these arguments further using more realistic simulated environments. To this end, we completed two sets of 36 simulations, each with 30,000 return scenarios. Each set of simulations is based on a different methodology for generating asset returns, i.i.d. returns or returns extracted from a block bootstrapping approach.[29] In the latter case, the methodology is as follows:

- Equity (using the S&P 500 Index) and fixed-income (using constant maturity 10-year US government bonds) total returns are initially drawn from historical series observed between 1955 and August 2017. We first randomly pick one start date and then pick the length of the block chosen according to a (0,1) uniform distribution while the length of the draw is determined according to a (p) geometric distribution.[30]

- To make long-term expected returns more realistic, the returns of equity and of fixed income have been adjusted such that the median compound annual returns are, respectively, 7% and 3%.[31]

The same mean parameters are used for the i.i.d. simulation. Furthermore, the volatility estimate used in the i.i.d. simulations is obtained from the 1955–2017 period from which the data were extracted for the bootstrap methodology. Obviously, any return asymmetry that may be present in the bootstrapping data is lost in the i.i.d. data.

---

[29]Bootstrapping is any test that relies on random sampling with replacement. Block bootstrapping is used when the data are correlated. The methodology tries to replicate the correlation by resampling blocks of data instead of single observations.

[30]The parameter « p » is determined according to the following formula:

$$\frac{1}{\max(\text{Last significant lag}, 6)},$$

where the last significant lag is determined using the maximum last significant lag among the following regressions:

1. Equity return regressed on its 36 lags.
2. Square of equity return regressed on its 36 lags.
3. Fixed-income returns regressed on its 36 lags.
4. Square of fixed-income return regressed on its 36 lags.
5. The product of the two returns regressed on its 36 lags.

[31]The setting of long-term expected returns is discussed in Chapter 6.

The block bootstrap allows for maintaining the patterns of relative volatility and relative correlations that have been observed in the past. It also allows for expected return scenarios coherent with reasonable expectations. Hence, half the scenarios have annualized equity returns greater than 7% and half are lower. The same logic applies to fixed-income annualized returns. Using this approach, we generated 30,000 scenarios, and the same scenarios are used for all glide path configurations. An analysis of the process indicates that the length of each block of return data extracted ranges from a few months to nearly 200 months with an average of 32 months.[32] Therefore, many patterns of shocks and recoveries are being captured.

Because the horizon is 35 years, 36 glide path structures have been considered. The first glide path assumes a stable 60/40 allocation with annual rebalancing even though we are using monthly return data and a monthly savings contribution. The second glide path assumes a 90/10 allocation during the first year and a transition to a 60/40 allocation over a period of one year. The third glide path assumes a 90/10 allocation during the first two years and a transition to a 60/40 allocation over a period of two years.

This process continues until a maximum transition period of 10 years is reached. For example, the 10th glide path maintains a 90/10 allocation for 10 years, transitions to a 60/40 allocation after 10 more years, and remains at a stable 60/40 allocation for the last 15 years. The last glide path maintains a 90/10 allocation for 35 years, with no time left to transition to a 60/40 allocation.

Therefore, our 30,000 return scenarios of equity and fixed income have been applied to 36 glide path structures on two sets of data. The amounts of savings are identical to those used previously for John. In other words, if the allocation is 60/40 and the returns are stable at 7% for equity and 3% for fixed income, the end wealth will be exactly what we calculated previously: $775,096 (see Table 3.1). Our objective is to measure the level of end wealth in difficult market environments represented at low quantile levels (1.0%, 2.5%, 5.0%, 10.0%, and 25.0%) for each glide path and each dataset. In other words, the 1% quantile level represents the 300th-worst final wealth scenario out of 30,000. The $775,096 represents a reference point for comparison purposes.

Figure 3.10 illustrates, from left to right, the level of final wealth observed according to the number of years of risk taking and at various quantile levels from 1% to 25%. Panel A presents the results for the i.i.d. approach, and Panel B for the bootstrap approach.

---

[32]All simulations were coded in MATLAB.

Figure 3.10.   Expected Wealth after 35 Years at Different Quantile Levels According to Number of Years of Risk Taking

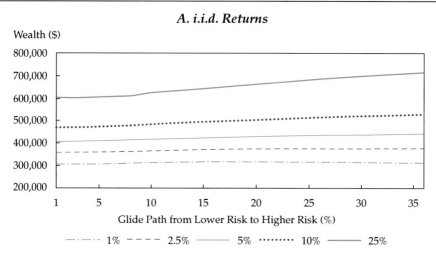

A. i.i.d. Returns

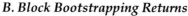

B. Block Bootstrapping Returns

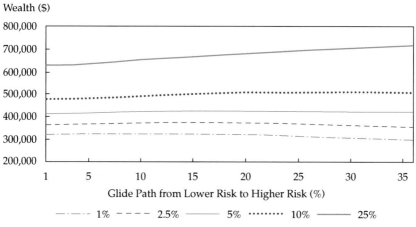

Bootstrap and i.i.d. results differ in two ways. When the number of years of risk taking is low (toward the left in the figures), the i.i.d. results lead to slightly lower levels of wealth at any quantile level. When the number of years of risk taking is high (toward the right in the figures), both datasets behave similarly at a higher quantile level, such as 25%. At lower quantile levels such as 1% and 2.5%, however, the bootstrap results would lead us to reduce the portfolio risk approximately 10 to 15 years before retirement, whereas the i.i.d. results would maintain the higher level of risk taking during the entire period.

The explanations for these results relate to some of the concepts discussed previously in this chapter. First, a higher level of risk taking should lead to greater wealth at higher quantile levels and lower levels of wealth at lower quantile levels. A wealth-smoothing effect occurs in the context of accumulation, however, which is implicitly a process that monetizes low-risk human capital wealth over time. This effect is reinforced by an implicit assumption of our simulation: the absence of correlation between capital market risk and income/human capital risk. The savings generated by John are stable in bull and bear markets. If income and capital market risk were highly correlated, the results could be different.

In the real world, portfolio wealth is subject to capital market risk, whereas human capital wealth is subject to the risk associated with an individual's ability to maintain savings effort. Fortunately, for many individuals, the risk of the former is likely greater than the risk of the latter. At one extreme, the human capital wealth of a tenured college professor is subject to low human capital risk. Some individuals may often change jobs but remain employed for much of their lives because their skill is in demand. Others may have challenges staying employed or generating a stable income.

Finally, self-employed households may have income that is highly volatile and correlated with equity returns. However, Cocco, Gomes, and Maenhout (2005) estimate relatively low correlations between income shocks and risky asset returns, supporting the argument for a greater allocation to risk assets early on.[33] Hence, the discount rate reflecting labor income risk varies across individuals depending on their education level, sector of activity, skill set, professionalism, and other factors.

To further clarify the effects of integrating human capital into the asset allocation decision, **Figure 3.11** illustrates the evolution of John's portfolio wealth using the same scenario as that reported in Chapter 2, which assumed a stable 60% allocation to equity (blue line) and certainty of returns. It also reports the present value of John's savings attributed to his human capital wealth (green line) using a low discount rate like that of a fixed-income asset. Using a low discount rate implies that John's ability to maintain his work income and savings until retirement is high and the correlation to capital market risk is low. As we would expect, John's portfolio wealth is very small initially but grows over time. Similarly, his human capital wealth is very high initially but decreases as he approaches retirement.

---

[33]Irlam (2017) also finds low correlations between labor income and equity markets.

Figure 3.11. Evolution of Portfolio and Human Capital Wealth and of Effective Exposure to Equity

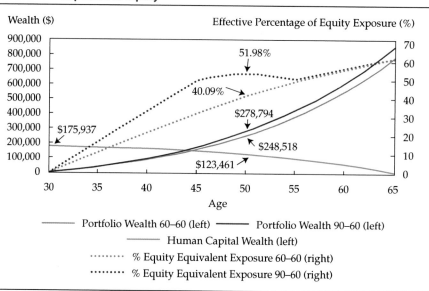

The dotted blue line illustrates the effective equity exposure as a percentage of the total of John's "life wealth" for the stable 60% asset allocation. For example, when John makes his first monthly savings contribution of $500, the value of his human capital is $175,937 (counting only the savings part of future labor income). Because the allocation to equity within the portfolio is 60%, John's effective exposure to equity is only 0.17%, or ($500 × 60%)/($500 + $175,937). When John reaches age 50, however, his portfolio wealth has increased to $248,518 and his human capital, as defined earlier, has declined to $123,461. Hence, his effective exposure to equity is then 40.09% – ($248,518 × 60%)/($248,518 + $123,461). Under this scenario, John's effective equity exposure will peak at 60% when he retires and has no human capital wealth left.

The fact that the effective exposure to equity is far less than the level targeted within the investment portfolio explains why several authors argue that investors should not only consider their human capital wealth as part of their allocation process but also use leverage to maintain a constant allocation against their total wealth, consisting of portfolio capital plus human capital. For example, Ayres and Nalebuff (2010) emphasize the role of the present value of lifetime savings, which they define as the sum of portfolio wealth and the savings part of human capital wealth. They argue that savers should have a constant asset allocation relative to lifetime savings, which implies a leveraged position in stocks when investors have low current savings and much higher human capital wealth.

Although we do not support using leverage for the average investor, the concept of targeting a more stable effective allocation to equity supports the principle of glide paths with a declining equity allocation. For example, Figure 3.11 also presents the evolution of John's portfolio wealth assuming a 90% equity allocation until age 50 and transitioning to a 60% equity allocation by age 60. The dotted red line presents the effective equity allocation. ("Effective" here means "including the savings part of human capital in the total portfolio.") The declining glide path allows John to achieve a higher effective equity allocation earlier, such as 51.98% at age 50, and maintain a more stable effective allocation in the last two decades, although the glide path could be calibrated more efficiently in the latter years to achieve an even more stable effective equity exposure.

If we understand the smoothing effect of human capital on wealth accumulation and consider that this effect becomes less important as the ratio of human capital to portfolio wealth declines, the glide path recommended to an individual who started saving 20 years before retirement should differ from the glide path recommended to an individual who started saving 35 years before retirement, even if both individuals are the same number of years from retirement.

Other simulations (not shown) indicate that an individual starting to save late could tolerate a higher level of risk taking for slightly longer than an investor who has already accumulated significant retirement wealth. This result is intuitive because the smoothing effect of accumulation on wealth is more significant at the beginning of accumulation than later. It implies that for a given investment horizon, if portfolio wealth has increased faster than expected, allocation to risky assets should be reduced,[34] and vice versa. Similarly, an investor whose savings capabilities increase more than expected could tolerate a higher level of portfolio equity exposure.

This discussion does not explain why the two return sampling methodologies (i.i.d. versus bootstrapping) lead to different levels of wealth (see Figure 3.10). Final wealth is usually lower using the i.i.d. method when the number of years of risk taking is low and higher when it is high. Because both sets of simulations are based on equity and fixed-income distributions having similar parameters for the first two moments (mean and standard deviation), the different results for the bootstrap approach must be explained by the other moments such as return asymmetry, by the autocorrelation of returns—such

---

[34]As indicated in Campbell (2017).

as long-run mean reversion—or by the correlation between equity and fixed income. They could also be explained by the time-varying volatility and correlations of the bootstrap data. For example, our data return series have a negative asymmetry, positive autocorrelations using monthly data, and negative autocorrelations using yearly data, indicative of longer-term price reversals. Although wealth levels are greater using the bootstrap data when the number of years of risk taking is lower, this fact does not change the observation that higher risk is sustainable. Finally, lower and declining levels of wealth when the number of years of risk taking is higher are likely explained by the negative asymmetry of equity returns.

3.7. Adjusting Glide Paths Dynamically

Incorporating human capital into the thinking about the accumulation process leads one to recommend a high level of equity exposure in the initial years. The relative importance of human capital and portfolio capital dictates how long a higher level of risk should be maintained and when a transition to a lower level of risk should start. Once portfolio capital becomes significant and the retirement horizon nears, other considerations such as individual risk aversion and drawdown risks become even more relevant. Although the glide path analyzed in Section 3.6 may represent an appropriate long-term solution in a general context that ignores information updates, is it possible to improve the distribution of expected outcomes using information updates?

Giron, Martellini, Milhau, Mulvey, and Suri (2018) propose a simple and efficient asset allocation strategy inspired by the CPPI method and compatible with a glide path approach. The strategy is a form of dynamic insurance in which the effective allocation to risky assets is determined by the distance between the current level of wealth and a floor level of wealth required to satisfy an essential yet affordable retirement income level. This distance sets the risk budget (RB_t) as follows:

$$RB_t = 1 - \frac{F_t}{W_t},$$

Eq. 3.2

where F_t is the floor below which wealth should not fall at time t (such as monthly) and W_t is the current level of wealth. If the current level of wealth is equal to or below the floor, no investment in risky assets would be allowed. This approach is consistent with the types of utility functions that will be recommended in Chapters 6 and 8 to evaluate the success of a retirement strategy or to optimize this strategy. As with traditional CPPI methodologies, the exposure to risky assets (w_t) is a multiple (m) of this risk budget. Hence,

$$w_t = m \times RB_t.$$ Eq. 3.3

Giron et al. (2018) apply the CPPI approach with two nuances, however. First, it is applied in the context of glide paths. Second, the approach is not designed to guarantee a minimum level of retirement income floor but to preserve a specific percentage of the wealth accumulated on a periodic basis (such as at the beginning of each calendar year). In other words, the floor level is reset every year, allowing the allocation to risky assets to revert to the allocation recommended in the glide path at the time of each reset.

The dynamic multiple (m_n) that Giron et al. (2018) recommend is derived from the allocation to the risky portfolio according to the glide path at the beginning of year n (TDF_{n-1}) and by the percentage of the purchasing power to be secured on a yearly basis (δ_{ess}).

$$m_n = \frac{TDF_{n-1}}{1 - \delta_{ess}}.$$ Eq. 3.4

For example, assuming the glide path recommends a 90% allocation to equity and the investor has an objective to preserve at least 80% of the wealth accumulated on a yearly basis, the equity multiple would be 4.5 or 90%/(1 – 0.80). Similarly, a 60% allocation to equity would lead to a 3.0 multiple. In this book, however, we make this calculation on a monthly basis.

Furthermore, a specific methodology must be established to determine the appropriate floor level (F). Many methodologies could be designed. In *Secure Retirement*, the floor level each month during a calendar year is established by multiplying the total wealth recorded at the beginning of the year (because of the annual reset) by δ_{ess} and adjusting each of the following 12 months by the variation in wealth that should be expected, assuming the expected new savings cash flows and a median portfolio return. This floor level is then compared with the current level of wealth (W_t) to determine the risk budget using Equation 3.2.

Although more detailed results are not presented here until Chapter 8, the Giron et al. (2018) strategy was replicated and tested with the example of John. Because of high portfolio turnover, we also tested a version of this strategy where the allocation to risky assets was bounded to a minimum of either 50% or 60% of the allocation recommended by the static glide path.

Figure 3.12.   Allocation to Risky Assets Using a Dynamic (CPPI) Process

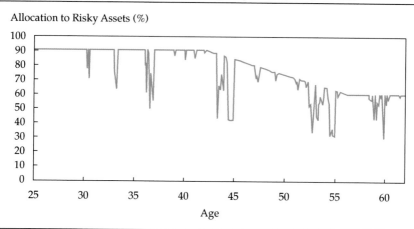

Figure 3.12 illustrates the effective allocation to risk assets for a single run of a Monte Carlo simulation assuming a 50% of glide path lower limit. Significant allocation change can still result from applying this approach, but the average decline in allocation over the entire period remains relatively small.

The strategy is highly efficient. The comprehensive case study in Chapter 8 demonstrates that the distributions of expected retirement income according to the scenario analyses for the dynamic glide paths with a zero or 50% lower-bound limit (as defined in the previous paragraph) stochastically dominate the static glide path approach. Furthermore, the average worst calendar year drawdowns across all scenarios were 30% less for the 50% lower-bound version and 35% less for the 0% lower-bound version than those of the static glide path. The 60% lower limit led to a similar distribution of expected retirement income, but the average of worst calendar year drawdowns was still lower by 25%. Disciplined risk management pays. The process is helpful not only during the initial stage of accumulation but also during the period of transition toward decumulation. In Chapter 4, we also evaluate the benefits of this approach during the decumulation period.

3.8.   Conclusion

By including human capital in the "life wealth" portfolio, we provide evidentiary support for maintaining a higher level of risk early and transitioning toward a lower level of risk as retirement approaches. Although it is possible to design a static default glide path that could be adequate for most investors, a more efficient solution is to adapt the risk level and glide path using information updates about performance or the ratio of portfolio capital to total capital. For example, investors who start saving later should have a different glide path than those who started saving early.

The results of the Monte Carlo simulations using i.i.d. data and bootstrap data are not that dissimilar. The i.i.d. data support maintaining a higher level of risk closer to retirement, however. Prudence suggests we should attribute more relevance to the bootstrap simulations that integrate dynamic changes in volatility and correlation. Also, we should remember a main argument of Pastor and Stambaugh (2011): We do not know the true expected returns of asset classes. Therefore, we may be underestimating portfolio risk. In this context, what truly matters is to use reasonable return expectations when calibrating our retirement model and to review these expectations carefully and periodically.

Combining (1) our understanding of how human capital's effect on portfolio risk influences the design of a static default glide path with (2) a dynamic strategy that adapts to the level of excess wealth, whether positive or negative, may lead to an even more efficient investment strategy.

Finally, it is useful to present the similarities between the conclusions reached thus far in Chapter 3 and the principles that support the management of the Canadian and Quebec Social Security systems. Both systems are fully or nearly fully funded. Both regimes' long-term liabilities are supported in part by portfolios of assets managed by Canada Pension Plan (CPP) outside of Quebec and Caisse de Dépôt (CDP) in Quebec. These portfolios cover no more than 20% to 25% of expected liabilities. The balance of 75% to 80% is to be met by participants' future Social Security contributions, a component of Canada's national human capital wealth.

The portfolios of assets in both regimes, excluding the human capital component, are managed with a higher level of risk taking than most traditional defined benefit plans. Fewer than 15% to 20% of assets are invested in fixed income. Equity and alternative assets such as real estate, infrastructure, and private equity account for most of the allocation. The higher level of risk taking within these portfolios is justified by the fact that participants are continuously paying financial contributions into the system. These contributions depend on three main factors: demography, level of employment, and workers' compensation. These aspects are assumed to be more predictable and

Figure 3.13. Rate of Return of the QPP Fund and Increase in QPP Total Contribution Earnings (1992–2016)

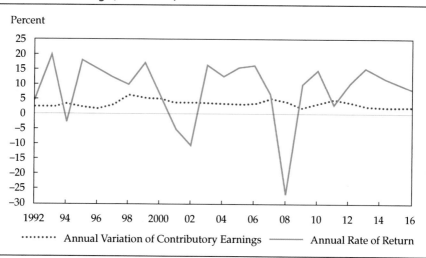

Source: Data from Retraite Québec.

therefore less risky than financial markets.[35] **Figure 3.13**, from an internal document of Retraite Québec,[36] the entity responsible for administering the Social Security system in Quebec, compares the volatility of work income and of portfolio returns. It is used to support the investment policy of investing 80% of the portfolio in equity, infrastructure, real estate, and private equity. The remainder is allocated to fixed income.

The management teams of both regimes are familiar with the concepts discussed in this chapter. The principles that apply to managing Social Security in Canada can be extended to managing individual retirement plans, whether within a 401(k) plan or in IRAs. Furthermore, the two Canadian regimes have put in place a set of rules designed to resolve underfunding

---

[35]The US Social Security system is underfunded, a topic discussed in Chapter 4. Furthermore, the assets within the US Social Security Trust Fund are entirely invested in special purpose Treasury securities. Finally, there is no mechanism in place to resolve the underfunding challenge, which can potentially affect Social Security payments within two decades. Congress must act preventively; otherwise, payments will have to be reduced. The situation is not as dire as this wording suggests if actions are taken quickly. The combination of a small tax increase and a modest cut in benefits (mostly by raising the full retirement age further) will cause the Social Security Trust Fund to be drawn down, but not extinguished, as baby boomers complete their retirements. After the baby boomers die, the country's average population age will be younger again, and Social Security will operate at a profit.

[36]The author is a member of the board of Retraite-Québec and president of its Investment Committee.

issues if they were eventually to occur—for example, because of a catastrophic market environment. The same prudence and set of rules can and should be incorporated in the design of private retirement solutions, as will be shown in several chapters of *Secure Retirement*. For example, Chapters 4, 5, 6, and 8 will raise the importance of (1) annuities and circumstances in which they may be most warranted, (2) the need for a decumulation engine that can reasonably adapt planned retirement income to unfavorable changes in economic circumstances, and (3) carefully and periodically evaluating whether changes to the savings plan and/or the planned retirement date are required.

4. Understanding the Decumulation Period

The decumulation phase presents even greater risk challenges than the accumulation phase. As individuals retire, their human capital wealth falls to zero or toward a much lower level, assuming they remain employed in some fashion. Therefore, the effective exposure to risky assets is no longer being reduced by human capital wealth to the extent that such wealth can be regarded as safe or of low variance. In principle, the level of risk taking within the portfolio should be reduced in such circumstances. Maintaining a low-risk portfolio for two decades or more, and consequently having a low expected return, can significantly affect the level and/or sustainability of retirement income.

Furthermore, individuals approaching their planned retirement age may be able to postpone retiring if unfavorable and unexpected circumstances occur. On the other hand, reentering the job market may be more difficult once they are retired. Retirees have less income flexibility. Consequently, a scenario in which retirement occurs too soon must be avoided. Finally, although individuals may have some control over retirement timing, their health and longevity remain uncertain. Being wrong about longevity and unlucky with respect to health issues can have disastrous consequences, depending on access to health care services, long-term care insurance, and quality of insurance coverage. Chapter 4 aims to expose the challenges associated with the decumulation phase and to introduce appropriate solutions to the low return expectations of traditional retirement strategies as well as the higher level of risk associated with the decumulation process. We also take this opportunity to explain some of the behavioral pitfalls associated with decumulation, a line of thought further refined in upcoming chapters. Chapter 4 assumes the decision to retire has already been made. The transition between accumulation and decumulation is addressed in Chapter 5.

4.1. Decumulation Is Riskier Than Accumulation

Two reasons explain why financial risk is usually greatest at the exact moment retirement begins. First, although our lifespan is unknown, the present value of expected income needs is highest at the moment of retirement.[37] Second, once an individual retires, market volatility no longer benefits the portfolio

---

[37]This statement assumes that significant expenses that could not be foreseen as of retirement, such as health care costs related to a severe illness, do not happen.

as it did in the initial part of the accumulation process. The reverse is occurring as the retirees draws income from the investment return and capital of their portfolio, so the savings rate is negative. The greater the market correction and the slower the recovery, the worse the effect on retirement income sustainability.

Table 4.1 illustrates the effects of an equity shock occurring in the first month of retirement. The base scenario assumes a portfolio with an initial value of $100,000 and a yearly retirement income equal to 5% of the initial amount, payable monthly at month end and subject to a 2% cost-of-living adjustment (COLA) once a year, or $417 per month initially. The portfolio is invested 60% in equity and 40% in fixed income, rebalanced monthly, with an expected yearly return of 5.4%. The table is designed to compare the end wealth after five years of a stable return scenario against other scenarios involving different equity shocks (either −20% or −40%) and different recovery patterns, such as

- a no-recovery scenario;

- a complete portfolio recovery spread evenly over the first year;

- a complete portfolio recovery spread evenly over the first five years; and

- a recovery occurring in the last four years, a scenario that assumes a 0% portfolio return from Months 2 to 12.

- A complete portfolio recovery occurring gradually within the first year, in which retirees do not rebalance their portfolios until the equity recovery is complete.

Table 4.1. Ending Wealth after Five Years Following an Equity Correction

	20% Equity Correction		40% Equity Correction	
	End Wealth	Percentage below Base	End Wealth	Percentage below Base
Base scenario	$100,443		$100,443	
No recovery	84,460	−15.9%	68,919	−31.4%
Recovery within one year	100,004	−0.4	99,464	−1.0
Recovery within five years	98,353	−2.1	95,784	−4.6
Delayed recovery	97,157	−3.3	93,965	−6.4
No rebalancing during recovery	91,565	−8.8	81,212	−19.1

no-recovery scenario implies that the annualized return over five years is 2.67% when assuming an equity shock of –20% and is –0.29% when assuming an equity shock of –40%. All other scenarios assume full recovery, so the annualized portfolio return is 5.4%.

Unsurprisingly, all equity shock scenarios lead to lower wealth than the base scenario, although the severity of the wealth decline varies significantly. A no-recovery scenario is obviously the worst case, but we are interested in evaluating the effect of different return patterns on the ending wealth level.

For example, a –20% equity shock followed by a full portfolio recovery within 12 months reduces ending wealth by only 0.4%. A slower recovery, such as within five years, further reduces ending wealth by 2.1%, and a delayed recovery reduces it by 3.3%. An equity shock twice as large has about twice the impact. Although an equity shock, even followed by a recovery, is not a pleasant outcome, it is not as dramatically bad as other possible outcomes. One of the biggest risks associated with a return shock is the possibility that the portfolio may not be rebalanced. In this last situation, the wealth loss is –8.8% and –19.1%, respectively, for the two equity shock scenarios.

An implicit assumption of most investment strategies is that the portfolio is periodically rebalanced. **Table 4.2** illustrates the effect of rebalancing following an equity decline of 40% as in Table 4.1 and assuming the fixed-income return remains stable.[38]

Table 4.2. Impact of Equity Shock on Rebalancing

	Portfolio Wealth	Equity	Fixed Income
Initial wealth	$100,000	$60,000	$40,000
Return month 1	–23.90%	–40.00%	0.25%
Wealth month end	$76,100	$36,000	$40,100
Monthly retirement income	$416.67		
Wealth after retirement income			
No rebalancing	$75,683	$35,803	$39,880
With rebalancing	$75,683	$45,410	$30,273

[38]Lussier (2013) investigated the benefits of calendar-, trigger-, and volatility-based rebalancing approaches. The approach assumed in this current example is monthly calendar rebalancing. However, Lussier and other authors find that less frequent rebalancing intervals, such as twice a year, can be even more efficient because this allows the portfolio either to benefit from favorable short-term positive market momentum because of rising exposure to performing assets or to reduce the impact of unfavorable short-term negative market momentum because of declining exposure to losing assets.

After one month, total wealth has been reduced to $76,100 and will be further reduced to $75,683 after the first retirement-income payment. The retiree must then decide whether to rebalance the portfolio. She may choose not to rebalance; in this case, the allocation to equity is no longer 60%. It is reduced to 47.3%. If the portfolio is rebalanced, the retiree must sell approximately $9,607 of fixed income to acquire equity. If she does not rebalance, the portfolio will not fully benefit from the equity return recovery.

Although conceptually easy, rebalancing during a difficult market environment is emotionally challenging. Consider the behavior of equity markets between March 2004 and February 2014. The annualized performance of equity markets between March 2004 and February 2009 was –7.3%, a poor performance largely attributable to the –43.6% equity return in the final 12 months during the liquidity crisis. Had an investor remained invested in the equity market for 5 more years, his annualized equity performance for this 10-year period would have been a respectable +7.6% because of the strong recovery that followed. Assume, however, that this investor panicked in February 2009, sold his equity to invest in cash, and reentered the equity markets only a year later. Although he was invested in equity for 9 out of 10 years, his annualized return would have been only 2.9%. Maintaining a strong equity exposure and rebalancing a portfolio in early 2009, after months of disastrous financial events not seen in decades, required courage and discipline, traits that even many investment professionals did not display.

The fear of rebalancing in crisis time is always an issue, but the fear is even greater during decumulation because the retiree is no longer adding to savings or is adding much less than during the accumulation phase. It is important to have an investment policy that is properly risk calibrated and to put in place processes that ensure its implementation. It is also important to design retirement strategies and processes that help manage those fears.

4.2. Impact of Return Shocks on Sustainability of Retirement Income

Let us reconsider the case of John. In our base scenario, John had accumulated portfolio wealth of $775,096 as of retirement. Assuming he maintains a 60/40 allocation generating a stable annual return of 5.4%, John could receive an annual retirement income of $53,412 paid monthly and adjusted annually to reflect a 2% COLA, and he could maintain this income for 20 years, until he reaches age 85. We can ask, however, how equity shocks would affect the sustainability of John's planned retirement income. Assume equity shocks of either –20% or –40% that can occur at any time between ages 65 and 85. In both cases, three recovery scenarios are considered: no recovery, a 12-month recovery delayed by 12 months, and a 60-month recovery delayed by 12 months.

Figure 4.1 illustrates on the vertical axis the decline in sustainability of retirement income measured in years for each of the two equity shock levels. Panel A shows that an equity correction of −20% with no recovery occurring early in retirement can amputate the sustainability of expected income by more than three years. The reduction is greater than six years for a −40% equity correction. As expected, the effect lessens if the correction occurs later—about half as much if it occurs after 8.5 years. An early shock with

---

Figure 4.1. Impact of an Equity Shock on Income Sustainability in Years According to the Timing of Shock

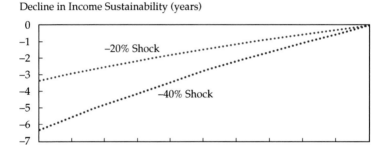

A. No Recovery

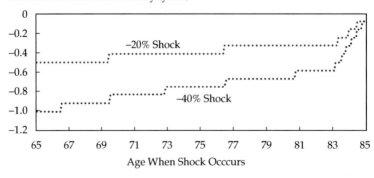

B. 12 Month Delay/12 Month Recovery

(Continued)

Figure 4.1. **Impact of an Equity Shock on Income Sustainability in Years According to the Timing of Shock** *(Continued)*

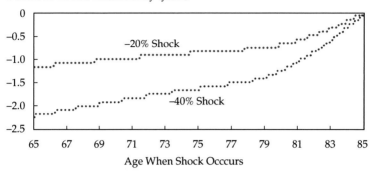

C. 12 Month Delay/60 Month Recovery

Decline in Income Sustainability (years)

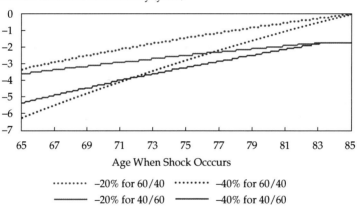

D. No Recovery 60/40 versus 40/60 Allocation

Decline in Income Sustainability (years)

no recovery can have significant consequences but implies that the expected long-term portfolio return is much less than 5.4%. Over 20 years, the annualized equity return assuming a –20% (–40%) equity correction would be 4.71% (3.95%), a relatively low long-term return assumption.

Panel B presents the same information as Panel A but assumes a full recovery after 24 months, consisting of a 12-month delay and a 12-month recovery. The effect is not significant if one assumes the retiree has a rebalanced portfolio. Panel C illustrates an even slower recovery over a period of six years. The impact of a –40% equity shock is relatively significant if it occurs in the initial years of retirement.

Two issues must be considered during the decumulation process. Being wrong about the long-term portfolio return has significant consequences. It is important to have realistic expectations about average long-term returns. Second, the consequence of a market correction with recovery can often be tolerated if the portfolio is rebalanced. However, we must still deal with the stress retirees will suffer if a financial crisis occurs during the decumulation phase, especially if it occurs early.

Before we consider the options available to help manage this concern, could the answer be to maintain a low-risk portfolio during the decumulation process? Panel D illustrates that a low-risk portfolio may not be the most efficient long-term solution. The figure compares the impact of an equity shock assuming a 60/40 allocation, as in Panel A, with the impact of the same shock assuming a 40/60 allocation. Unless the shock is significant and occurs early, a low-risk portfolio does not offer better income protection. The lesser impact of the equity shock on portfolio returns in the case of a 40/60 portfolio is neutralized by the lower expected return during all other months.

Nevertheless, most glide path products advocate an equity allocation ranging between 40% and 55% as of retirement, between 30% to 40% 10 years after retirement, and declining further to between 24% and 40% after 20 years and beyond. The effect of a conservative glide path on expected income can be significant. For example, assuming identical wealth at retirement, stable returns, and a 60/40 allocation, a retiree calibrating withdrawals to have enough capital until age 85 would run out of money 21 months earlier with a 40/60 allocation. The effect of lower returns becomes even more unfavorable if greater longevity is assumed. For example, if the retiree calibrated her withdrawals for age 90, she would run out of capital 33 months earlier. At age 95, it would be 48 months. Therefore, the pattern of returns and the level of returns matter greatly in decumulation.

Although a low-equity allocation may be warranted to reduce financial risk and help manage fears, are there mitigating aspects? Also, how do we account for the risk that we may live longer than average life expectancy indicates? To answer these questions, we must first increase our understanding of life expectancy, of annuities, and of the important role of Social Security for most retirees.

4.3. Understanding Life Expectancy

Four basic principles related to life expectancy must be considered in the retirement-planning phase:

- On average, women live longer than men.

- On average, the longer you have lived, the older the age you are expected to reach.

- Longevity is uncertain. Although we can estimate longevity, there remains considerable uncertainty regarding this estimate.

- Considerable differences in life expectancy exist among industrialized countries and even within a country according to socioeconomic status.

4.3.1. Women Live Longer.

According to research by Assari (2017) at the University of Michigan, "Women experience higher stress, more chronic disease, more depression, more anxiety and are more likely to be victims of violence." Yet, without exception, women live longer than men in all countries. In the United States, the life expectancy of men at birth is nearly four years less than that of women.[39] Several factors explain this observation, including the following:

- Women have biological advantages that put them at a lesser risk than men of developing cardiovascular issues.

- Women are more health aware and better communicate their problems, which helps the process of diagnosis.

- Women engage less in risky behavior.

- Men are more likely to commit suicide.

In this book, we take for granted that women live longer than men and concentrate on the implication of this fact. Although the social safety net does not discriminate based on this evidence—for example, women do not receive lower Social Security payments than men even though they are expected to live longer on average—this longevity difference will affect other aspects of retirement income for women, such as the cost of purchasing an annuity outside of an employer-sponsored qualified plan. Currently US laws do not allow gender discrimination in such a plan.[40]

4.3.2. The Longer You Have Lived, the Older the Age You Are Expected to Reach.

Life expectancy is not independent of how old you already are. For example, although the life expectancy of women at birth

---

[39]Social Security, Actuarial Life Table, "Periodic Life Table 2014."

[40]According to Charles E. Lynch (2012) of Retirement Management Services: "Employer-sponsored qualified plans offering annuities must abide by Equal Employment Opportunity Commission (EEOC) rules, which state that 'the employer will be liable for sex discrimination if it provides different coverage to employees of each gender on the basis of gender.' So, a $100,000 lump sum would have to provide the same monthly pension regardless of the gender of the retiree. Compared to the annuity market outside of 401(k) plans, a gender-neutral annuity within a 401(k) plan would give men too little per month and women too much for the same lump sum conversion."

Figure 4.2.   Expected Longevity of Males and Females Relative to Current Age

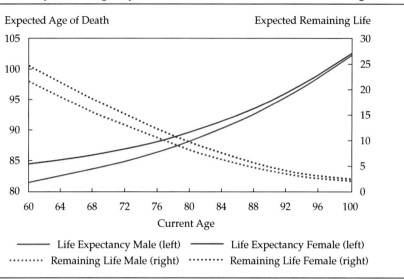

Expected Age of Death   Expected Remaining Life

———— Life Expectancy Male (left)   ———— Life Expectancy Female (left)
········· Remaining Life Male (right)   ········· Remaining Life Female (right)

is 81.6 years, it is, respectively, 85.9 and 90 years for 65-year-old and 80-year-old women. **Figure 4.2** presents on the left axis the life expectancy of men and women in the United States based on their current age, starting with age 60.

Life expectancy at birth is irrelevant to the average individual planning for retirement. As individuals near retirement, their expected longevity is already several years longer than that initial projection. Furthermore, as years pass, retirees must adjust to the possibility that each passing year increases their expected age of death. Life expectancy increases at a decreasing rate as we age, however. The right-hand axis of Figure 4.2 indicates how many more years the average man and women are expected to live for a given current age. This illustration shows that, although aging increases the *total* number of years we are expected to live, it also reduces the *remaining* number of years the average man or woman is expected to live.

4.3.3. Longevity Is Uncertain. A retirement strategy cannot be designed simply based on average life expectancy. **Figure 4.3**, Panel A indicates the likelihood that a man or woman age 65 or 80 will live to age 85 or older.

At age 65, men have a 22% probability of living to 90. For women at the same age, the probability is 36%. Once men and women reach age 80, however, these probabilities rise to 36% and 46%, respectively. A retirement

Figure 4.3. Longevity Likelihood and Probabilities

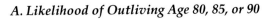

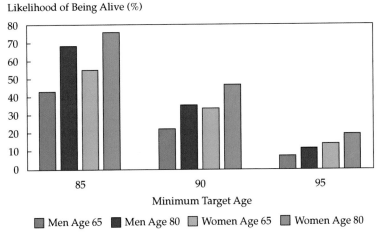

A. Likelihood of Outliving Age 80, 85, or 90

Likelihood of Being Alive (%)

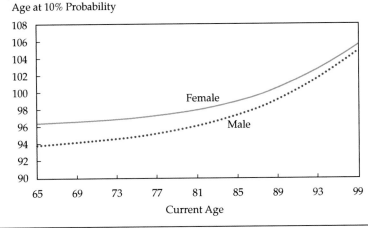

B. Expected Longevity When Probability of Survival Is Approximately 10%

Age at 10% Probability

plan must account and adjust for the possibility that we may live considerably longer than expected.

Aging also reduces the uncertainty about how many more years we should be expected to live. As an example, the fact that we are 85 years of age and no longer 65 years of age does not increase substantially the likelihood that we will live to be 120. Panel B illustrates, for any current age between 65 and 100, the age at which the probability of survival is approximately 10%. The figure shows the data separately for women and men. Women age 65 have a

67

10% probability of living beyond age 96. Once they are 90 years old, however, they have a 10% probability of living beyond 100. Therefore, when a retiree is 65, we must plan for the possibility that he or she may live two to three decades. When this individual reaches age 90, we can plan for a shorter horizon. This information will help to dynamically calibrate a retirement strategy as the retiree ages.

4.3.4. Life Expectancy Varies across a Country and across Socioeconomic Groups within a Country.
The citizens of many countries have greater life expectancies than those in the United States. **Table 4.3** presents the life expectancy at birth and as of age 65 for men and women across several countries.

The United States ranks 31st in the world in life expectancy at birth and 28th for individuals age 65. Japan is first overall. Although studies confirm that the US disadvantage extends across all ages, much of the difference can be explained by a higher incidence of death at a young age. For example, a study by Fenelon, Chen, and Baker (2016) shows that, respectively, 50% and 20% of the difference in life expectancy of US men and women relative to other industrialized countries can be explained by a greater level of motor vehicle traffic crashes, homicide- and firearm-related injuries, drug poisoning, pregnancy complications, and infant mortality. There is also a higher prevalence of preterm births, obesity, and diabetes during childhood.

These factors matter less, however, to the life expectancy of individuals already 65 years old. For example, although the average differences in life expectancy at birth for men and women between Canada and the United States are, respectively, 3.3 years and 2.5 years, they are, respectively, 1.1 and 1.2 years at age 65 because the aforementioned factors have less effect

Table 4.3. Life Expectancy in Years in Four Countries

	At Birth		Age 65	
	Men	Women	Men	Women
United States	76.9	81.6	83.3	85.9
Canada	80.2	84.1	84.4	87.1
United Kingdom	79.4	83.0	83.7	86.0
Japan	80.5	86.8	84.4	89.2

Note: Life expectancy data for the United States may differ from that reported previously because it originates from a different source.
Source: World Health Organization (www.worldlifeexpectancy.com/world-life-expectancy-map) 2015 data.

on individuals who have already reached age 65. Still, a gap remains and has been investigated in many studies (e.g., Avendano and Kawachi 2014). For example, the United States has a greater level of mortality attributed to infectious diseases, ischemic heart diseases, diabetes, and respiratory issues (women only).

Lifestyle and socioeconomic or public policy issues have been identified among the main culprits, but life expectancy remains a complex and multidimensional issue. For example, studies show that the quality of care in the United States may not be the cause—indeed, survival rates for several chronic conditions may be better in the United States than in other high-income countries—but insured as well as uninsured Americans experience poorer health than Europeans. Although this US health disadvantage appears to characterize all socioeconomic classes, it is likely more prevalent among the poor and least educated. Access to health care compared with other industrialized countries appears to be a factor.

This set of circumstances implies that the mortality tables used to design and calibrate public pension plans such as Social Security and private defined benefit plans may not be appropriate to a specific investor/retiree. Each of us is unique. Some of our health advantages or disadvantages over others may be driven by genetics or socioeconomic status, attributed to our own behavior, or simply affected by good or bad luck. Brown and McDaid (2003) found 12 variables that were significant in post-retirement mortality analysis: age, alcohol use, education, gender, health behavior (lifestyle and use of health services), income, marital status, obesity, occupation, race and ethnicity, religion (participation), and smoking. Furthermore, Brown and Scahill (2010) indicate that "for some variables, the mortality profile of the preferred risks (e.g., high education, high income) is less than 50% of the mortality of the impaired risks (e.g., low education, low income)." They found the mortality rates for males at ages up to 64 and females at ages up to 60 that are in the top quartile of income to be half the rates of those in the bottom quartile of income. Although we concentrate in this chapter on the life expectancy of the average man or woman, we come back to the issue of "mortality distinctiveness" in Chapter 7.

4.4. Understanding Annuities

Annuities are contracts issued by insurance companies that provide a stream of regular income either immediately or at some point in the future in exchange for a lump sum payment or series of payments. Our interest lies in single premium immediate annuities (SPIAs), which pay a steady income to start now for as long as you live in exchange for a single payment; and

single premium deferred annuities (SPDAs), which pay such an income starting at a later predetermined date.[41] For example, assume that a $100,000
annuity contract purchased at age 65 offers an immediate and annual payout
paid monthly of 6.37% with no COLA. Therefore, the annuity would pay an
income of $530.33 per month ($100,000 × 0.0637/12) starting now for life.

Although annuities may seem to be complex instruments, the price of an
annuity is simply the present value of an expected stream of cash flows just
like any other financial product. Five sets of parameters need to be considered:

- The annuity payment received periodically (AP_t). In this case, the amount
  is fixed every month at $530.33.

- The survival probabilities of the annuity's beneficiary(ies) at each period
  (SP_t), estimated from actuarial tables.

- The discount factor used for the present value of each annuity payment
  (DF_t).

- The annuity features incorporated in the contract, such as COLA, minimum guaranteed period in the event of early death, or whether the contract covers a single annuitant or a couple (joint life). The annuity features
  can affect both the annuity payment and the probability of that payment.
  For example, an annuity with a 10-year certain feature implies the payout
  will be made by the insurer in the first 10 years whether the annuitant is
  alive or has died (in which case the payout is made to the annuitant's beneficiaries). Furthermore, a joint life annuity is likely to pay for a longer time.

- The overhead costs of the insurer. These consist of upfront sales charges,[42]
  as well as ongoing administration and profit charges.

- If we ignore the overhead costs for now, the cost of an annuity can be
  summarized as

$$\text{Cost annuity} = \sum_{t=1}^{T} APt \times SPt \times DFt. \qquad \text{Eq. 4.1}$$

Equation 4.1 has several implications:

- Annuities are more expensive for women than for men, implying a lower
  payout rate, because women usually have higher survival probabilities.
  These instruments are even more expensive if they are joint annuities

---

[41]The relevance of variable annuities is discussed in Chapter 6.
[42]According to immediateannuities.com/annuity-commissions/ these sales charge vary between
1% and 5% for SPIAs and SPDAs. We assumed charges of 3% in our models.

purchased by a couple, implying that the annuity pays if either one of the two annuitants is alive.

- Annuities are more expensive and, as such, have a lower payout rate when interest rates and corporate credit spreads are lower, implying that the discount factor is higher. Insurance companies invest the annuity premium in a fixed-income portfolio that incorporates government and corporate securities.

- The cost of an annuity depends on the annuity payment features:

  - The cost is greater, implying a lower initial payout rate, if the annuity contract incorporates a COLA that will raise the annuity payment over time.

  - The cost is greater, implying a lower payout rate, if the annuity payment is guaranteed for a specific period. For example, if the payment of $530.33 in the previous example is guaranteed for 10 years or 120 months, the survival probability is replaced by 100% for those first 120 months because the payments are guaranteed to be made to the successor(s) whether the annuitant is alive or not.

  - The cost is greater, implying a lower initial payout rate, if the annuity contract starts paying at a younger age, such as 60 instead of 65, because more annuity payments are expected to be made and the survival probabilities associated with those payments are higher.

  - The cost is less, implying a higher payout rate, if the annuity is deferred. A deferred annuity starts paying at a predetermined future date. The payout rate is higher because the annuitant will not receive any payment during the deferred period, implying the first payouts to be made are further affected by the time value of money and are associated with lower survival probabilities.

Annuities vary in price across insurers. Insurers may use different mortality tables, have investment portfolios that lead to different discount factors, and may be less or more commercially aggressive in terms of pricing at different points in time.[43] In this chapter, we use the model described in

---

[43]For example, the website immediatennuities.com provides annuity pricing from the top insurers. When comparing the best payout of a life annuity and of a life annuity 10-year certain, the payout could almost be identical even though the annuity with the 10-year certain payout should be more expensive and have a lower payout. The two quotes are likely from different companies that use different valuation terms. Therefore, it is important to shop for annuities across insurance providers.

Equation 4.1 but adjusted for upfront and ongoing fees, and we rely on the same actuarial tables as the previous section. **Table 4.4** presents the payout rates of different annuities for men and women currently age 65 according to the model and to the market as reported by WebAnnuities Insurance Agency on 13 February 2018 (see immediateannuities.com).

"Life" in Table 4.4 means payment for the life of a "single" annuitant (i.e., an individual annuitant who may or may not be married) with no death benefit. "Life + 10-Year certain" means income for life with income guaranteed to the annuitant's beneficiaries until the end of the first 10 years of the contract.[44] "Life + 10-Year certain + 2% COLA" implies that the income will also be adjusted annually upward by 2%. "Life deferred 10 years + Cash refund" means income starts in 10 years and payments to the annuitant or successors will at least equal the nominal amount paid for the contract. The last annuity is like the 10-year annuity but starts income in 15 years. For example, an annual payout of 12.5% implies that it would require eight years before retirement income is equivalent to the contract value that has been paid.

Table 4.4. Annuity Payouts and Value of Guaranteed Component (as a Percentage of Premium) for an Individual Age 65 as of 13 February 2018

	Men			Women		
	Model	Market	PV/C	Model	Market	PV/C
Life	6.85%	6.50%	0%	6.15%	6.19%	0%
Life + 10-Year certain	6.47	6.37	59.4	5.94	6.13	54.5
Life + 10-Year certain + 2% COLA	5.36	—	53.8	4.83	—	48.4
Life deferred 10 years + Cash refund	12.41	12.33	73.2	10.89	11.14	72.0
Life deferred 15 years + Cash refund	21.03	18.37	67.6	17.42	16.96	66.4

---

[44]A life + 10-year certain contract is the equivalent of buying 10 strips of zero-coupon bonds that will pay the exact amounts guaranteed in the first 10 years with a life annuity deferred by 10 years. When an annuity purchase is considered, both options should be evaluated to determine their relative cost efficiency. Also, combining zero-coupon bonds with deferred annuities will improve the portfolio liquidity, because the guaranteed-income components represent a large proportion of the market value of an immediate annuity 10-year certain. As of the time of this writing, we determined that purchasing a strip of zero-coupon bonds combined with a 10-year deferred annuity was 2% cheaper than buying solely an immediate annuity with a 10-year guaranty. It also reduces the amount committed to buying annuities by nearly 60% because more of the investment is applied to buying the zero-coupon bonds.

Although we are satisfied with our model's accuracy, we expected to observe some differences in pricing between the model and the insurance market. WebAnnuities Insurance Agency at immediateannuities.com reports the best pricing available among different insurers, and pricings do differ significantly across insurers. The most significant difference between the model and the insurance market is the payout rate for 15-year deferred annuities for men. The model payout is significantly higher. It is likely that insurers adjust their mortality tables for the likelihood that men buying 15-year deferred annuities are healthier than the average individual in the general population. Brown (2011) estimates that adverse selection—that is, the fact that annuities tend to be purchased by individuals expected to live longer—is responsible for an 8% to 12% reduction in annuity payouts.

The table also presents the present value of the income (PV/C column) that is guaranteed to be received by the successors in the event of death. One drawback of annuities is the risk that the annuitant dies soon and therefore the income payout stops early, which explains why an annuity can offer high payout rates. To minimize regret in the event of death, annuity contracts can include a minimum period of guaranteed payments or a minimum cumulative payment such as the total premium paid by the annuitant. Therefore, Table 4.4 also indicates the present value of the guaranteed income to be paid as a ratio of the total premium. This ratio varies from 53.8% and 73.2% for men to 48.4% and 72.0% for women.

Finally, the pricing difference between a life annuity with or without a 10-year certain period is smaller than the model suggests, making the 10-year certain option very cheap and valuable as of 13 February 2018.[45] Finally, the 2% COLA option reduces the model payout in the first year from 6.47% for men to 5.36% and from 5.94% to 4.83% for women, although the dollar payout will then be adjusted by 2% annually.

Annuities are often shunned by investors. The so-called annuity puzzle refers to the low level of annuity use observed among retirees. The reasons most mentioned to explain this observation are liquidity, opportunity costs/ regrets and other behavioral explanations, and financial conditions.[46]

Liquidity: The capital invested in a standard life annuity is no longer available to the investor—for example, for emergencies or a large purchase. As Ameriks and Yakoboski (2003, p. 18) state, "There is an inherent tradeoff between maintaining a stock of assets and supporting a flow of income." In their opinion, annuities are valuable because they allow retirees to achieve the greatest efficiency in spending money throughout retirement.

---

[45]We should not assume the insurance market is currently pricing efficient.
[46]Much of the literature review that follows is inspired by Collins, Lam, and Stampfli (2015).

Ameriks, Caplin, Laufer, and Van Nieuwerburgh (2008) suggest, however, that "retirement security can be summed up simply as 'having the resources you need, when you need them.'" Therefore, annuities can act as a partial solution to security only when emergencies arise. They could even exacerbate financial distress. Turra and Mitchell (2008) conclude that annuities become less attractive to people facing a liquidity shock such as medical expenses. Although we agree with these observations, which we will support later in Chapter 4 and in Chapter 6, we are not advocating for complete annuitization of wealth or even that annuities are appropriate for all individuals.

Opportunity Costs/Regret and Other Behavioral Explanations: Life annuities are irreversible transactions. If the annuitant dies early, she and her successors, may have received only a small fraction of the premium paid. Also, higher-returning but riskier assets may have become highly profitable after the annuity was purchased; an annuity is essentially a 100% allocation to fixed income. Finally, the retiree may have a bequest motive such as leaving part of her wealth to her heirs or to a charity.

Even in the absence of a bequest motive, there has been significant resistance by individuals to acquiring annuities. Long-term insured income streams for retirees are largely dominated by Social Security and DB pension plans. Given that DB plans are in decline and US Social Security will face its own funding challenge, it has become even more important to understand the potential benefits of annuities and overcome the reluctance to use them.

Hu and Scott (2007), among many others, address the behavioral aspects, mainly mental accounting and aversion to losses, that cause most investors to ignore annuities. Mental accounting refers to the fact that risky outcomes can be framed narrowly instead of broadly. In the context of annuities, it means that retirees perceive annuities as a narrow gamble, such as "Will I live long enough to make back my initial investment?" instead of more broadly as a tool to optimize intertemporal consumption and avoid end-of-life penury. This observation may support a preference for annuities that integrate a minimum period of guaranteed income even though such annuities are simply a combination of zero-coupon bonds—the guaranteed portion—and a deferred annuity with no such guarantee. Again, it is an issue of mental accounting.

Hu and Scott (2007) also use the work of Tversky and Kahneman (1992) on cumulative prospect theory (CPT) to show how aversion to losses can explain avoidance of annuities.[47] The theory argues that decision weights may not be equal to probabilities. Lower-probability events may be overweighted, and higher-probability events may be underweighted. It also implies that extreme gains or losses are weighted more heavily than medium-sized gains or losses, even assuming that probabilities are equal. Loss aversion reduces the attractiveness of annuities because the aversion to loss from possible early death is exaggerated. At the same time, longevity annuities, with their payouts deferred far in the future, may appear as an attractive gamble because the apparent payout yield is significant relative to the premium, much like a lottery ticket. Financial advisors must manage these perceptions of retirees.

The risk of regret can be reduced through an appropriate level of annuitization—that is, by not putting all the eggs in one basket—and specific annuity features such as a minimum-income guarantee. Even if minimum-income guarantees are suboptimal, they may be necessary to convince investors to accept annuity contracts as a component of their retirement strategy. In other words, they may be less suboptimal than not buying annuities at all. In the next section, we show that the risk of regret must be evaluated in the context of the entire asset allocation and decumulation process. The behavioral aspects that lead retirees to ignore annuities must also be fought through the way portfolio management decisions and the overall decumulation process are framed.

Financial Conditions: Annuities are often considered unattractive in a low interest rate environment. Albrecht and Maurer (2001) conclude that annuities purchased in low interest rate environments produce modest payouts that can be matched through self-annuitization of an asset portfolio. Poterba (2001) also questions the benefit of acquiring annuities in a low interest rate environment. He also believes it may be unwise to acquire all of one's annuity position at the same time because the payout is significantly affected by the prevailing yield curve. In contrast, Orszag (2002) argues that annuities are more attractive than bonds in low interest rate environments because the annuity mortality premium—that is, the effect of declining survival probabilities on the annuity payout, which can be thought of as the risk-sharing

---

[47]Tversky and Kahneman developed the CPT risk decision model in 1992. This model is a further development of prospect theory, which assumes losses and gains are valued differently and thus individuals make decisions based on perceived gains instead of perceived losses. It is also known as loss-aversion theory and implies that when confronted with two equivalent choices, individuals will prefer the option presented in terms of potential gains to the one presented in terms of possible losses. The difference between CPT and the original prospect theory is that weighting is applied to the cumulative probability distribution function, not to the probabilities of individual outcomes.

part of the annuity contract—accounts for an increasing percentage of the payout as the annuitant ages.

Finally, Beshears, Choi, Laibson, Madrian, and Zeldes (2012) confirmed many of the foregoing concerns through two surveys administered to 5,130 participants, but they also found that although only 21.2% of participants would opt for full annuitization of their wealth balance at retirement, another 58.9% of respondents would select partial annuitization when offered. Also, less than a fifth of respondents would select a constant payout, 32% would prefer an annuity with a COLA, and 50% an annuity with a COLA combined with real payout growth.

4.4.1. Fees Embedded in Annuity Prices. Dellinger (2011) describes the fees related to annuity pricing. First, insurers apply a spread between the return earned on the underlying portfolio of assets—usually a mix of fixed-income instruments—and the rate credited on the liability. This spread covers the ongoing costs and margin of profits. An upfront charge may be applied to cover acquisition expenses such as wholesaler compensation, financial adviser sales compensation, policy issuance, record setup, and other policy acquisition expenses. We estimated these costs. More specifically, we calculated the present value of the dollar payout of the annuities presented in **Table 4.5** as a ratio of the present value (PV) of the theoretical payout that could be expected in the absence of any fees.[48] The first number is the ratio that would be obtained if we complete the calculation using the Social Security mortality tables.

An 86.3% ratio for a straight life annuity for men implies that 13.7% of the price paid by the annuitant covers the present value of all fees. Results appear to indicate that annuities that defer payouts—either because of a COLA option leading to smaller initial payouts or because of a full-deferral period—are more expensive.

The effective cost, however, is likely less than shown in this table. As indicated, the annuity pricing computed in Table 4.5 is derived from the Social Security Life Table. It is likely that annuities are purchased by individuals who have a greater longevity than the general population. If longevity is underestimated, implicit costs are overestimated. According to Yermo (2001), half the "apparent" cost of annuities is in fact explained by adverse selection. Adverse

---

[48]This calculation assumes the cost structure is identical across annuities. Pricing in Table 4.5 is obtained using a corporate yield curve, not the Treasury curve often used to calculate the money's worth ratio (MWR), which compares the expected present discounted value of payouts with the premium cost of the annuity. Using a Treasury curve increases the level of the ratio. Hence, our ratios are lower than what is often reported in the literature but more coherent with what we understand of these products' cost structure.

Table 4.5. Ratio of Present Value of Cost-Adjusted Annuity over Present Value of No-Fee Annuity According to Social Security/Society of Actuaries Mortality Tables

	Men	Women
Life	86.3%/91.3%	85.5%/87.6%
Life + 10-Year certain	85.4%/89.8%	84.4%/86.6%
Life + 10-Year certain + 2% COLA	86.5%/90.2%	85.6%/87.3%
Life deferred 10 years + Cash refund	79.4%/83.0%	78.6%/80.4%
Life deferred 15 years + Cash refund	76.1%/81.1%	75.4%/77.9%

selection could also explain why deferred annuities appear relatively more expensive than immediate annuities. The second number in each cell indicates what the ratio would be if the mortality rates were derived from the Society of Actuaries (SOA) mortality tables for healthy annuitants (discussed in Chapter 7).

4.4.2. Factors Affecting the Decision to Acquire Annuities and the Type of Annuity (Immediate vs. Deferred). As previously indicated, there is significant disagreement about the use of annuities in a low interest rate environment. To complete our understanding of annuities, we studied several scenarios reflecting potential regret and market conditions when acquiring annuities:

- compromise between immediate and (far) deferred annuities,

- relative efficiency of investing in fixed income instead of acquiring an annuity in a lower versus higher interest rate environment,

- relative efficiency of investing in fixed income instead of acquiring an annuity in a rising interest rate environment, and

- relative efficiency of investing in fixed income instead of acquiring an annuity in different real-return (i.e., inflation-adjusted) environments.

These scenarios are analyzed in Appendix I. Overall, despite concerns that annuities are unattractive in low-yield environments, our results show that they may be attractive. One reason is that annuities can be acquired to substitute for a portion of the fixed-income portfolio. This is in fact the approach used in *Secure Retirement*. Another reason is that the presence of annuities significantly reduces the income risk of the retiree, much as human capital does, especially in the first few years of retirement. Finally, the appendix shows the effects of both the yield curve and the longevity curve on annuity pricing.

The next section addresses the risk effect of annuities in a more complete portfolio setting. One aspect we consider in Section 4.5 is that an annuity investment should not be considered in a vacuum. It must be evaluated in the context of an investment portfolio designed to meet the retiree's total inflation-adjusted income needs. The fact that an immediate annuity generates income that will reduce the cash drain on the investment portfolio, compared with a deferred annuity, implies that the decision to invest in an annuity and the type of annuity to be acquired cannot be made independently of the asset allocation decision for the liquid asset portfolio. For example, can the retiree support a more aggressive allocation to risky assets within the liquid asset portfolio if he purchases an immediate or deferred annuity? What is the long-term effect of such a choice from a risk and return perspective?

4.5. Handling Risks in Decumulation

There are three major challenges in decumulation: the financial risk related to the level and patterns of portfolio returns, the uncertainty about longevity, and the evolution of income needs. These issues may be unimportant for individuals generating a retirement income from all income sources that is at least twice as large as their expected needs, but few people are in such a position. For many individuals, a thin and unstable demarcation exists between wealth surplus, in which portfolio assets can adequately cover income needs over a lifetime, and wealth deficits, in which portfolio assets are insufficient. Among other reasons, this situation occurs because needs rise or fall to meet available resources. This implies, as advised in this book, that periodic monitoring of the retiree's funded status is required.

4.5.1. The First Challenge: Level and Pattern of Expected Returns and the Role of Annuities. The risk that individuals face in retirement is not only that they may suffer a market correction early, when its effect is maximized, but also that they may fear rebalancing their portfolio. Although a competent adviser can help navigate this trouble period, it is worthwhile designing a strategy that motivates the retirees to remain disciplined. Telling retirees that markets usually recover following a correction may not be enough or even accurate. The traditional advice in decumulation is to run a low-risk portfolio. **Figure 4.4** presents five distinct glide paths currently proposed by large asset managers.

The initial allocation at age 65 varies from 40% to 54% and ends between 20% and 40%. All proposed glide paths have an allocation to equity lower than or equal to 40% 10 years post retirement. Average equity allocations vary between 33.7% and 42.2% if the individual dies at 85 and between 30.1%

Figure 4.4. Five Known Decumulation Glide Paths

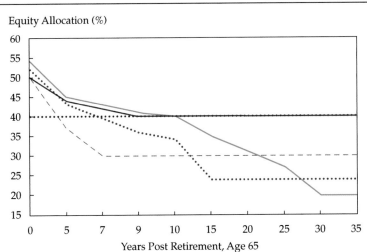

and 40% if the individual lives until 100. A low-risk portfolio is meant to help investors deal with high-risk environments that will occur from time to time during retirement, but the long-term expected return on such a portfolio may be too low. Running a low-risk portfolio for what could be a period ranging from 20 years to 35 years is a very long time.

Life annuities can play an efficient role in managing financial risk and some of the longevity risk when full annuitization is not wanted or desirable because of other factors. As early as 1965, Yaari (1965) showed that retirees unconcerned with a bequest motive should annuitize their retirement savings. The literature differs, however, on when and how much to annuitize. One group of experts argues that investors should annuitize as much as is required to achieve a minimum standard of living target, assuming enough wealth has been accumulated, while keeping only the surplus wealth exposed to the hazards of financial markets. Another group believes that annuitization should be postponed for as long as possible until "some" optimal threshold is reached. Obviously, there are also intermediate views that recommend gradual and partial annuitization considering factors such as age, expected retirement income, and bequest motives. For example, models in Brown (2001) and Davidoff, Brown, and Diamond (2003) suggest that individuals with greater wealth benefit less from owning annuities. They argue that market incompleteness (e.g., the illiquidity of annuities) renders annuitization of a large proportion of wealth inadvisable. Wealthy individuals are less likely to exhaust their financial resources, more likely to take risks and more capable of taking them, and also more likely to have a bequest motive.

The evolution of the trade-off between maintaining a higher-risk portfolio and buying annuities can be explained in the following way. As explained by Babbel and Merrill (2007), a portfolio of risky assets offers the expectation of a higher return than an annuity initially. By postponing the purchase of annuities, individuals have the chance of improving their lifestyle beyond their income target, an eventuality that disappears once full annuitization is completed. Similarly, Milevsky (1998) argues that because buying annuities is an irrevocable decision, investors should delay this decision for as long as possible, because immediate annuitization may impose unacceptable constraints on future consumption, provided the risk of failing to acquire adequate lifetime income remains within tolerable levels.

As we age, however, and in the absence of a bequest motive, annuities become cash flow valuable. As the individual's survival probabilities decline, the annuity payout increases. For example, Kapur and Orszag (2002) introduced the concept of the annuity premium, defined as the spread between the annuity payout yield and the long-term fixed-income yield. They recommend annuitization once the annuity premium exceeds the expected equity risk premium.

On the basis of the material already covered, an appropriate decumulation strategy would have to satisfy the following requirements:

- help maintain a high level of expected investment income,

- reduce the effects of a market correction, especially if it occurs early,

- allow for enough liquidity in the portfolio balance to meet unexpected income needs, and

- help manage the fears of retirees during financial crises, thereby improving the likelihood that the rebalancing strategy will be followed with greater discipline.

A way to satisfy several of these four requirements may be to incorporate immediate nominal annuity contracts—these are not inflation adjusted—with a minimum payout guarantee into the retirement portfolio mix. A nominal annuity brings the benefit of a high payout rate when it is needed the most, early in the retirement phase. The guarantee—such as a 10-year certain payout—helps manage regret risk, and its implicit cost is reasonable, given that a new retiree's survival probability is highest during those initial years. Another approach is to include deferred annuities combined with portfolios of zero-coupon bonds.

Furthermore, the presence of annuities can help justify a g
tion to risky assets in the residual portfolio, which helps main
level of sustainable income. For example, as already shown, mar
have an equity allocation in the 40% range or below during the retirement
phase. We also understand that retirees fear the possibility that riskier assets
may become highly profitable after annuities are acquired.

Consider three portfolios: the 40/60 and 60/40 equity/fixed-income portfolios and a 70/30 liquid assets/annuity portfolio in which the liquid assets
are allocated on a 60/40 equity/fixed-income basis. This latter portfolio is
equivalent to an initial allocation of 42/28/30 to fixed income, equity, and
annuity. Assume the expected fixed-income return is 3%; the expected equity
return is 7%, of which 2% is from dividends and 5% from capital gains; and
the payout on a life annuity 10-year certain is 6.37%. Finally, assume an individual expects to spend 5% of her overall wealth initially. **Table 4.6** presents
the expected cash return from all sources—interests, dividends, and annuity income—and expected total return, including capital gains, of the three
portfolios.

The 40/60 portfolio is less risky than the 60/40 portfolio, but the expected
total return is less than the 5% spending target. Even assuming a stable return,
the investor would gradually drain her capital. Although a 60/40 allocation is
more likely to cover the desired payout in the long term, it does expose the
retiree to greater downside risk and more stress. None of the glide path strategies surveyed advises a 60% allocation to equity.

The integration of an annuity component into the overall portfolio generates greater cash income and total expected return in the initial years.
Although the residual portfolio ex annuity has a 60/40 allocation, the implicit
exposure to equity is much lower once the market value of the annuity contract is considered. Assuming a market shock occurs, the annuity approach
can better meet the participant's income needs than even a 40/60 portfolio

Table 4.6. Cash Return and Total Expected Return of Three Portfolios (Equity, Fixed Income, and Annuity)

Expected Returns from …	40/60/0	60/40/0	42/28/30
Interest income	1.8%	1.2%	0.84%
Dividend income	0.8	1.2	0.84
Annuity income	0.0	0.0	1.91
Total cash income	2.6	2.4	3.59
Capital gains	2.0	3.0	2.1
Total return	4.6	5.4	5.69

while having less effect on the retiree's capital, because the annuity strategy generates more cash income. Furthermore, in comparison with a 40/60 allocation and as calibrated, the annuity component is replacing part of the fixed-income component, even allowing for a small increase in the equity component. This approach does not compromise the long-term return from equity.

It is also important to pay attention to the way the strategic advice is being framed. One requirement of prospect theory is specifying a reference point, a status quo scenario. For example, if we were to argue in favor of introducing an annuity component within the strategic allocation, it might be preferable from a behavioral standpoint to use the annuity portfolio as the reference point instead of a traditional portfolio solution.

To illustrate the benefit of annuities, consider John's situation again. In our base scenario, John had accumulated a portfolio wealth of $775,096 at his intended age of retirement (65). **Figure 4.5**, Panel A compares the evolution of his wealth during the decumulation period, assuming stable returns and two of the portfolios mentioned, 40/60 (red line) and 42/28/30. The figure presents three lines for the latter: portfolio wealth only, considering the 60/40 equity–bond allocation; portfolio wealth plus the value of the guaranteed portion of the annuity contract; and portfolio wealth including the full estimated market value of the annuity contract (the 42/28/30 portfolio). Calculations assume spending equal to 4.5% of initial retirement wealth, adjusted yearly for inflation.

Before the retiree reaches age 65, all scenarios are based on the same wealth accumulation. The drop of the solid blue line at age 65 illustrates the purchase of the annuity contract, and the dotted line incorporates the value of the annuity's guaranteed portion.[49] The dashed line illustrates that, although the annuity contract does not guarantee a payout beyond age 75, it does have a significant market value. In market value terms, the 42/28/30 portfolio with an annuity has a greater market value than the 40/60 portfolio as of age 71.5 years. Because the presence of the annuity allows for a riskier portfolio of liquid assets, the equity/bond component of the 42/28/30 portfolio compounds faster and eventually reaches a higher value, at approximately age 82.6 years. Finally, assuming a rosy scenario of stable returns, the 40/60 portfolio can support John's income needs until age 98.2 years, and the portfolio with an annuity has significant remaining wealth at the same age.

---

[49]The dotted line illustrates the approximate value of the portfolio wealth if the guaranteed portion of the annuity were replaced by zero-coupon bonds and the life annuity 10-year certain were replaced by an annuity deferred by 10 years.

Figure 4.5. Evolution of Wealth

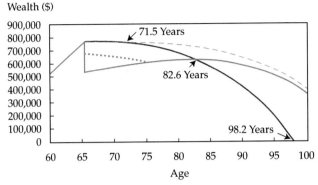

A. Assuming Stable Returns, 4.5% Income Payout

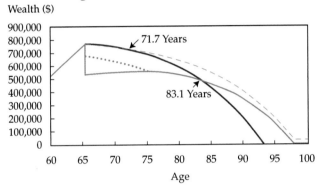

B. Assuming Stable Returns, 5.0% Income Payout

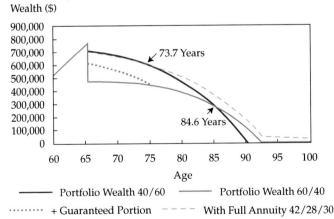

C. Assuming a −20% Equity Shock, 5.0% Income Payout

Panel B illustrates the effect of a higher income payout rate (i.e., spending rate) of 5%. A higher income payout increases slightly the age at which the two strategies break even in terms of wealth: 71.7 years if the market value of the annuity is considered and 83.1 years otherwise. This result is to be expected because a higher payout reduces the long-term benefits of reinvesting. The higher income payout also decreases the sustainability of the decumulation. The 40/60 portfolio exhausted its wealth at age 93.3, whereas the equity/bond component of the 42/28/30 portfolio exhausted its wealth at age 98.2. However, the annuity would cover approximately 20.1% of income needs if the retiree were still alive.

Panel C adds the effect of a 20% equity correction that occurs in the first month of retirement, with no recovery. The effect of a shock on wealth is similar conceptually to that of an increase in the payout rate. It will move the breakeven ages between the two strategies forward because the income payout is exhausting a smaller amount of capital. The 40/60 portfolio is exhausted after 90.1 years, and the equity/bond component of the 42/28/30 portfolio is exhausted after 92.3 years. The results also mean that the annuity will become the sole source of income earlier (at 92.3 years instead of 98.2 years). When portfolio wealth is exhausted, the annuity payout will cover 22.6% of income needs. Finally, a much larger equity shock with no recovery, such as −40%, would be required to exhaust the capital in both strategies at about the same age (approximately 87.1 years) and for the annuity contract to become the sole source of income even earlier. If living longer than savings allow and maintaining a minimum guaranteed income are our main concerns, then annuities are helping meet these concerns.

We now evaluate the benefit of annuities under conditions of uncertainty, in which positive and negative return surprises can occur at any time during the decumulation process and with different circumstances and varying levels of severity. The following analyses are based on the same bootstrap Monte Carlo return generation methodology as that described in Chapter 3.

Table 4.7, Panels A and B, present the likelihood that John will *not* exhaust his capital at ages 85 and 100, assuming two different equity/fixed-income allocations, five scenarios of annuity purchase, and two scenarios of income payout (i.e., spending) rising with inflation.

Assuming a 4% income payout, the probability of not exhausting capital by age 85 is high in all cases. At age 100, a 40% equity allocation, as recommended by many decumulation glide paths, has a greater risk of not meeting the long-term horizon than a 60% allocation; but the stress, or variability, associated with a 60% allocation is greater. However, a 30% annuity purchase combined with a 60% equity allocation in the remaining assets—the

Table 4.7. Probability of Not Exhausting Capital

| | Age 85 | | Age 100 | |
| | Equity Allocation | | Equity Allocation | |
Annuity Allocation	40%	60%	40%	60%
A. 4% Income payout				
0%	97.4%	97.3%	62.4%	71.9%
10%	98.1	98.0	65.1	74.0
20%	98.9	98.6	68.4	76.7
30%	99.4	99.3	72.4	79.7
40%	99.8	99.7	77.3	83.3
B. 5% Income payout				
0%	85.2%	87.2%	34.2%	47.9%
10%	85.8	87.8	34.0	47.8
20%	86.5	88.3	33.8	47.7
30%	87.4	89.0	33.6	47.4
40%	88.5	89.9	33.2	47.2

equivalent of a 42/28/30 allocation to equity, fixed income, and annuity initially—has a 79.7% likelihood of not exhausting its capital at age 100.

The results for the 5% income payout are as expected. A higher income payout increases the likelihood of exhausting the capital. Furthermore, the presence of annuities does not support higher probabilities of success or nonexhaustion, given that a higher income payout cannot easily be met by a lower-risk portfolio, although the annuities will keep paying once the capital is exhausted. However, the issue is not whether a 60/40 allocation with no annuity component is preferable—because the higher income payout may be deemed too risky—but whether a 60/40 allocation associated with an annuity purchase is preferable to a 40/60 allocation. Again, the former remains preferable. Moreover, while the probability of exhausting the capital may be similar with or without an annuity component at age 100, a larger annuity component will cover more of the income needs if the individual is still alive at an advanced age.

To complete this section, **Figure 4.6** presents the probabilities that John will be exhausting his savings year by year for the 40/60 allocation and the 60/40 allocation (within unannuitized assets) combined with 30% in an annuity for both 4% and 5% income payouts. As expected, the annuity approach usually has a higher probability of not exhausting John's savings.

Figure 4.6. Probability of Not Exhausting Capital at Different Ages with 4% and 5% Income Payout

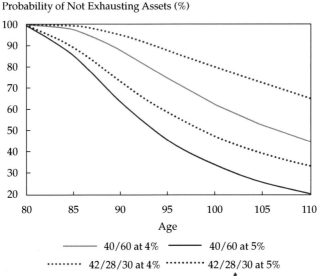

Furthermore, we must always remember that the annuity will keep paying when savings are exhausted. In fact, if it could be shown that full annuitization leads to a 100% probability of achieving the desired level of income, other factors such as legacy objectives, liquidity concerns (loss of flexibility), behavioral aspects (regret), or perhaps financial conditions (low interest rates) would be required to justify partial annuitization.

4.5.2. The Second Challenge: Uncertainty in Life Expectancy.

Milevsky and Huang (2011) define longevity risk as the risk of living longer than expected and of depleting financial resources. Incorporating an annuity component helps manage the risk of decumulation in two ways. It increases the expected sustainability of the income payout and keeps contributing to the income of the retiree after savings are fully exhausted. Unless full annuitization is considered, however, this approach does not fully protect the retiree from catastrophic return scenarios that could deplete savings in less than 15 to 20 years, nor against living longer than expected.

One of the many challenges of decumulation is the frequent assumption that we pursue a fixed policy of income payout adjusted for inflation. Abbas and Matheson (2005) advise that targets may have to be revised to reflect updated information concerning wealth and liability values: "Pursuing a fixed goal may be operationally motivational when things are going smoothly, but when major impacts, such as setbacks or new opportunities, create a need to reevaluate alternatives, the normative approach demands determining new targets. Simply maximizing the probability of reaching the old target is no longer optimal." This advice is echoed by Waring and Siegel (2015), who provide a mechanical rule for updating spending, given new information about the portfolio value and rates on Treasury inflation-protected securities (TIPS). It also implies that monitoring and periodically updating the retiree's financial situation are essential. In other words, the type of information provided by Table 4.7 and by Figure 4.6 should be recomputed as the retiree ages and circumstances change.

Some literature is concerned with the "normal" path of expenses of individuals as they age, an aspect considered in the next section. However, individuals must have a policy guiding how the income payout could be adjusted in the event of severe and prolonged market corrections and longer expected longevity, the aspect considered here.

It would be easy to simply advise that in the event of a portfolio correction of –20%, the income payout should be adjusted down by 20% to maintain the same sustainability. Many individuals, however, could not tolerate such an adjustment or adjust their lifestyle as quickly as necessary. They might also have fixed commitments. A decumulation policy should consider the tolerance level of retirees in adjusting their income needs. At the same time, we must account for the likelihood that an unfavorable portfolio performance may reverse and that life expectancy is reduced as we age. As discussed earlier, the longer we live, the less likely we are to live another 15 years but the older the age we are expected to reach.

Milevsky and Huang (2011, p. 45) believe that "the optimal forward-looking behavior in the face of personal longevity risk is to consume in proportion to survival probabilities—adjusted upward for pension income and downward for longevity risk aversion—as opposed to blindly withdrawing constant income for life." Frank, Mitchell, and Blanchett (2011) also argue in favor of dynamically managing the withdrawal rate as a retiree continues to live beyond expected longevity. The implementation proposed in Chapter 6 reflects these views. In this chapter, we explore a specific withdrawal approach, a decumulation engine.

A decumulation engine should periodically reevaluate whether the current level of income payout can be maintained or should and could be adjusted—downward or upward—and, if so, when the adjustment should potentially start.

A decumulation "engine" is, of course, a metaphor. It is in fact a set of formulas or recommendations regarding spending, asset allocation, and so forth; it does not do the work for you. It is also easy to override by not following the

87

recommendations. If a financial adviser or investment management firm with authority over the account uses the engine, that organization may do the work for its clients, but many investors will not like the lack of flexibility in such an arrangement. When discussing the outcomes from using a decumulation engine, then, these caveats need to be kept in mind.

The engine would require

- having information such as expected long-term returns and risk of asset classes;

- applying longevity risk for any given age;

- integrating all sources of income in the decision-making framework, such as from annuities, Social Security, and DB plans;

- defining a tolerance for adjusting income payout in case of unfavorable return scenarios, such as maximum of 10%; and

- incorporating a buffer when the initial income payout is set, such as 5%— for example, avoiding a situation in which a slight decline in expected return immediately triggers a payout adjustment.

The engine would also require that we define an acceptable probability level of not achieving our income-for-life goal either because the level and patterns of market returns are disappointing or because we live longer than expected. Hence, we need to incorporate both return and longevity uncertainty in the overall probability of not meeting our expectations.

For example, our retiree may be willing to accept a 20% probability of not fully achieving his goal. The decumulation engine is inspired by an approach described in Milevsky and Robinson (2005), which is further explained and tested in Chapter 6. It combines the uncertainty surrounding both portfolio returns and longevity, assuming for now a maximum probability of failure of 20%. In John's case, targeting a 20% probability of not achieving his initial goal leads to a recommended initial payout of 4.76%, or $36,925. We consider the effects of incorporating such an engine on the level of income that can be sustained relative to the target and in the context of specific return shock scenarios. In Chapter 6, this method is used again, but in the more realistic context of stochastic returns.

All examples assume a financial crisis leading to a 20% portfolio loss with no recovery in the first month of retirement. **Figure 4.7**, Panel A reproduces part of Figure 4.5, Panel C but adds another piece of information: the income paid to John as a percentage of the original target income as of retirement. The 60/40 portfolio with an annuity has exhausted its assets as of age 94.5.

This result is reflected in the target income ratio, which suddenly drops from 100% to slightly more than 20%, all of which is provided by the annuity income. Because the annuity payout is not inflation adjusted, the target income ratio further declines over time.

But what if we applied Milevsky and Robinson's decumulation methodology specifying, as indicated, an acceptable probability of failure of 20%? Figure 4.7, Panel B illustrates the consequences of applying the decumulation engine if we were to impose no constraints on the level of income adjustment.

Figure 4.7.   Evolution of Wealth

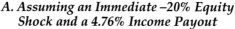

A. Assuming an Immediate –20% Equity Shock and a 4.76% Income Payout

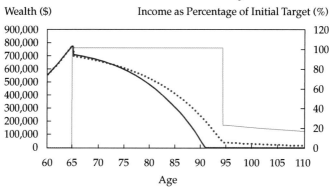

B. Assuming a –20% Equity Shock, a 4.76% Income Payout, and a Decumulation Engine with a 20% Acceptable Probability of Failure

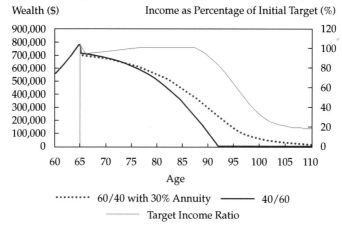

(Continued)

Figure 4.7.   Evolution of Wealth *(Continued)*

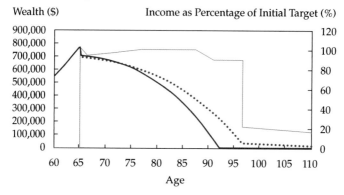

C. Evolution of Wealth Assuming a –20% Equity Shock, a 4.76% Income Payout, a Decumulation Engine with a 20% Failure Level, and a 10% Real Income Decline Tolerance

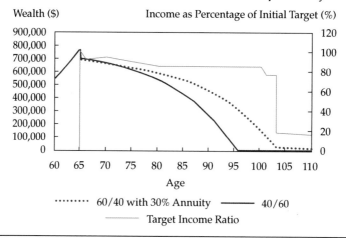

D. Evolution of Wealth Assuming a –20% Equity Shock, a 4.76% Income Payout, a Decumulation Engine with a 20% Failure Level, a 10% Real Income Decline Tolerance, and a Consumption Adjustment

Assuming no recovery, the decumulation engine recommends gradually reducing dollar income withdrawals to 94.5% of targeted income (on a 12-month rolling basis), with a full real-income recovery occurring by age 76.7. By age 87.6, income would gradually decline again, and this decline would reach 10% of targeted income by age 90.8 and 32% by age 94.5 (at which assets would have been fully depleted without the decumulation engine). Although not illustrated, if the same shock of –20% had occurred after 10 years instead of after one month, no income adjustment would have been required until age 92.2.

We could also consider the –20% shock scenario in the context of a recovery lasting 24 months but delayed by 12 months (not shown). In this case, the income withdrawals would have been reduced to approximately 93.7% of targeted income as of age 66.4, but full target consumption would resume by age 67.3.

Some retirees, however, may not want to consider an income adjustment of more than X% from their target. In this case, the decumulation engine would maintain a higher income level for a longer period, but the retiree faces the risk of total ruin much sooner, except for the annuity payment that remains. Figure 4.7, Panel C presents the same scenario as Panel B, with the added constraint of not decreasing payout by more than 10% in a year. The portfolio would be fully exhausted by age 96.5.

At this point, we are still not trying to determine what an appropriate level of retirement income risk is. We are simply presenting methodologies that can help with this process. These examples illustrate the usefulness of having a decumulation engine that can appropriately smooth the pattern of income adjustment when facing uncertain returns and can provide relevant protection within the income constraints that are imposed. Small income adjustments planned well in advance can improve the solvability of a problem in retirement planning.

4.5.3. The Third Challenge: Evolution of Income Needs. Several factors affect our income needs as we cross into retirement. Assuming a specific level of household expenditure before retirement, a lower level of income would be required after retirement to cover the same expenditures. For example, part of the income earned before retirement is required to cover Social Security contributions and other savings plans. Furthermore, retirees have access to extra tax deductions, and Social Security benefits are partially or fully tax free. These aspects and others are important to consider when calibrating a retirement plan.

The objective of this section is to understand what happens to the expenditures basket of individuals as they retire and over time. Until now, we have assumed that whatever target level of income was set as of retirement, this number would increase yearly by the inflation rate. If expenditures do not follow this pattern, however, any deviations can significantly affect, either positively or negatively, the retirement strategy's sustainability.

Most earlier studies examining the transition from work to retirement found a decrease in household expenditures within the first two years after retirement, ranging from a low of about 4% to a high of 17%. These studies usually used food expenditures as a proxy for consumption expenditures, but food is a very restrictive definition of consumption expenditures. Using a broader definition of consumption data from the Consumer Expenditure Survey (CEX) that incorporates housing costs, food, transportation, apparel, medical care, entertainment, and other items, Fisher, Johnson, Marchand, Smeeding, and Torrey (2005) find that consumption expenditures fall by about 2.5% in the first year of retirement but then continue to decline by approximately 1% a year afterward. For example, in the 10 years after retirement for cohorts of individuals who retired at ages 65 and 69, declines in consumption ranging from 1% to 8% were observed. Over 15 years, declines of 13% to 18% were observed, suggesting an average decline of 1% per year.

Hurst (2008) observed that the decline in spending during retirement is mostly limited to the categories of food and work-related expenses. Approximately 20% of the declining expenditures on food can be attributed to increased shopping diligence, resulting in lower prices paid for the same good, whereas the 80% is attributed to more time spent cooking at home. Some expenses do increase during retirement, however, such as those for entertainment and travel (Aguiar and Hurst 2008). If the pattern of expenditures is as described, Blanchett (2014) argues, the cost of funding retirement could be far less than assumed by traditional models.

Although this information is important, one should not rely fully on an expected expenditure decline to justify saving significantly less. Every individual is different, but if the assumption of declining consumption expenditure were valid, it would provide the required income flexibility to face the financial shocks that we addressed in the prior section. The best approach would be for each household to properly monitor the structure of expenditures as retirement nears, such as in the last 5 to 10 years, to better understand consumption patterns and what to expect after retirement. Therefore, although designing a pension plan on the assumption that the level of required income is likely to decline significantly in the first 15 years may not be prudent, some reduction in planned consumption could be justified. Chapters 7 and 8 further explore this aspect.

Finally, another aspect is very important to US individuals: health expenses. According to Hurd and Rohwedder (2006), households differ a great deal in the change in expenditure associated with retirement, and much of this heterogeneity is explained by individuals who retire involuntarily because of deteriorating health. Furthermore, Medicare does not cover all health services and does not pay 100% of the cost of services it does cover. Remaining costs must either be covered with supplemental insurance or paid out of pocket. This potential cost burden adds considerable uncertainty to the retirement-planning process, especially for some US individuals, but likely less for Canadians or Europeans.

Figure 4.7, Panel D presents the same information as Panel C but assumes a gradual reduction of income needs at a rate of 1% per year over the first 15 years. Therefore, the adjusted income target as of age 80 is 85% of the target as of age 65 (in real dollar terms). Although the decumulation methodology recommends some adjustments below the adjusted income target in the initial years, these adjustment never require reducing consumption by more than 4% on a rolling 12-month basis. Finally, the retiree easily reaches age 100 while meeting the adjusted income needs.

4.6. Understanding Social Security

The US Social Security program plays an important role in the retirement income of most Americans. Social Security payments represent a significant portion of many retirees' retirement income and, like annuities, can significantly affect the recommended asset allocation of private savings.

Social Security is designed to replace a portion of wage earnings. Although in this book we do not aim to explain all the intricacies of Social Security income calculations, we do present some of the main characteristics of the Social Security program:[50]

- The age at which beneficiaries are eligible for full Social Security benefits is gradually being raised. Americans who will turn 62 in 2018 (i.e., those born in 1956) will need to wait until age 66 and 4 months to claim their full Social Security retirement benefit. Full retirement age (FRA) will increase by 0.2 years every year until it reaches 67 in 2022.

- Beneficiaries can claim Social Security benefits as early as age 62 but no later than age 70. If a claim is made before FRA, full benefits are reduced by 0.56% for each month for the first 36 months prior to FRA. Any additional month is reduced by 0.42%. If benefits are claimed after FRA, full benefits are increased by 0.67% for each month.

- As of 2018, benefits cover the first 90% of monthly wage income of $895, 32% of income above that amount up to $5,397, and 15% of excess income above that second amount, up to $10,700, beyond which no additional benefit is paid.[51] The first two amounts, called the bend points, are

---

[50]Those intricacies have been properly coded, however, in the simulations of Chapter 6 and 8.
[51]This amount, indexed for inflation, was correct when this chapter was written. As of 2019, the maximum amount of taxable earnings was $132,900, or $11,075 per month.

indexed according to the average wage index. The last amount is the maximum taxable earnings (MTE) figure, which determines the maximum amount on which the Social Security payroll tax is applied. The coverage factors are 90%, 32%, and 15%; MTE is also the maximum coverage amount.

- Benefits are based on the highest 35 years of indexed wages. Prior wages earned by the beneficiary are also indexed according to the average wage index to calculate earned benefits. If the beneficiary did not contribute for 35 years, the calculation will be based on some years of zero earnings.

- Benefits are adjusted yearly, starting at age 63, according to the growth in the Consumer Price Index for Urban Wage Earners and Clerical Workers.

- Social Security affords significant spousal benefits. These benefits can affect the retirement strategy in the context of a household approach. This aspect is discussed in Chapter 7.

The maximum amount that can be received monthly by a beneficiary is less than could be expected from the foregoing bend points, the MTE amount, and the coverage factors. There are two main reasons. First, wages earned after age 60 are no longer indexed for calculating initial benefits. Second, the MTE does not necessarily increase in line with the average wage index.

There is also another aspect of potentially significant importance. Like the Canadian and Quebec Social Security programs, the US program is funded through Social Security contributions and the Social Security Trust Fund. Unlike the Canadian programs, however, the reserve assets have been invested over time in relatively low-yielding special issue bonds—instead of a diverse portfolio of fixed income, equity, and real assets such as real estate, infrastructure, and private equity—and the trust fund is underfunded. It is expected to be depleted completely by 2034 despite changes made to the FRA.

For example, Reynolds (2017) estimates that Social Security taxes will have to increase from 12.4% to 16.4% in 2034 if action is delayed until then and all current benefits are maintained. The required increase would be 3.3% if the tax were raised in 2026 and 2.6% had the tax been raised in 2018. If no actions are undertaken by Congress, such as higher Social Security taxes or further increasing the FRA, Social Security benefits will be reduced by approximately 23% in 2034, or else the shortfall will have to be paid from general government revenues, an action currently not permitted by law. If the benefit reduction occurs, millennials will either receive reduced benefits when they retire or will be funding an even greater part of the benefits of earlier generations. We come back to this aspect in Chapter 8.[52]

It may be interesting to understand the effects of Social Security from John's point of view, assuming that he is single. Hence, we have three goals in this section.

- First, evaluate the effect of Social Security on John's overall asset allocation. Social Security is the equivalent of an inflation-adjusted annuity. It has a market value that can be estimated using the same pricing mechanism used to evaluate an annuity with a COLA.

- Second, even if John intends to retire at 65, he may decide to trigger Social Security benefits earlier or later. Because it is possible to estimate the benefits that John will be receiving at different ages of implementation, it is also possible to evaluate the IRR from the decision to postpone receiving Social Security under different longevity assumptions.

- Third, Social Security affects John's overall financial risk as he ages. It improves the sustainability of his decumulation strategy.

Figure 4.8, Panel A illustrates John's asset allocation, including all the components of his resources. As of age 65, John has accumulated the same private wealth shown in our earlier scenario assuming a stable 60/40 allocation and stable returns: $775,096. The figure illustrates his nominal wealth accumulation and shows the allocation between equity and fixed income. It also shows the effect of the 30% of total wealth allocated to the purchase of an annuity with a 10-year payout guarantee; the guaranteed and unguaranteed portions are shown separately. Finally, the diagram shows the implicit market value of the Social Security benefits starting at age 50, assuming John would choose to trigger these benefits when he retires. By the time John retires, the FRA will likely be 67 years under the current rule. Although an individual cannot collect the present value of future Social Security benefits in cash, the diagram shows what the benefits are implicitly worth to John using actuarial principles. Finally, the calculations assume that retirement income (consumption requirement) is set at 75% of John's work income as of retirement, adjusted for inflation.

---

[52]Although a federal program, Social Security does not guarantee benefits. According to the opinion of the Supreme Court in *Fleming v. Nestor*, the Court held that entitlement to the benefits is not a contractual right. Benefit levels are what Congress says that they are. See www.ssa.gov/history/nestor for reference.

Figure 4.8. Asset Allocation Including Social Security

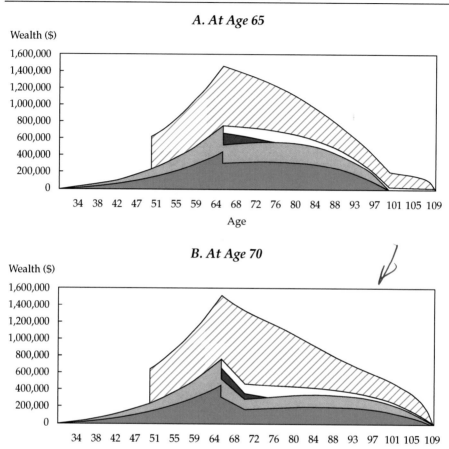

Three observations can be made from this figure:

- Social Security is an important wealth component for John. When he turns 65, it will account for 48.1% of his total wealth.

- The allocation to equity looks small in this context. Once the annuity has been purchased, it represents less than 22.1% of total wealth.

- The market value of Social Security declines over time but not as fast as that of the annuity for two reasons. First, Social Security benefits are adjusted for inflation. If John were to live a very long life, his nominal

Social Security benefit could increase substantially over 30 or 40 years. Second, the older we are, the longer we are expected to live, indicating that the probability that John will be alive at age 102 is greater when John is already 95 than when he is 85. Although this is true in the context of both the annuity and Social Security, these higher probabilities as John ages apply to the inflation-adjusted benefits of Social Security, in contrast to the annuity payouts, which do not rise with inflation. Hence, Social Security is an efficient type of longevity insurance.

Most glide paths recommend a declining equity allocation during retirement as we age. Social Security, however, much like annuities, supports maintaining a stable allocation to equity within the liquid asset portfolio. Both are a form of fixed-income asset and provide longevity insurance. Also, nominal annuities support a higher equity allocation because their higher payouts help withstand the very negative effect of early return shocks, whereas Social Security provides long-term inflation protection. In other words, our allocation to equity (S) in retirement, assuming some human capital (HC) remains, is determined by

$$\frac{S}{S + B + \text{Annuity} + SS + HC_s}, \qquad \text{Eq. 4.2}$$

where B and SS represent the bond and the Social Security allocation.

Panel B presents the same information as Panel A but assumes that Social Security benefits are delayed until age 70. Postponing Social Security improves the sustainability of the retirement strategy, but it will contribute to draining the portfolio of liquid assets and could lower legacy wealth. Nevertheless, **Figure 4.9** illustrates this compromise solely in terms of the internal rate of return (IRR) from the decision to postpone Social Security benefits to age 66, 68, or 70 against taking those benefits at age 65, assuming the full retirement age is 67. Postponing benefits to either age 66, 68, or 70 generates a zero annualized IRR if one lives to age 80.4, 81.1, or 82.6—in other words, that is the breakeven age—and a positive one after that. The IRRs, expressed as an annual rate, surpass 4% between ages 86 and 89. The IRR from postponing Social Security to age 70 if the individual retires at age 67, living off other (non–Social Security) resources for those three years increases beyond 4% at age 89.75. (This last strategy is not shown in the diagram.)

Even if we concluded that from an IRR perspective, Social Security benefits should be postponed, it is not obvious that postponing to age 70 is optimal in all cases. We will gain a better understanding of the effects once we

Figure 4.9. IRRs of Claiming Social Security at Ages 66, 68, and 70 According to Longevity

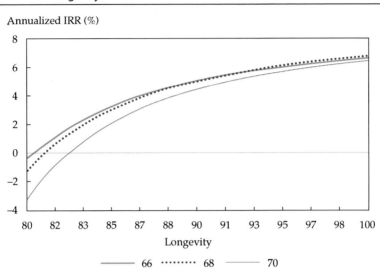

4.7. Conclusion

fully integrate the Social Security decision into our simulations and take into account uncertainty about longevity.

Decumulation is a more challenging process than accumulation because the options available to retirees are more limited and the uncertainty is greater and more impactful. Retirees can decide when to retire but have less control over how long they will live. They might conceivably benefit from market volatility during the accumulation process, because it could help smooth financial risk, but they will be penalized by the market volatility during the decumulation period. Retirees have greater control over how much to save pre retirement than how much to spend post retirement because they will need a specific level of income to sustain their accustomed lifestyle or even just to meet fixed commitments. They likely have low tolerance for a significant reduction in retirement income and face the greatest emotional and financial risks close to retirement.

In Chapter 4, we discussed how to approach the decumulation process. Insurance solutions in the form of annuities are available, but they require the retirement challenge to be framed broadly because individuals have behavioral impediments that are obstacles to annuity-based solutions. As indicated, the proper comparison is not how a 60/40 portfolio allocation combined with annuities will perform against a 60/40 portfolio without annuities, because in the absence of an annuity, investors will likely hold a more conservative allocation. Furthermore, for the average retiree, the emphasis should be on resolving the financial and emotional stress that comes with longevity, not on the opportunity cost that results from dying early. How we frame the retirement solution is extremely important.

The Social Security program plays an important role in retirement planning for most individuals, although the United States has concerns about the sustainability of the existing benefit terms.

We did not explicitly cover the dynamic glide path strategy tested in Chapter 3 in the context of accumulation. We did evaluate the strategy in the context of decumulation, but it did not lead to an improvement in the distribution of expected income compared with a situation in which the strategy is applied only during the accumulation process. At most, it had a relatively neutral effect.

It may be that the dynamic glide path strategy is not as effective once the allocation to the risky component is already lowered. It may also be that the presence of annuities already contributes to a significant reduction of risk. Finally, the strategy may not be as effective in the context of decumulation, when the contribution of human capital has gone to zero. We performed additional simulations and confirmed that the efficiency of the dynamic glide path approach is reduced in the presence of an annuity component.

Finally, there is no financial strategy that guarantees that the target income pattern will be met unless the retiree has significant excess wealth. Although the purpose of *Secure Retirement* is to help maximize the level of income that can be achieved from a given level of wealth, retirees need access to financial tools that help them calibrate their expected income according to the sometimes disappointing reality of financial markets. Decumulation is a multidimensional issue and must be supported by appropriate simulation tools and applications.

5. Understanding Transition Factors for Long-Term Investors

The transition period from accumulation to decumulation can be stressful for future retirees, especially without proper guidance. Chapter 5 is concerned with specific aspects of risk transition affecting the asset allocation decision in the long term. Four topics are discussed.

Chapters 3 and 4 evaluated the effects of return shocks, often linked to equity, on investors' future wealth and their ability to meet income goals in retirement. A frequent assumption of many of these analyses is that low returns associated with a shock will eventually mean revert, at least on average, resulting in a favorable wealth outcome. Chapter 5 reviews the evidence on mean reversion and the implications of this assumption, especially as retirement nears.

Second, it was assumed until now that asset portfolios were built from two components only: equity and nominal bonds. Several glide path products, however, recommend an allocation to real (i.e., inflation-indexed) return bonds. Chapter 5 discusses the pertinence of using nominal bonds versus real-return bonds versus cash.

Third, the goal of any investor before retirement is to accumulate as much wealth as possible, given the individual's level of risk aversion. As one transitions into retirement, however, and into a decumulation period, when the purpose is to generate an income that rises with inflation, the real rate of return may become even more relevant to the allocation process after retirement.

Fourth, in Chapter 4 we introduced nominal annuities as an asset component. It was assumed that the full amount of the intended annuity exposure is purchased as of the retirement date. In the context of stochastic returns, however, it may be advisable to spread annuity purchases over time.

5.1. Conceptual Impact of Return Mean Reversion and the Evidence

If returns show a mean reversion, the idea of time diversification is legitimate. The debate on the evidence related to mean reversion, however, is not resolved. As indicated by Spierdijk and Bikker (2012), the cause of this debate is the lack of a long enough historical time series of equity returns to statistically support the argument for mean reversion. A hundred years of historical data and few significant equity shocks are not enough to achieve statistically significant conclusions when equity valuations may take many years to revert to their "fundamental" level. According to Cecchetti, Lam, and Mark (1990), "All we can do is wait" for longer data series to become available, although more powerful tests have been designed since their study.

Another take on this question is offered by Samuelson (1994), who points out that no matter how long the period, there is only one sample of the past, and the conditions that produced that sample will not be repeated in the future. So it is unknowable whether future stock valuations will mean revert. Goetzmann and Ibbotson (2006) point out that some degree of mean reversion is tautologically observed in markets that survived to the present, so any forecast of mean reversion is an implied forecast that the market with which you are concerned will survive.

The earlier work on absolute mean reversion—that is, mean reverting against an unspecified mean value—is attributed to Poterba and Summers (1988), who find positive autocorrelations of returns over periods of less than a year and negative autocorrelations over periods of three to eight years, supporting the hypothesis of mean reversion at longer horizons. The variance of eight-year returns, compared with four-year returns, is about half of what would be expected if returns were i.i.d. Fama and French (1988) also find that mean reversion explains 25% to 40% of the variation in three- to five-year equity returns. Both studies rely on data from the 1926–85 period. Bennyhoff (2008) compares the risk of holding US stocks over 1926–2006, assuming different investment horizons. He finds the average standard deviation of yearly returns is 18.55%. If the returns were i.i.d., the 30-year returns would have a standard deviation of $18.55\%/\sqrt{30} = 3.39\%$; the actual result is 1.38%, suggesting mean reversion. We caution, however, that there are only two *independent* 30-year periods in the 80 years studied, and the rolling returns that Bennyhoff studied have peculiar statistical properties that come from counting the same subperiods over and over, making his conclusion shaky.

Such conclusions have been criticized by McQueen (1992), who believes the evidence for mean reversion is overstated because it is overly influenced by highly volatile periods such as the Great Depression and World War II. Finally, Campbell and Viceira (2002) also evaluated the annualized standard deviation of k-period returns of equity but also of other assets such as rolled T-bills, long bonds, and five-year bonds. They find that equity risk declines with k, T-bill and long-bond risks increase, and five-year bond risk declines. The usefulness of these findings is discussed in more detail when the choice among cash, nominal bonds, and real-return bonds is discussed in the next section.

Others have looked at the idea that mean reversion occurs around a fundamental value proxied by valuation ratios such as the historical average dividend yield or P/E of the country one is analyzing, or the valuation ratios of a world index. Campbell and Shiller (2001) and Coakley and Fuertes (2006) conclude that financial ratios tend to mean revert. Using data from 1900 to 2008, Spierdijk, Bikker, and van den Hoek (2012) also find evidence of mean reversion in 17 countries and conclude that mean reversion occurs more rapidly in periods of high economic and political uncertainty such as the Great Depression, the oil crises of 1973 and 1979, and Black Monday in 1987. They also document that half-lives of shocks, the period it takes for country indices to absorb half of a shock, ranged between 2 years and 22.6 years. Balvers, Wu, and Gilliland (2000) found half-lives ranging between 2.4 and 5.9 years with a 90% confidence interval. Both findings would lead one to recommend longer transition periods (many years) from higher to lower risk in glide paths, especially if significant wealth has already been accumulated.

More recently, Mukherji (2011) used a nonparametric block bootstrap method to evaluate the mean reversion hypothesis for both large and small company stocks in the US market using data from 1926 to 2007. He finds strong evidence of mean reversion for small stocks over the entire period and over the subperiods 1926–1966 and 1967–2007. Also, although he finds strong evidence of mean reversion for large stocks over the entire period, the evidence is weaker for the period 1967–2007.

5.1.1. Why Would Equity Returns Mean Revert? Robert Shiller (1981, pp. 433–434) stated that "measures of price volatility over the past century appear far too high—5 to 13 times too high—to be attributed to new information about real dividends." GMO's Jeremy Grantham (2012) argued the market is 19 times more volatile than is justified by the underlying economic engine. Is this indicative of a failure of the efficient market hypothesis (EMH)?

"Excess" volatility could be explained by irrational or even rational behavior. Tversky and Kahneman (1981) present evidence that individuals overreact to new information. Poterba and Summers (1988) attribute mean reversion to the irrational behavior of noise traders, whereas others attribute it to overreaction to financial news and fads. In contrast, Statman (2005, p. 36) believes that investors are neither rational nor irrational but simply normal: "Normal investors are affected by cognitive biases while rational investors are not." This belief certainly justifies the need for investment tools that enforce or support greater discipline and help manage emotions through quality information and feedback mechanisms.

Rational explanations, which do not contradict the EMH, have also been theorized. Assuming all available information is incorporated in equity prices, security valuation is determined by expected returns. Rational pricing may lead to time-varying expected returns. Wide fluctuations in expected returns may be caused by uncertainty about the economy's survival, according to Kim, Nelson, and Startz (1991). For example, mismanagement of the liquidity crisis by central banks in 2008 could have led to greater and more persistent structural consequences.

Rather than theorize further about the potential causes of mean reversion, it may be more effective to evaluate its effect on wealth accumulation during several historical market drawdowns.

5.1.2. Anatomy of Drawdowns and Recoveries. If annualized equity risk were greater at short horizons but less at long horizons, allocating more to equity when retirement is still far away would make sense. It is even more defensible if lower-risk human capital is considered, given the wealth accumulation benefits from the interaction between periodic savings and market volatility.

Figure 5.1, Panel A identifies all the historical periods from August 1926 to December 2017 that were characterized by an initial equity drawdown of at least −10% in the US market.[53] There were 17 such periods, lasting from 0.5 years to 15.3 years. The largest drawdown was triggered by the Great Depression: It was −82.5%! The drawdown started in August 1929 and ended in June 1932. It then took nearly 13 years to neutralize those losses on a total return basis.

Therefore, although 62% of monthly equity returns were positive over those 91+ years (from 1926 to 2017), investors have spent 53% of this entire period either in drawdowns of 10% or more or waiting to recover from these drawdowns. The inflation-driven environment of the 1970s and early 1980s also led to many drawdowns of shorter duration.

Figure 5.1, Panel B presents similar information but identifies the length of the period triggered by an initial drawdown of 10% in which the duration of the drawdown and recovery is determined by the time required to achieve a return that would at least have been equal to the risk-free rate. The risk-free rate approximates the rate of inflation or a little more (so we can tell roughly how long a recovery was needed to make the investor whole in real terms). The vertical axis shows the nominal compound annual return over each period. In environments where the risk-free rate is close to zero, the duration

---

[53]The data are based on the US equity market factor as defined by the firm AQR. The market factor is adjusted for the risk-free rate.

Figure 5.1. Recovery Periods

A. All Drawdowns of –10% or More since August 1926

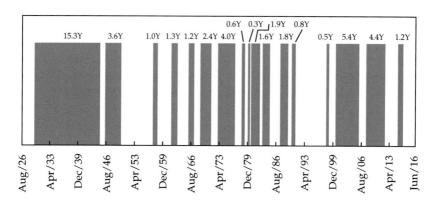

B. All Drawdowns of –10% or More since August 1926, Defining Recovery as Matching the Risk-Free Rate of Return

Annualized Absolute Compounded Returns (%)

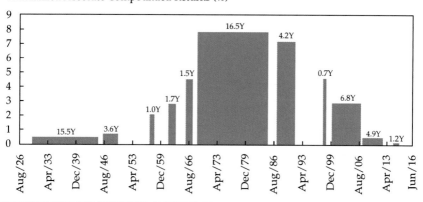

of drawdowns is similar to those in Figure 5.1, Panel A. High short-term interest rates in the 1970s and 1980s, however, mean that it took 16.5 years after a drawdown started in November 1968 for investors to start outperforming the risk-free rate, assuming no fees. This result is for total returns including dividend income, not price-only. Thus, an inflation-driven environment adds challenges to equity management. The findings in Panel B also mean that equity investors spent 64% of all months since 1926 attempting to match the risk-free rate once a 10% drawdown was triggered.

These figures also illustrate the importance of remaining invested consistently in the market. For example, the average annualized equity return was 9.9% during this period. If a hypothetical long-term investor missed out on the best 12 months of returns generated over those 91+ years, that investor's annualized return would have been reduced to 7.4%. Consistency is key, and successful market timing in the financial industry has little empirical support.

This data seems very depressing at first glance. In Chapter 3, however, we argued that an investor's performance in a wealth accumulation process can be enhanced by the price volatility in financial markets. For example, even though it took 15.5 years during the Great Depression for equity markets to deliver a total return greater than the total return of the risk-free rate, the IRR of an investor in accumulation was likely very different.

Therefore, **Table 5.1** presents the same information found in Figure 5.1, Panel B for each drawdown and recovery situation (start date, end date, duration, and annualized risk-free return over the period) as well as for the size of the drawdown. It also indicates by how much the IRR of an investor in accumulation would have surpassed the risk-free rate during each period, assuming different scenarios of initial wealth and periodic savings. Five accumulation scenarios are considered: no initial wealth, and initial wealth equal to 50%, 100%, 200%, or 400% of the contributions (in real dollars) that will be made during the drawdown and recovery period. In other words, we consider different scenarios of the relative importance of human capital and portfolio capital wealth, so we can observe differences in the way this ratio affects wealth building, given the return shocks during the accumulation phase.

In all cases, we assume monthly savings contributions will rise with the inflation rate. This assumption implies that during the deflationary period of the Great Depression, nominal contributions declined; they roughly doubled during the inflationary period of the 1970s.

From Table 5.1, we can conclude that the worst drawdowns usually occur within three years of the previous market peak. The one exception is the 5.8-year drawdown that occurred starting in 1968. The market did not recover its 1968 level in total return terms, plus an additional return at the riskless rate, until 1985. The reversion pattern is good news for investors in accumulation facing horizons of several decades. Second, an investor with small initial wealth fared very well during those periods. For example, although the annualized risk-free rate from 1929 to 1945 was a paltry 0.5%, an investor gradually saving into this market would have achieved an excess annualized return on savings of 8.6% or 9.1% in absolute total. For an investor with no initial wealth on the day of the initial drawdown, the least profitable period in excess return terms would have been 1968 to 1985, although the nominal

Table 5.1. Excess Return above the Risk-Free Rate for Portfolio in Accumulation during Different Drawdown Periods

Start	End	Duration in Years	Size Drawdown	Duration in Years	Risk-Free Return	Nominal Excess Return above Risk-Free Return				
						No Wealth	50%	100%	200%	400%
Aug-29	Feb-45	15.5	-82.5%	2.8	0.5%	8.6%	4.5%	3.2%	2.1%	1.3%
May-46	Dec-49	3.6	-24.1	1.0	0.7	10.7	6.0	4.2	2.7	1.6
Jul-57	Jul-58	1.0	-15.0	0.4	2.1	26.9	13.6	9.4	6.1	4.0
Dec-61	Aug-63	1.7	-23.1	0.5	2.8	16.9	8.6	5.9	3.7	2.3
Jan-66	Jul-67	1.5	-15.4	0.7	4.5	17.0	9.6	7.2	5.3	4.0
Nov-68	May-85	16.5	-35.6	5.8	7.8	4.6	2.5	1.7	1.1	0.7
Aug-87	Oct-91	4.2	-29.7	0.2	7.2	7.6	3.8	2.6	1.6	1.0
Jun-98	Feb-99	0.7	-17.7	0.2	4.6	30.5	17.1	13.0	9.7	7.6
Aug-00	May-07	6.8	-45.0	2.1	2.9	9.8	5.2	3.6	2.3	1.4
Oct-07	Sep-12	4.9	-51.6	1.3	0.5	10.6	5.7	4.0	2.6	1.6
May-15	Jul-16	1.2	-10.9	0.7	0.2	13.3	7.5	5.6	4.1	3.1

return would still have been 4.6 percentage points above the risk-free return of 7.8%! The performance of an investor in a process of accumulation no longer appears so bleak.

Figure 5.2 provides a perspective on these numbers in the context of John, who started savings at age 30 and plans to retire at age 65. It illustrates the evolution of the ratio of portfolio wealth to remaining contribution in real terms, assuming a stable return scenario. It shows that John would reach a ratio of portfolio wealth to human capital wealth of approximately 50% at age 40, 100% at age 45, 200% at age 50, 400% at age 55, and more than 10 to 1 at age 60.

Table 5.1 and Figure 5.2 show that an investor who is 15 to 20 years from retirement may not have to fear holding a portfolio of risky assets even in the event of a severe market correction. By buying at low prices, this investor may still benefit from a drawdown even if financial markets do not fully mean revert. However, the same investor should be worried about a pattern of return events similar to those observed over 1929–1945 or 1968–1985 if fewer than15 years remain to retirement, given that significant wealth has already been accumulated and the accumulation process is drawing to a close. For example, midway through these two periods, the IRR would have been –1.0% in the first case and +2.2% in the second, assuming the risk allocation had not been reduced. These returns are lower than the risk-free rate in both periods. Furthermore, if the allocation to risky assets is significantly reduced over the period, the return recovery will be more difficult. Hence, investors face a trade-off among

- maintaining higher risk during the accumulation process for as long as possible to benefit from higher returns,

Figure 5.2. Evolution of the Ratio of Portfolio Wealth to Human Capital Wealth

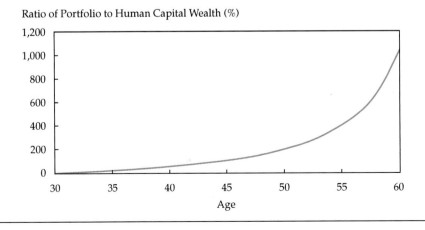

- having less risk to protect portfolio wealth as the decumulation phase approaches, and

- implementing a risk reduction path over a period long enough to recover the wealth lost during a drawdown period with as much in risky assets as prudent management allows.

The transition is complex.

Furthermore, we cannot ignore the behavioral aspect of this transition. As Bennyhoff (2008) framed the risk issue, which of the following better describes the volatility experience of an investor with a 30-year horizon: the standard deviation of the full 30 years or the average standard deviation year by year? Not all investors with a 30-year horizon can extricate themselves from "live" volatility in short intervals. At the very least, investors would need consistent benchmarking of their current situation against their long-term goal.

Fortunately, a risk management process, such as the dynamic glide path proposed in Chapter 3, helps to mitigate the risk of a significant drawdown during the transition phase. It may reduce the size of drawdowns by temporarily accelerating the decline in active equity exposure and allow the equity exposure to revert to the allocation proposed by the glide path once the floor guaranty has been reset (as illustrated in Figure 3.12), allowing the portfolio to more fully capture a return recovery.

5.2. Choice among Cash, Nominal Bonds, and Real-Return Bonds

"As a matter of fact, what investment can we find which offers real fixity or certainty of income? … As every reader of this book will clearly see, the man or woman who invests in bonds is speculating in the general level of prices, or the purchasing power of money."

—Irving Fisher, 1921

Holders of fixed-income instruments are exposed to credit risk, real-return risk, and inflation risk. Let us initially concentrate on the latter two risks. Assuming an investor has a 30-year horizon, short-term instruments such as T-bills will protect only against short-term inflation risk, and even then, the protection is imperfect. Although the annualized return of T-bills over the period 1927–2017 was +0.46% above the CPI–All Urban Consumers, there were significant discrepancies at 30-year horizons. T-bills undercompensated for inflation by –1.92% annually for the 30-year period ending in March 1963—a period that started at the bottom of the Great

Depression—and overcompensated by +2.11% for the 30-year period ending in June 2010, in the aftermath of the 1970s inflationary period. T-bills do not guarantee long-term inflation protection because we cannot assume the real rate necessarily remains positive.

On the other hand, an investor in a 30-year bond could achieve a real return above expected inflation but is exposed to unexpected inflation. Although the coupon reinvestment rates will likely increase in the presence of unexpected higher inflation, the higher coupon rates will be more than neutralized by the capital losses on the bonds themselves.

Most of the literature supports the view that the true risk-free fixed-income asset for a conservative long-term investor is a long-term inflation-indexed bond, removing the inflation uncertainty. As Campbell and Viceira (2002) point out, however, most professionally managed portfolio solutions allocate significantly to nominal bonds, whereas inflation-linked bonds usually play a smaller role and are introduced either when the individual approaches retirement or during retirement. Hence, conventional investment advice seems to imply that inflation risk is well managed and that concern about significant upward inflation surprise is unwarranted. Considering the long horizon of retirement planning, it appears inappropriate to rely on current short-term economic and monetary policy wisdom to establish an investment strategy.

Before questioning current practice, we need to realize that long-term inflation-linked bonds (ILBs) present issues for investors:

- First, buyers of long-term ILBs are "fixing" the real rate of return on their investment for potentially several decades. This move may represent a great opportunity at times when the real rate is significant, but accepting a real rate of less than 1% above inflation (the current rate available on these bonds) for decades on a 30-year financial instrument may not be the best alternative. This problem can be ameliorated by investing in an inflation-linked bond *fund*, but funds too have their problems (e.g., variable yields, tax consequences).

- Second, although corporations issue ILBs, these are usually of shorter maturities—such as 5 to 10 years—and the market is still relatively small. Hence, investors are usually restricted to investing in TIPS, so they do not earn the credit spread a corporate investment-grade portfolio could provide.

- Third, TIPS provide their return compensation in a very specific way. Not all the expected return is paid through the coupons, and part of the compensation is received through an adjustment of the face value of the bond. This means investors may have to sell a portion of their TIPS holdings to generate the desired income. This is especially true in the case of TIPS held in a taxable portfolio because the adjustment to the face value is taxable in the year it occurs (PIMCO 2017).

Consider the following example. As of 6 April 2018, the yield on the 30-year TIPS was 0.92%, whereas it was 3.02% on the 30-year nominal T-bond. This indicates that TIPS are priced as if investors expected a breakeven inflation rate of 2.1%. Investors will realize a return of inflation plus 0.92% by acquiring the TIPS. If they believe inflation will be less than 2.1%, the nominal bond will be preferable; if they believe inflation will exceed 2.1%, the TIPS will be preferable. If real rates increase, both the TIPS and the nominal bond will be negatively affected.

The timing of the compensation for both bonds is very different, however, even if we assume the inflation rate is exactly as expected. Consider a simplified example of an ILB and a nominal bond, both of five-year maturity, assuming yearly coupons of 1% and 3%, respectively—implying a breakeven inflation rate of 2.0%—and realized inflation scenarios of 1%, 2%, and 3%.[54]

The example in **Table 5.2** shows the nominal bond will pay the same cash flows whatever the realized inflation. These cash flows will have different real values (i.e., purchasing power), however, depending on what inflation rate actually occurs. It also shows the ILB will deliver the same IRR as the nominal bond if the realized inflation is equal to the breakeven inflation as of the time the ILB is purchased. The yearly cash flows of the ILB are lower, however, except at maturity when they are higher.

In summary, three points can be made:

- T-bills do not guarantee inflation protection because the real rate is uncertain.

- Long-term nominal bonds are subject to significant uncertainty regarding realized versus expected inflation.

- Long-term ILBs require the investor to fix or lock in the real rate of return, and the market for corporate ILBs is underdeveloped.

A possible compromise would be to maintain a portfolio of medium-term bonds having a corporate credit component. For example, the US Aggregate Core Index currently has a duration of less than six years with 38% in US T-bonds. A medium-term bond portfolio offers the following benefits:

- The relatively short duration of the bonds allows the investor to reinvest the income from the portfolio relatively quickly at the new prevailing rates.

---

[54]Coupons are normally paid semiannually.

Table 5.2. Cash Flow Generation of Nominal Bonds and Inflation-Linked Bonds under Different Scenarios of Realized Inflation

	Nominal Bond	ILB					
Coupon Rate	3.0%	1.0%		1.0%		1.0%	
Realized Inflation	1.0%	1.0%		2.0%		3.0%	
Year	Cash Flows	Cash Flows	Nominal Value	Cash Flows	Nominal Value	Cash Flows	Nominal Value
0	−1,000.00	−1,000.00	1,000.00	−1,000.00	1,000.00	−1,000.00	1,000.00
1	30.00	10.00	1,010.00	10.00	1,020.00	10.00	1,030.00
2	30.00	10.10	1,020.10	10.20	1,040.40	10.30	1,060.90
3	30.00	10.20	1,030.30	10.40	1,061.21	10.61	1,092.73
4	30.00	10.30	1,040.60	10.61	1,082.43	10.93	1,125.51
5	1,030.00	1,061.42	1,051.01	1,114.91	1,104.08	1,170.53	1,159.27
IRR	3.00%	2.00%		3.00%		4.00%	

- It allows the investor to benefit, on average, from the term premium.

- It allows the investor to generate a higher return than Treasuries by participating in the credit spread on quality fixed-income assets.

This approach is consistent with Campbell and Viceira (2002), who conclude that when comparing the annualized standard deviation of return over horizons of various lengths, the volatility of rolled T-bills and long bonds held to maturity increases with the time horizon whereas the volatility of five-year rolled bonds decreases. To further evaluate this approach, we compare six fixed-income alternatives under two extreme scenarios of an interest rate environment assuming an investment horizon of 30 years. The six fixed-income alternatives are

- money market (MM) instruments,

- 2-year rolled constant maturity T-bonds,

- 10-year rolled constant maturity T-bonds adjusted toward 2-year maturity between Years 21 and 30,

- 30-year rolled constant maturity T-bonds adjusted toward 2-year maturity between Years 2 and 30,

- a 6-year rolled constant maturity portfolio with an investment-grade credit component adjusted toward a 2-year maturity between ages 25 and 30, and

- the US Aggregate Core Index.

The first yield environment is the one observed between September 1981 and September 2011, representing the largest decline in bond yields in more than 100 years. For example, the 10-year bond yield was 15.84% at the beginning of the period, whereas it was 1.92% at the end. The second environment is the reverse bond yield environment, starting at 1.92% and ending with 15.84%. **Table 5.3** presents the annualized returns assuming two cash flow scenarios: a single initial cash flow and a second scenario in which a periodic monthly savings contribution is increased by the rate of realized inflation. In the case of the US Aggregate Core Index, the reverse scenario is not considered because properly computing returns accurately from the information available would be difficult.

Table 5.3 presents relevant information such as the standard deviation of monthly returns and the excess return (those above inflation) of each fixed-income portfolio under a declining or rising yield environment. The table shows these results for both a single initial cash flow and periodic monthly

Table 5.3. Performance of Various Fixed-Income Strategies in Rising and Declining Yield Environment (Single Cash Flows vs. Monthly Contributions)

		MM	2-Year Treas.	10-Year Treas.	30-Year Treas.	6-Year with Credit	Agg. Index
	Standard Deviation	0.24%	0.78%	2.19%	2.50%	1.65%	1.42%
				Excess Return			
Single cash flow	Yield declining	1.88%	3.71%	6.95%	**7.32%**	6.15%	6.29%
	Yield rising	**1.88%**	1.66%	0.37%	1.07%	1.24%	
Periodic contribution	Yield declining	0.50%	1.93%	3.84%	**4.88%**	**3.58%**	3.70%
	Yield rising	**3.18%**	2.90%	1.21%	3.08%	**3.38%**	NA
Duration	Minimum	0.08	1.64	4.93	6.48	3.69	NA
	Maximum	0.08	1.99	9.05	20.51	5.70	NA
	Average	0.08	1.87	7.28	13.01	4.90	NA

contributions. Table 5.3 also specifies the minimum, maximum, and average duration of each portfolio observed at specific points in time over the entire period.

If a single cash flow is considered, the MM portfolio generates the same excess return (1.88%) in both environments, given that the maturity of the instrument is monthly. As we increase the maturity/duration of the portfolio, we observe a widening gap in excess return between the declining and the rising yield environment, making a longer bond strategy a riskier gamble when starting from a low-rate environment. If we consider periodic contributions, however, the portfolio that generates the most stable patterns of excess returns is the mid-duration portfolio with an investment-grade credit component. It is an appropriate solution if the objective is to avoid putting too much confidence in our forecasts of real returns and inflation. Although not a perfect inflation hedge, it adapts quickly to a changing yield environment and offers a credit spread on quality assets that could compensate, in part, for unexpected inflation.

5.3. Impact of the Real Rate of Return on the Investment Decision Process

The return above the inflation rate is what allows investors to improve their well-being. A 4% fixed-income return in a 2% inflation environment is preferable to a 4% return in a 4% inflation environment. How does this fact affect the process of allocating across various financial assets, such as equity, fixed income, bonds, real-return bonds, and annuities, especially as retirement nears? What factors have the greatest effect on the level of real returns in the long run?

5.3.1. Real Interest Rates in the Long Run.
Real interest rates are affected by transitory and fundamental forces. Transitory forces include factors such as movements in oil prices and currency shocks. Fundamental forces are related to the level of savings and investment. Yi and Zhang (2016) of the Federal Reserve Bank of Minneapolis completed a study on the evolution of real rates in 20 countries since the mid-1950s. Their measure of real rates is based on the long-run average of the real yield on a short-term, risk-free asset.

Their analysis shows that the median of real rates, calculated across all countries, fluctuated by about 4 percentage points from its low to its high. The median rate was near zero in the mid-1950s, negative in the mid-1970s, strongly positive in the late 1980s and 1990s, and negative again recently. It has since risen to about zero. Furthermore, the recent period shows a significant decline in the range of real rates across those 20 countries, from a high of 5% in the 1980s to less than 1%.

According to the IMF (2014), "Economic and financial integration has increased sufficiently during the past three decades or so for real rates to be determined largely by common factors." Much of the decline from the mid-1980s to the early 1990s has been attributed to monetary policy improvements, whereas further decline in the late 1990s was attributed to fiscal policy improvements. Three factors since the early 2000s explain the further decline in real rates: the substantial increase in savings in emerging market economies, an increasing gap between global nominal savings and nominal investment since the early 2000s in advanced economies, and an increase in demand for safer assets among emerging market economies. Bernanke (2005) pointed to rising savings by an aging population in several industrialized countries and to a "glut in global savings" concentrated in emerging market economies. Although the real rate could rise from its low current level, the authors of the IMF report believe conditions for a return to the real rates that prevailed in the 1980s and early 1990s are not present.

Not all analysts fully agree. Hamilton, Harris, Hatzius, and West (2015) discuss the danger of mistaking short-run headwinds for permanent weaknesses. Although collapses in business cycles have not recently been followed by big and swift recoveries, as they once were, a secular stagnation of real rates is not a foregone conclusion.

Nevertheless, the issue is not whether we can reliably forecast how real rates will evolve but, rather, whether we can determine how the asset allocation process should be influenced by lower or higher real rates at the time important investment decisions have to be made.

5.3.2. Real Interest Rate and Asset Allocation.
The minimum performance objective for long-term investing is to outperform inflation. The excess return investors can achieve above inflation is a function of three parameters:

- real rate of interest, defined (as we did earlier) as the excess return of a short-term risk-free instrument above inflation;

- term premium, which is the excess return a quality asset of longer maturity can offer above the short-term risk-free rate (such as the rate on a 10-year Treasury minus the rate on T-bills); and

- risk and liquidity premiums.

Bernanke (2015) says the term premium reflects a buffer to compensate for two key risks: the change in the supply and demand for bonds and inflation. As discussed earlier in this chapter, the main risk associated with buying long-term bonds is being wrong about future inflation. The larger the term premium, the greater the protection investors receive against faulty inflation assumptions. As in Figure 4.5, Panels A and B, we compared the benefits of generating retirement income from bonds and annuities assuming two different real interest rate environments and found that although a higher real rate is beneficial to both strategies, the benefits are greater for the longer-duration asset—that is, the annuity—assuming the inflation expectations are approximately right.[55]

Figure 5.3 illustrates the history of the real return—defined as the spread between T-bills and inflation over the previous 12 months—and of two term premiums, the spread between the 10-year rate and T-bills and between the 30-year rate and the 10-year rate. In the 1980s and 1990s, investors had significant opportunities to invest in an environment of high real returns. Such an environment favored longer-duration assets. The environment of recent years has been less favorable to longer-term assets because the term premiums barely compensate for a negative real rate. We can conclude that an environment of higher real rates and term premiums allows for longer-duration assets and/or a greater allocation to fixed income and annuities. The asset allocation methodology should adjust to this reality.

Figure 5.3. Real Return and Term Premiums

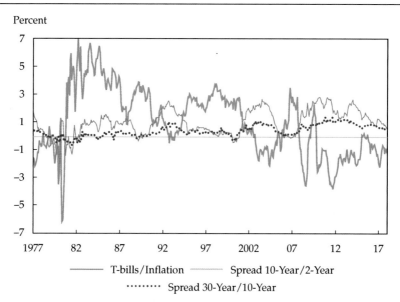

---

[55]In Figure 4.5, the fixed-income asset and the annuity (as of the age of 65) had durations of approximately 7 and 9.25 years, respectively.

5.3.3. Buying Annuities in Uncertain Return/Yield Environments:
A Tale of Two Johns. John "A" retired in December 2006 at age 65. He had saved $775,096 in his 401(k) plan. The rate on 10-year T-bonds at that time was 4.6%. John "A" invested 30% of his assets to purchase a SPIA with a 10-year payout guarantee. John allocated $232,529 to the annuity and invested the balance of $542,567 in a fixed-income and equity portfolio. The annuity payout (not indexed) was 7.5%.

John "B" retired in February 2009 at age 65. When John "A" retired, John "B" was still in a savings phase. John "B"'s portfolio had a cumulative wealth of $692,472, approximately the same amount that John "A" had saved two years prior to his retirement. By the time John "B" retired, the 10-year rate was only 3.0%, versus 4.6% when John "A" retired. The payout John "B" could get on an annuity was only 6.8%, even though credit spreads were significantly wider.

This was not the only issue facing John "B", however. By the time he retired, John "B" was caught in the most significant financial crisis in recent history. Even though John "B" continued to invest nearly $1,000 of savings every month until his retirement in February 2009, the total value of his assets plunged by nearly 20%. Although the same circumstances applied to John "A," John "A" had already purchased his annuity and obtained a much higher payout guarantee.

Table 5.4 compares the income situation of John "A" and John "B" as of February 2009. By that time, John "A" had gone through two years of annual retirement income at a level of 4% of his total wealth as of December 2006, inflation adjusted. He had also received two years of annuity payout.

Purely for reasons of timing, John "A," who is now age 67, can count on an expected annuity and investment income of $3,241 per month, whereas John "B" can expect only $2,698, which is 16.8% less than John "A"'s income.

When annuities are part of the portfolio recommendation, acquiring the intended annuity exposure over time may be the preferable strategy, especially

Table 5.4. The Impact of Retiring at the Wrong Time on Retirement Income

	John "A"		John "B"		
	Notional Annuity	Asset Portfolio	Annuity Income	Portfolio Income*	Total Income
John "A"	$232,529	$397,161	$1,453	$1,787	$3,241
John "B"	166,862	389,344	946	1,752	2,698

*Expected income assuming a 5.4% annual return.

if the allocation is significant. An equity shock not only depletes the portfolio value, affecting the amount of annuity income that can be purchased, but also can be accompanied by a significant bond yield decline, thereby reducing the payout that will be offered on the annuity. Although the effect of the decline in yield may be compensated by capital gain on the fixed-income portfolio, the hedge will be imperfect because the annuity likely has a longer duration than the bonds.

No one should attempt to time the appropriate moment to acquire annuities perfectly. On the other hand, although deferred annuities (i.e., annuities that begin their payout after a delay) offer a greater cash payout, the IRR of the annuity is less than the expected return on an equity/fixed-income portfolio. Hence, it may not be advisable to purchase deferred annuities too early.

What if both John "A" and John "B" had purchased their annuities in the last five years before retirement with the objective to own approximately 30% of their wealth in annuities as of retirement—six annuities in total? In the context of John "A," this approach would have had very little effect on his situation. His expected income as of February 2009 would have remained almost the same. John "B", however, would have improved his expected monthly income to approximately $2,880. The expected income gap compared with John "A" would have been reduced to approximately –11.5%.

5.4. Conclusion

Transitioning toward retirement is complex and risky. We want high returns so that we can accumulate as much wealth before retirement as possible, but we must be concerned with bad luck and bad timing just before we retire. The human capital component does not provide the same risk-adjusted benefits as we near retirement. Our understanding of drawdowns and recoveries indicates that such a transition must be relatively long. The dynamic glide path methodology discussed in Chapter 3 mitigates some of this risk.

The literature supports ILBs as the appropriate long-term inflation hedge. Many glide paths proposed in the industry increase the ILB component as retirement approaches. ILBs are not without their limitations, however. They predetermine the investors' real return for a long period and make it difficult to extract a credit premium that a high-quality corporate bond component could provide. A portfolio of medium-term bonds with a quality corporate credit component appears more appropriate for protecting against inflation and real-return uncertainties. It reduces the need to make another allocation decision as retirement nears.

Not all investors retire in an equal opportunity environment. Some retirees will face more favorable circumstances, such as a high real return and term premium, but others must navigate less favorable conditions. Although we cannot easily forecast if a retiree will benefit from a high real-return and/or term premium environment when asset allocation decisions have to be made, we understand that such a favorable environment would favor longer-duration assets. The proposed allocation close to retirement will be affected by the real-rate environment. A higher real rate close to retirement supports a transition toward longer-duration assets and/or a greater allocation to fixed income and annuities.

Finally, annuities are an effective component for many retirees. They offer a high payout and allow investors to maintain a riskier risk profile in the remaining portfolio. The timing of an annuity purchase, however, can have long-term consequences. It may be preferable to spread the purchase of annuities over several years.

6. Calibrating a Retirement Strategy

We have covered enough material in the previous chapters to support the development of an integrated retirement-planning process that can meet as efficiently as possible the goal(s) of a retiree in an uncertain world. **Figure 6.1** presents a diagram of the variables involved in the retirement-planning challenge during the accumulation, transition, and decumulation phases discussed in Chapters 3, 4, and 5. The figure specifies which components are under an individual's control—or at least somewhat under his control—and which are not.

Chapter 6 addresses three topics. First, we present the two main conceptual approaches of retirement planning—shortfall and life-cycle—used in the design of retirement solutions, as well as the methodologies and results of several empirical studies. Second, we discuss the components and design of objective functions that could be used to represent, as best as possible, the interests of investors/retirees when confronted with intertemporal choices. (We use the term "interests" purposely. The objective of a retirement-planning exercise should be to help individuals make appropriate decisions,

Figure 6.1. Variables of the Retirement Planning Challenge (Simplified Version)

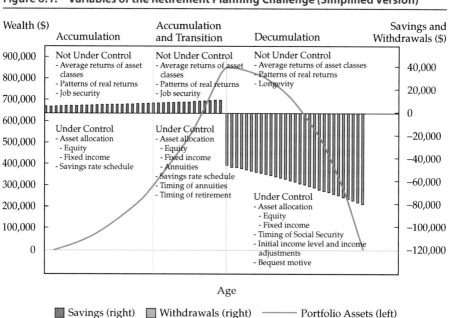

not necessarily to cater to misguided fears. In other words, the process designed to support individuals in this difficult task should have an educational component that leads to more rational and informed decisions that are in retirees' best interests.) Third, we apply a more comprehensive Monte Carlo simulation approach to the example of John.

6.1. Retirement Planning: Which Process?

Milevsky (2011) makes an important point that must be understood before we move forward—namely, that the cost of providing an adequate retirement income is not magically reduced by overestimating expected returns: "You can't tweak expected return assumptions until you get the number that you like. ... Assuming a more aggressive rate of return—or planning some arbitrary age [of death]—and then claiming that retirement has suddenly become cheaper is a dangerous fallacy."

This raises the issue of the *sustainability* and *feasibility* of retirement. Feasibility is about the portfolio's ability to fund the desired cash flows. Is the retirement income objective reasonable and rational considering the current wealth, human capital potential, other sources of income, and reasonable expectations of returns and inflation? Sustainability is about the likelihood that the income objective can be met in the long run considering parameter uncertainties such as asset returns and longevity. Answering the sustainability question requires a risk model and perhaps even adaptive asset allocation and consumption models.

Implicit in the material discussed thus far is that the primary objective is sustaining a retirement income target, not maximizing wealth as of retirement. Retirement income models fall in two categories. *Life-cycle* models integrate the dynamic of retirement planning, attempting to proactively tailor to investors' circumstances (e.g., changes in income expectations or decumulation needs) and financial markets (e.g., unexpectedly low or high portfolio returns). The solution is often derived from an optimization process and requires an objective function designed to maximize lifetime utility of consumption. *Shortfall minimization* models estimate the likelihood of not achieving a minimum income or wealth objective. Several iterations may be required to evaluate shortfall risk, given different portfolio risk profiles. Such models rely on backtests of historical returns, bootstrapped reshuffling of historical returns, and Monte Carlo simulations. We have used all three methods in previous chapters.

Both types of approaches have their detractors, although characteristics of both can be combined. The shortfall approach is easier to explain, but proponents of an expected utility approach criticize the shortfall approach for

121

being too narrow. The life-cycle approach can be more comprehensive and adaptive but also can be more complex to implement and to explain to investors. It requires that we identify a utility function that adequately represents the structure of investors' preferences and risk aversion—how they react to positive and negative surprise according to specific contexts—and that we properly calibrate this function to each investor.[56]

A shortfall approach may also require a way to explicitly (using a function) or implicitly (using graphic representations or other means) evaluate the "utility" of investors so as to compare different retirement-planning options. Measuring utility appropriately is a challenge. Rabin and Thaler (2001, p. 225) conclude that "people do not display a consistent coefficient of relative risk aversion, so it is a waste of time to measure it." Yook and Everett (2003) found only a 56% correlation among six different questionnaires designed to evaluate the risk aversion of 113 part-time MBA students. We also know that individuals will answer differently depending on how a question about risk is framed—for example, as a loss versus as a gain. Hence, it may be necessary to find intuitive ways to present the risk profiles of retirement-planning alternatives in ways investors can easily understand even if utility functions are used to help narrow these choices.

6.1.1. Shortfall Approach. The shortfall approach is concerned primarily with preventing or estimating the likelihood of falling short of an income objective under a predetermined spending policy. It usually prescribes a portfolio with a significant equity allocation to generate a higher expected income combined with disciplined rebalancing and income withdrawal processes. The analysis can be based on historical returns or on a Monte Carlo simulation.

The most talked-about shortfall approach is the 4% rule of William Bengen (1994). Using data from Ibbotson since 1926, Bengen simply evaluated the number of years (capped at 50) a portfolio could sustain an inflation-indexed payout initialized at X% of the wealth achieved as of retirement, assuming the first withdrawal occurs during any year between 1926 and 1976. Because the data coverage ended in 1992, well short of a 50-year horizon for a 1976 retiree, Bengen extrapolated missing returns using an average rate of 10.3% for stocks, 5.2% for fixed income, and 3% for inflation—not a process we would methodologically advise. Assuming a 50/50 allocation to equity and intermediate-term

---

[56]Calibrating a utility function to a specific investor is a difficult task that few advisers even attempt. The current advancements in machine learning, however, will allow us to more precisely evaluate investors' risk aversion based not only on their profile (income, education, health, profession, and so on) but also on actions and decisions they have made in the past in specific circumstances. Machine learning may even allow for preemptive communications from advisers to investors, minimizing the risk of impulsive behavior.

Treasuries, he found that a 3% withdrawal policy would never fail; a 4% policy was reasonable, because it would never lead to a withdrawal period of less than 35 years; but a 5% policy was too aggressive. Recently, Bengen advised that he had revised his recommendation to a 4.5% rule.[57]

Others have used a similar approach to establish similar rules supported by Monte Carlo simulations, allowing for a greater number of investment return paths to be considered and for the calculation of shortfall probabilities. Blanchett (2013) tested for constant dollar withdrawal rates ranging from 3% to 10% and determined that the 4% rule could lead to a 9% likelihood of failure over a 30-year horizon.

Milevsky and Robinson (2005) recognize that concentrating solely on the withdrawal rate is unwarranted. In their opinion, the three main levers available to prevent financial ruin are retirement age, asset allocation, and spending target. Asset allocation alone cannot solve bad spending decisions. They recommend controlling for retirement success by appropriately setting the retirement date and allowing for some flexibility in reducing the retirement income target if necessary.

It is interesting that Milevsky and Robinson (2005) are using a closed-form analytical formula that integrates a standard lognormal distribution for returns and an exponential lifetime mortality rate estimate. With proper calibration, this approach can be used to quickly estimate a probability of shortfall, prior to having the results of a more comprehensive Monte Carlo simulation. It can also be used, as they propose, to investigate the effect of incorporating annuities into the retirement solution. This approach was used in the decumulation engine application in Chapter 4.

Table 6.1 compares the resulting shortfall probabilities for an individual age 65, assuming different payout levels—from 3% to 6% in real terms—and portfolios having different risk levels. The table confirms that even if the payout rate is low, the all-fixed-income approach can lead to a higher probability of not meeting the payout target. In other words, a low-return/low-risk portfolio does not generate enough cash flow in most circumstances to meet the target. Portfolios strongly tilted toward fixed income can have substantial probabilities of failure when dealing with long horizons. A higher payout target increases the probability of shortfall, but a higher-risk portfolio is more likely to meet the target. In the case of a 4% to 5% payout, a 60/40 portfolio allocation appears preferable.

Frank, Mitchell, and Blanchett (2011) are also concerned about limiting shortfall probabilities but address the issue with a more dynamic approach.

---

[57]"The '4% rule' is actually the '4.5% rule.'" —William Bengen, architect of the Safe Withdrawal Rate: earlyretirementdude.com/summary-tuesdays-reddit-interview-inventor-4-rule/

Table 6.1. Shortfall Probabilities Using a Closed-Form Approach

Payout Rate	Allocation, Equity/Fixed Income			
	0/100	40/60	60/40	100/0
3%	15.4%	5.6%	4.8%	6.4%
4%	26.8	12.1	10.3	11.9
5%	39.0	20.5	17.6	18.4
6%	50.6	30.1	26.0	25.5

Note: Using average real returns corresponding to compounded nominal returns of 7% for equity return and 3% for fixed-income return and volatility of 20% for equity and 8% for fixed income.

They propose to set the failure probability at a level consistent with the retiree's risk tolerance but manage the payout rate dynamically to maintain the same shortfall probability at any age. This is consistent with the principle of the decumulation engine discussed in Chapter 4, and it will be further refined in the Monte Carlo simulations in this chapter. It is, of course, possible to eliminate the risk of shortfall entirely by having spending move directly with market values, as Waring and Siegel (2015) demonstrate; but most investors are not prepared to adjust spending by the large needed amounts.

Moreover, Pye (2012) explains that many individuals simply have not saved enough to cover their income need with a 4% payout rate. Furthermore, he argues that a fixed payout rate cannot be the optimal solution. For example, someone retiring in the early 1990s could easily have maintained a high payout such as 7.5% through 2010, when Pye's article was published. But an individual retiring in 1966 would have been unable to maintain a 4% payout consistently. Pye believes that an income retrenchment policy must be implemented in the event of substantial market declines. In addition, the initial payout should be set at a level that is unlikely to require significant downward adjustments as the retiree ages.

In the last decade, more authors have raised the need to either reassess the retirement income target or annuitize a portion of the portfolio to better manage shortfall probabilities. Davis (2010) cautions against using set payout rules when facing time-varying parameters. He recommends completing a periodic review of investors' circumstances and adjusting when required. Tahani and Robinson (2010) also argue that adjusting retirement income is the most important tool in reducing the risk of shortfalls.

We have already discussed in Chapter 4 some evidence related to the evolution of retirees' spending habits. Although we recommended that individuals should not plan on saving significantly less because they may spend

124 © 2019 CFA Institute Research Foundation. All rights reserved.

less as they age, the possibility of spending less can represent a valuable buffer against an unfavorable return environment. Milevsky (2012, p. 83) states that according to data from the US Department of Labor, "by 65, retirees are spending between 50% and 70% of what they did at 50. By 80 it has dropped to under 60%" for most retirees.

Pang (2012) looks to annuities, in combination with mutual funds, as a tool to minimize shortfall risk. His objective is to minimize the weighted probability of real income and residual wealth falling below specific thresholds. Pang also believes buying annuities in a low interest rate environment itself presents a significant risk, however—a concern we do not particularly share if annuity investments are substituting for fixed-income assets—but he argues, as we noted, that delaying the purchase of annuities may expose the individual when a severe market correction occurs.

Zahm and Ameriks (2012) look at the internal rate of return (IRR) of annuities using the median life expectancy as the horizon for the calculation. They find, unsurprisingly, that IRRs are usually less than those of 10-year Treasuries. As was implied in Chapter 4 and will become clear in Chapter 6, however, this finding ignores the benefits of annuities when considered in combination with other portfolio assets and the fact that half of all individuals will live past the median age.

Finke, Pfau, and Williams (2012) criticize the shortfall metric, which in their opinion puts too much emphasis on retirement income to be paid when survival probabilities are low. For example, if the target shortfall horizon for a 65-year-old retiree is 30 years and the probability of living beyond age 95 is only 10%, we are putting much pressure on the portfolio's ability to generate income for a low-probability event. Although we agree in principle with their argument, we should not ignore the possibility that an individual age 65 may rationally be just as concerned with a shortfall at age 80 than she is of falling short in the coming year. Hence, the weights we should attach to the utility of retirement income in future years should not necessarily be those derived from mortality tables. A retirement plan should be designed so that the fear of being unable to maintain an appropriate standard of living in the coming years does not affect the ability to enjoy life now. We will discuss this aspect again as we address the proposed objective function.

6.1.2. Life-Cycle Approach. The life-cycle approach is interested in the dynamic of intertemporal consumption. In its simplest form, it seeks to find the "optimal" asset allocation and consumption path to maximize lifetime utility in an environment characterized by uncertain asset returns and uncertain longevity. For example, Equation 6.1 shows a standard representation of a common utility-maximizing value function as of the date of retirement or any date thereafter, assuming no bequest motive:

$$\max U_x = \sum_{t=0}^{T-x} \beta_t \times p_t \times u(C_{x+t}),$$

Eq. 6.1

where x is the current age, T is the age at which the likelihood of death is almost certain, such as 120, β_t is the retiree subjective discount factor, p_t the conditional probability that the retiree at age x is alive at age $x + t$, and $u(C_{x+t})$ is the utility derived from consumption—no matter how that utility may be measured. In this context, the objective is to dynamically manage the asset allocation and withdrawal schedule during retirement to maximize overall utility over time, considering the current level of overall wealth. The challenge is even more complex in the context of taxation, other financial objectives, health coverage concerns, guaranteed income, households/dual consumption, bequest motives, the fact that the planning process starts well before retirement, and finally the challenge of adequately measuring the preferences of investors. The subjective discount factor is discussed in the next section.

Utility-based analysis has been used to maximize specific objective functions within life-cycle models. Samuelson (1969) and Merton (1969) have shown that under restrictive assumptions, such as constant relative risk aversion (CRRA) utility, i.i.d. returns, finite or infinite lifetime, and a risky (μ) and risk-free asset (r), the optimal allocation is independent of age and wealth and is solely attributed to the expected return on both assets, the volatility of the risky asset (σ^2), and the risk aversion parameter (γ):

$$\frac{(\mu - r)}{\sigma^2 \gamma}.$$

Eq. 6.2

In contrast, however, Collins, Lam, and Stampfli (2015, p. 71) concluded Part II of their comprehensive literature review titled *Longevity Risk and Retirement Income Planning*, which inspired several segments of this book, with the following:

> The trend in recent academic literature is away from building models that assume CRRA utility, normal distribution of asset returns, time-invariant volatility and correlation parameters, constant inflation, and fixed withdrawal formulas. Indeed, it is somewhat surprising that the practitioner-oriented literature continues to produce a multitude of articles seeking optimal spending and asset management strategies derived from portfolio models

embracing such assumptions. Advances in retirement income risk modeling are striking in terms of both the complexity of the models and the scope of insights engendered.

However, many of the case studies offered in the literature do not comport comfortably with likely spending patterns faced in retirement. Retired investors rarely spend according to constraints established either by shortfall probability estimates or according to autopilot formulas like the 4% adjusted-for-inflation rule. Furthermore, the utility-based analysis underpinning many life-cycle models generates optimal consumption rules based on the form of a possibly linear utility function rather than on the practical choices and exigencies that the investor encounters. Financial planning recommendations flowing from such risk models appear to be highly sophisticated, but investors should be mindful that such recommendations often arise in highly artificial contexts.

In other words, many models have implicit or explicit assumptions that are not realistic, a concern we seek to minimize in the framework presented in this chapter and especially in Chapter 8 as we apply our framework to the overall picture facing a retiree. Despite this concern, Sheikh, Roy, and Lester (2015) completed a commendable exercise of balancing withdrawal amounts over time, considering return and longevity uncertainty using a dynamic programming approach.[58] The authors present a decumulation model that accounts for wealth and lifetime income from sources such as a defined benefit (DB) pension plan, Social Security, or annuities. They use an Epstein–Zin-type function and integrate information related to wealth, consumption, survival probability, joint stock/bond real return distribution using the J.P. Morgan non-normal framework, a risk aversion parameter, and elasticity of intertemporal consumption. They solve for asset allocations and withdrawal rates starting at age 60 to maximize expected utility for men, women, and couples of different wealth levels at different ages and with different lifetime income. **Table 6.2** summarizes some of their results. We can make these observations:

- For a given level of wealth and guaranteed (annuity-like) lifetime income,
  - older retirees can support a higher withdrawal rate,
  - older retirees can support a higher bond allocation (less risk), and

---

[58]Dynamic programming is a recursive optimization approach that is efficient but computationally intensive. It seeks to simplify a complicated problem by breaking it down into simpler subproblems. The methodology can be quickly overloaded if the number of independent portfolio dimensions is increased.

Table 6.2. Optimal Withdrawal Rate and Bond Allocation as a Function of Age, Wealth, and Lifetime Income

Age	Wealth ($ M) and Lifetime Income ($)	Couples		Males		Females	
		Withdrawal Rate	Bond Allocation	Withdrawal Rate	Bond Allocation	Withdrawal Rate	Bond Allocation
65	0.5 M & 20,000	5.8%	24%	6.4%	21%	5.9%	20%
65	0.5 M & 50,000	6.1	0	7.2	0	6.6	0
65	2.5 M & 20,000	5.3	47	5.5	46	5.1	46
65	2.5 M & 50,000	5.5	38	5.9	36	5.5	35
75	0.5 M & 20,000	7.6	29	8.4	26	7.7	25
75	0.5 M & 50,000	8.1	2	9.8	0	8.8	0
75	2.5 M & 20,000	6.8	49	7.1	48	6.5	47
75	2.5 M & 50,000	7.2	41	7.7	39	7.1	38

- males can support a higher withdrawal rate than females or couples.

This is because of declining survival probabilities as one gets older and a shorter life expectancy for males.

- For a given age and wealth,

    - individuals benefiting from a higher level of guaranteed lifetime income can sustain a higher withdrawal rate, and

    - retirees with greater guaranteed lifetime income can have a more aggressive asset allocation.

This is because of the lower risk related to lifetime income, such as Social Security or income from a DB plan. Lifetime income acts like human capital and is even less risky (because human capital involves the risk that you can lose your job). It reduces the income risk during retirement and allows for a lower allocation to fixed income in the portfolio and greater withdrawal rates.

- For a given age and level of guaranteed lifetime income,

    - withdrawal rates at higher wealth levels should be less than at lower wealth levels, and

    - wealthier retirees should be more conservative.

This is because retirees with greater wealth already have a higher nominal level of withdrawal and derive lower utility from higher consumption. It is also because negative returns carry greater pain than the satisfaction provided by equivalent upside performance once basic consumption needs are satisfied.

Sheikh, Roy, and Lester (2015) also tested their approach against the 4% rule. They find their approach leads to a significantly higher certainty equivalent. They conclude, "A dynamic approach helps to address these challenges, adeptly balancing the management of longevity and lifestyle risk in a more prudent manner throughout a broader array of market cycles" (p. 25). Appendix II summarizes several studies based on different contexts, measures of utility, and methodologies. For example, it presents the results of a 2018 study by Irlam that may be the first to apply a deep reinforcement learning approach to the issue of retirement planning, allowing for significantly faster testing and implementation. Several of these studies inspired the general approach for the design of utility functions that is applied in this book.

6.2. Subjective Discount Rate and Probability of Survival

Before we propose a utility function that could be used to design a retirement program, we need to address two usual components of such function: the subjective discount rate and the probability of survival. Both components attribute less utility to future cash flows than to current cash flows, but for different reasons. We also need to discuss the type of utility function that is favored.

6.2.1. Subjective Discount Rate and Choice of Utility Function.

The subjective discount rate is intended to measure how we value the intertemporal choices we make as individuals, such as consuming less now to consume more in the future. Rae ([1834] 1905) was among the first economists to examine the sociological determinants of these choices. In the 19th and early 20th centuries, intertemporal choices were thought to arise from various psychological motives (Frederick, Loewenstein, and O'Donoghue 2002). In 1937, however, Samuelson introduced the discounted-utility (DU) model, which assumes that all "psychological and rational" motives underlying intertemporal choices can be summarized by a single parameter, the discount rate. The model also implicitly assumes that individuals are unconcerned with their time pattern of utility. A variable utility profile has the same value as a fixed utility profile if the two profiles lead to the same discounted utility. In the DU model, single-period utilities are simply additive. It would be reasonable, however, to expect retirees to seek some stability in their expected consumption profile.

Although Samuelson had reservations about this model's validity and never endorsed it as a normative model—his intention was solely to offer a generalized model of intertemporal choices—its simplicity gave it wide acceptance. Looking back at Equation 6.1, you can see that the DU model implies that the discount factor (β_t) integrates all the diverse motives of intertemporal choices:

$$\beta_t = \left(\frac{1}{1+k}\right)^t,$$

Eq. 6.3

where k represents the individual's rate of time preference.

According to Frederick et al. (2002), most analyses of intertemporal choices assume diminishing marginal utility, but we should not confuse diminishing marginal utility with positive time preference, which is implied by a positive discount rate. The former leads individuals to spread consumption over time, whereas the latter supports attributing more value to current consumption. Although diminishing marginal utility seems justified, however, the assumption of positive time preference could be challenged.

Many empirical analyses have been conducted in recent decades to better understand how individuals deal with intertemporal choices. This work generally supports the principle of "hyperbolic" discounting—that is, the idea that individuals apply lower discount rates to faraway rewards rather than to near rewards, whereas the DU model assumes a constant rate. When Thaler (1981) asked subjects to choose between $15 now and $X 1 month, 1 year, or 10 years from now, the median responses were implicit annualized returns (i.e., discount rates) of 345% over 1 month ($20), 120% over 1 year ($50), and 19% over 10 years ($100). Frederick et al. also mention, however, that the observation of lower discount rates at longer horizons is largely attributed to studies that incorporate time horizons of less than a year.

The DU model also contradicts such other empirical observations as these:

- Losses are discounted less than gains.

- Small amounts are discounted more than large amounts.

- Greater discounting is applied to avoid a delay rather than to accelerate.

- An improving sequence of outcomes is usually preferred to a declining sequence having the same DU.

- Individuals prefer to spread consumption, implying further that we cannot assume independence of utility benefits across different periods.

A significant issue in optimizing intertemporal choices is how to deal with self-awareness (or lack thereof), inconsistencies, and issues of self-control. For example, some individuals are aware that they lack self-control over their spending. Self-awareness may lead such individuals to invest a portion of their assets in annuities. which limits their ability to spend too quickly; or they may buy a house, which imposes forced savings. Others may lack the sophistication to recognize their own self-control issues. These individuals need tools and public policies to guide them even if they do not realize that they need these tools and policies. Furthermore, it may be necessary to optimize the design of these tools and policies to improve awareness and education.

In any case, both self-aware and naive groups of individuals need proper tools to help them calibrate their actions and receive the necessary periodic feedback. Without adequate tools and a good process, no one is sufficiently well equipped to handle a lifetime of intertemporal consumption challenges. There are simply too many dimensions to consider.

We have already indicated that individuals may be concerned with the pattern of their utility. Duesenberry (1952), Pollak (1970), and Ryder and Heal (1973) introduce the idea of habit formation, which may explain why consumption adjustments following a shock may be initially sluggish but will then adapt in the longer term. For example, Ryder and Heal account for habit formation by introducing a state variable representing an exponentially weighted sum of prior consumptions.

Models referring to intertemporal choices presume that any new option available to an individual is integrated into that person's existing long-term plan. This presumption is attractive but difficult to implement in real life. The evidence shows that individuals are unable or unwilling to reevaluate their entire stream of consumption properly each time a new option is considered or a change of circumstance occurs. They will usually focus on what has changed instead of reevaluating their entire situation.

Consequently, consistent with prospect theory (PT), a conceptually distinct form of habit formation is to express utility as a deviation from a reference point or expected target. Utility is measured using a value function that penalizes negative deviations more than it rewards positive ones. It also exhibits diminishing sensitivities to the magnitude of both gains and losses, implying implicitly larger discount rates for smaller deviations than larger ones.

Figure 6.2 contrasts the concept of a standard utility function reflecting decreasing marginal utility of wealth with that of a value function. The value function reflects asymmetry between losses and gains relative to a reference point when assessing value. As we can see, the shape of the PT value function's curve is similarly concave in the gain space but is convex in the loss space. Experiments in behavioral economics usually show that losses loom larger than gains by a factor of about 2.

In this respect, Loewenstein and Prelec (1992) completed some of the most important work on DU anomalies. They show that applying such a framework to intertemporal choices makes it less desirable to transfer positive or negative excess consumption (against a benchmark) from one period to another. For example, accelerating consumption implies early utility/value gains made at the expense of lower utility/value later in life. The shape of the PT function, however, implies that those early gains will be of smaller magnitude than the losses that will occur later. It also implies that an individual would prefer to spread gains over time but concentrate losses. Although the former may be a reasonably acceptable behavioral assumption, the latter may not. Furthermore, the shape of this function also opens the door to the possibility that individuals may express their preferences differently if the same

Figure 6.2.   Utility Function vs. PT Value Function

A. *Utility Function*

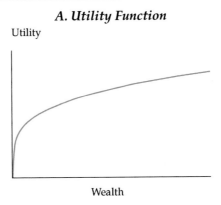

B. *Value Function*

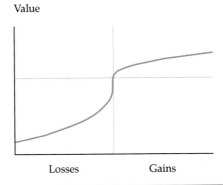

issue is presented in terms of gains instead of losses—for example, by presenting a situation as a gain instead of loss avoidance. Evidence shows that framing has a significant effect on the decision process.

At least two other issues need to be addressed: investors' expertise and changing utilities. For example, if an individual prefers having $1,000 now rather than $1,200 in one year in a 3% return environment, is it because he rationally integrates other considerations or because he is simply ignoring capital market reality? When asked about his intertemporal preferences for $1,000 now versus $1,000 + $X a year from now, does he rationally integrate inflation expectations in determining his subjective discount rate? At the very minimum, the subjective discount rate in a nominal dollar world should equal the rate of expected inflation, but it is not obvious that it should be much greater than inflation during retirement.

The literature also discusses how the marginal utility of receiving $1,000 now may be less than the marginal utility of receiving the same real amount in 10 years because the individual's baseline consumption may be greater then. We do not often reflect, however, on the utility derived from a specific reward while employed versus the utility derived from receiving a similar reward when retired and living off our savings. Could the utility we derive from a specific reward change (upward or downward) as we approach or are in retirement?

The complexity of human behavior, needs, and concerns means it is difficult to reduce the rationalization of intertemporal choices to a single discount rate or even a hyperbolic discounting process. We are not advocating that all the parameters of the utility function we will propose should be accepted by everyone but simply that the function should be transparent and reflect reasonable behavioral expectations.

6.2.2. Probability of Survival. There is rationality to the idea that value attributed by a 65-year-old individual to the real retirement income desired at age 75 should be less than the value attributed to the real retirement income desired for next year, because the probability of being alive at age 66 is greater than the probability of being alive at age 75. In the United States, the probabilities for the average male would be approximately 98.4% and 79%, respectively. Hence, if we consider a utility function such as that described in Equation 6.1, all other things assumed to be equal, the expected utility derived from a cash flow at age 75 would be 79/98.4 of the utility derived from the same real cash flow at age 66.

As previously indicated, whether we should adopt a strict Cartesian view of how survival probabilities should be integrated into a utility function has been little studied. (A Cartesian view suggests a mechanistic interpretation of how survival probabilities affect utility.) Declining survival probabilities support a higher level of initial consumption, given that the likelihood such a level will have to be maintained is declining. In other words, if you knew you were going to die in exactly two years and had no bequest motive, you might decide to spend all your assets during these two years.

Two issues concern individuals in retirement, however. First, assuming the retirees do not have access to a generous inflation-adjusted DB plan that covers most of their needs in combination with Social Security, most individuals will live off their Social Security benefits and private savings. Doing so creates significant uncertainty for retirees because the level and pattern of asset returns are unknown, unless a fixed-income strategy involving low risk and low return is followed. Second, longevity and health bring considerable uncertainty, and many individuals such as John may ask the following question: Even though the average male age 65 has more than a 50% probability of dying before age 84, what if I live to be 84 or more? Should retirees be willing to increase their level of consumption based on the likelihood that they may be dead by age 85 or earlier? There is no perfect recommendation, but we will assume that retirees are concerned about meeting their income needs for the better part of a "reasonable" life expectancy, to be defined in the next section. We expect this reasonable age to be much greater than the median age, however. In other words, an age corresponding to a survival probability of less than 50% would be used. Given that many people do live far beyond their life expectancy, how can we make this approach work? The key is to adjust this reasonable age dynamically as the retiree ages.

6.3. Designing an Objective Function

A PT value function is used to adjust the reasonable age of life expectancy. We use a function that measures satisfaction relative to an income objective. More specifically, we use two income objectives: a preferred income objective (PIO) and an essential income objective (EIO). Hence, the utility function is calibrated after we ascertain the following information:

- EIO: What is the amount of inflation-adjusted core retirement income that the individual could reasonably target and achieve with reasonable certainty? This amount must be consistent with accumulated wealth and expected longevity. Assume this amount is $50,000.

- PIO: What amount of excess income would the individual like to achieve if possible? Say the amount is $60,000.

These initial parameters are very important and should be established with the help of a financial adviser. Likely this exercise should be completed as a two-step process: first, fixing these two initial parameters as best as possible; then, refining them once analytical results providing probability estimates are obtained.

In *Secure Retirement*, we assume the PT value function is calibrated such that the utility derived from achieving the EIO is nil. The utility derived from achieving an income gain of up to $10,000 against the EIO, however, is only half the loss of utility derived from achieving an income loss of the same amount. Relative losses are weighted twice as much as gains. **Figure 6.3** illustrates what a PT value curve may look like in this situation. As can be seen, the slope of the value function is significantly steeper for negative deviations than positive ones, more so when deviations are small. Another user

Figure 6.3. Example of a Calibrated PT Value Curve

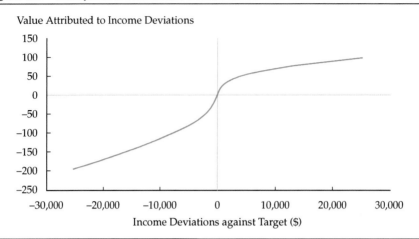

may choose different assumptions, but these assumptions are reasonable for a behavioral point of view. In Chapter 8, we use different types of implementation of this principle.

This function estimates the utility derived from consumption at a specific point in time. Three aspects can affect how total utility is valued and distributed in an intertemporal framework, as in Equation 6.1:

- subjective discount rate

- survival probabilities

- evolution of income needs

Any of the following changes in parameters would cause the initial income assumption to increase: a higher discount rate, lower survival probabilities, or an expected decline in future income needs relative to current income needs. Based on the preceding discussions, the value function integrates the following assumptions:

- The subjective discount rate is an imperfect tool for properly calibrating investors' preferences, especially during a retirement phase. What discount rate should be set? Is the individual sophisticated enough to properly understand this rate's significance? Can we design tests to appropriately estimate what this rate should be? In *Secure Retirement*, we prefer to rely on more objective measures to express intertemporal preferences. Hence, the discount rate will equal the rate of inflation—the real rate is zero.

- The survival probabilities used in the value function reflect the desire of individuals *not* to outlive their savings, for a reasonable expectation of longevity. Hence, at any given age after retirement, we assume a survival probability of 100% for all years until some predetermined lower survival probability, such as 25%, is reached. The actual survival probabilities will be used for all remaining years. For an individual such as John, assuming he retires at 65 and is currently 65, this approach would imply using a 100% survival probability up to approximately age 91.7 and then using the actual probabilities thereafter. Once John reaches age 85, the break-even age will be closer to 95. This "step function" approach is not consistent with mortality experience but is useful because it protects retirees from overspending early in retirement because of overconfidence about their mortality expectation.

- Because the utility derived from consumption at a specific point in time is measured in reference to an income/consumption objective, it is important to properly estimate how this objective may evolve as the retiree ages. There is also literature on how the average individual's expense basket evolves as that individual ages, ignoring for now health-related aspects. Although, as indicated previously, we do not necessarily recommend fully incorporating this aspect into planning, it may be reasonable to assume some expense reduction if a proper analysis of past expense patterns has been conducted. The simulations that follow will allow for such adjustments.

In other words, we favor calibrating the more objective aspects of the process, such as survival probabilities and consumption patterns, rather than subjectively adjusting the discount rate when dealing with intertemporal preferences. Other users may prefer a different set of assumptions, but in the end, it is about having reasonable assumptions.

6.4. Calibrating a Retirement Solution for John: A Monte Carlo Approach

In the remainder of Chapter 6, we will evaluate several environments of accumulation and decumulation for John.[59] The different simulations become gradually more realistic, although much less comprehensive than the work presented in Chapter 8. For example, we ignore the effects of taxation, dynamic annuity allocation, the asset location decision, dynamic glide paths, and ownership of real estate assets.

---

[59]All return scenarios generated to complete the Monte Carlo are obtained using the same block bootstrapping approach and assumptions described in Section 3.6.

6.4.1. Simulation Set 1. Assuming a 60/40 fixed allocation, John's expected wealth at age 65 is $775,096. Assuming that as of age 65 John requires an annual initial payout of either 4% or 5% of this amount, adjusted thereafter for inflation, we present the probability that the income objective would not be fully met at ages ranging from 85 to 110. We also present the same probabilities if 10%, 20%, 30%, or 40% of the accumulated wealth as of retirement had been invested in a single premium immediate annuity (SPIA). Finally, we look at the same probabilities assuming a glide path transition from 90% toward 60% in equities during the accumulation period and the same dollar payout as under the 60/40 fixed allocation. This glide path remains for other simulations to follow. **Table 6.3** presents the results.[60]

There are three conclusions:

- The glide path as opposed to the 60/40 allocation leads to higher probabilities of success, especially if the target payout ratio is 5%.

- The presence of an annuity does not significantly change the probability of success. The annuity would still provide income, however, even if the portfolio and the annuity cannot fully meet the income requirement.

- A 5% payout does significantly reduce the probability of success relative to a 4% payout. This outcome confirms the results of several studies indicating that a payout of 5% in the absence of a dynamic decumulation strategy may be too high.

6.4.2. Simulation Set 2. The second set of simulations looks at the effect of adjusting the savings rate during the accumulation period if, for example, the wealth accumulated by John at age 50 was less than the expected wealth. In this case, John would increase his savings rate to target the same expected final wealth as of age 65. The adjustment is limited, however, to an increase of no more than 20% of the annual amount saved. For example, because John's saving rate under our base scenario is 10%, the savings rate could not increase to more than 12%. This scenario is meant to recognize that in the real world, some further sacrifice may be needed and planned for if financial markets do not deliver a favorable environment during the accumulation period but an individual has limited ability to save much more. **Table 6.4** presents the impact of adjusting the savings rate at age 50 when wealth is less than the expected amount. It should be compared with Table 6.3, Panel C, where the glide path and payout are identical.

---

[60]The probabilities of success in Table 6.3, Panels A and B, are lower than those presented in Table 4.7, Panels A and B, because in Chapter 4 we considered only the uncertainty of returns during the decumulation period.

Table 6.3. Probability of Success

% Annuity	Age					
	85	90	95	100	105	110
A. Constant 60/40 allocation and 4% payout						
0%	84%	76%	68%	63%	58%	55%
10%	84	76	69	63	59	55
20%	83	76	69	64	60	56
30%	83	75	69	65	61	57
40%	82	75	70	65	61	58
B. Constant 60/40 allocation and 5% payout						
0%	72%	61%	53%	48%	43%	39%
10%	71	61	53	48	43	40
20%	70	60	53	48	44	40
30%	69	60	53	48	44	41
40%	67	59	53	48	44	41
C. 90/10 toward 60/40 glide path and 4% payout						
0%	87%	80%	74%	69%	65%	62%
10%	87	80	75	70	66	63
20%	87	80	75	71	67	64
30%	86	80	75	71	68	65
40%	86	80	76	72	69	66
D. 90/10 toward 60/40 glide path and 5% payout						
0%	77%	68%	61%	56%	52%	49%
10%	76	68	61	56	52	49
20%	76	68	62	57	53	50
30%	75	67	62	57	53	51
40%	74	67	62	57	54	51

Although the savings rate adjustment was limited to 20%, the effect is perhaps less significant than could have been expected, given that the increase in the success rate is only 2 to 3 percentage points, or slightly more when the payout rate is 5%. The savings increases added nearly $31,000 in total contributions, which represents 3.6% of expected wealth as of retirement. Savings that occur late in the process, however, benefit less from compounded returns. This addition, for instance, would be expected to add approximately $46,000

Table 6.4. Probability of Success: Glide Path and 4% Payout

	Age					
% Annuity	85	90	95	100	105	110
0%	89%	83%	77%	72%	68%	64%
10%	89	83	77	73	69	65
20%	89	83	78	73	69	67
30%	88	83	78	74	70	68
40%	88	83	78	75	71	69

of wealth, but this amount is not enough. For example, the data in Figure 3.10 show that even at the 25th percentile level, a glide path with a transition starting at age 50 has an expected wealth at age 65 of nearly $200,000 less than expected wealth at the 50th percentile level. Under adverse financial situations, the required increase in savings would have to be very significant to meet the initial target.[61]

The alternative to saving more is spending less in retirement. That is, when the financial environment is unfavorable, it may become necessary to review the income objective's feasibility. Further analyses of the simulation results show that the cap adjustment of 20% is easily reached in most scenarios where the accumulated wealth was below the target at age 50.

6.4.3. Simulation Set 3. As Social Security is added to the equation, we replace the objective of a target payout ratio of 4% or 5% of accumulated wealth with an income replacement ratio of 70% of work income. We assume that the Social Security payment will not be reduced because of the possible eventual depletion of the Social Security Trust Fund. The potential impact of the depletion in the absence of a political solution will be tested in Chapter 8. Panels A and B of **Table 6.5** present the results when Social Security is received at either age 65 or 70.

The effects of postponing the initial Social Security claim are especially significant if the retiree is expected to live beyond age 85. Because Social Security is adjusted for inflation, it is an efficient source of longevity insurance. If Social Security payments were to be reduced in the early 2030s by 20% or more, however, it could affect the decision to postpone Social Security. Preliminary analyses indicate the trade-off may no longer be worthwhile for

---

[61]A 90–60 glide path has an expected wealth of $850,968 as of retirement. Figure 3.10 shows the expected wealth at the 25th percentile level to be approximately $670,000. This means that despite an expected supplementary gain of $46,000, quite a few scenarios fall short of the wealth objective.

Table 6.5. Probability of Success: Glide Path with 70% Target Income

	Age					
% Annuity	85	90	95	100	105	110
A. Social Security at 65						
0%	80%	72%	65%	59%	55%	52%
10%	80	72	65	60	56	53
20%	79	71	65	60	57	53
30%	78	71	65	61	57	54
40%	77	71	65	61	58	55
B. Social Security at 70						
0%	87%	82%	77%	74%	70%	68%
10%	86	81	77	74	71	69
20%	84	80	77	74	72	70
30%	83	79	77	74	72	70
40%	81	78	76	74	73	71

an individual expected to live to age 85 but still worthwhile if a longer life is expected.

6.4.4. Simulation Set 4. Some situations may have no better alternative than postponing retirement in the event of insufficient wealth. The simulations in **Table 6.6** look at the effect of postponing retirement by as much as 24 months on the probability of failure. The trigger for deciding to postpone retirement is wealth more than 5% below the expected level. Retirement is postponed by one month for each 0.5% wealth deficit beyond 5%. Maximum postponement occurs when the wealth level is 17% below expectations.

The analysis indicates that postponing retirement is necessary in nearly 40% of all scenarios. Therefore, it is unsurprising that the probability of meeting the income objective at age 100 increases from approximately 59% to 74% in Table 6.5 to more than 90%. The tables also show that postponing retirement by up to two years, although unpleasant for some, is one of the most effective steps to ensure income sustainability.

6.4.5. Simulation Set 5. Even if an individual is well prepared for retirement and has purchased some annuities to reduce the potential impact of financial crises, the financial environment during retirement could still be unfavorable. This last set of simulations evaluates the impact of a decumulation engine whereby the probability of failure has been set at 20% and the reduction of retirement income limited to no more than 10% in any one year.

Table 6.6. Probability of Success: Glide Path with 70% Target Income and Mechanism for Postponing Retirement

	Age					
% Annuity	85	90	95	100	105	110
A. Social Security when retirement occurs						
0%	98%	96%	93%	91%	88%	87%
10%	98	96	94	91	89	88
20%	98	96	94	92	90	89
30%	98	97	95	93	92	90
40%	99	97	96	94	93	91
B. Social Security at 70						
0%	98%	96%	95%	93%	92%	90%
10%	98	97	95	94	93	92
20%	98	97	96	95	94	93
30%	98	97	96	95	95	94
40%	98	98	97	96	95	95

Table 6.7 presents the impact of applying the decumulation engine. Because the option to postpone retirement leads to a significant improvement in the probability of success, the decumulation engine is tested without the option to postpone retirement. Hence, Simulation 4 evaluated the probability of success assuming retirement may be postponed but the inflation-adjusted retirement income target remains the same. Simulation 5 evaluates the probability of success assuming retirement may not be postponed but the retirement income target could be reduced by up to 10% in specific circumstances. A reduction of less than 10% is still counted as achieving the income target. Two conclusions can be reached. First, the decumulation engine considerably improves the probabilities of success against the status quo at age 100 (see Table 6.7), although it implies that we are willing to accept a potentially lower retirement income. Furthermore, it is not quite as efficient as considering the option to postpone retirement by as much as two years. Clearly, both options should always be part of the retirement tool kit. We also looked at the percentage of simulation scenarios where the decumulation engine was triggered. **Table 6.8** presents the results at ages 70, 85, and 100 for Social Security at 65 and at 70.

Although the decumulation engine increases the likelihood of meeting a minimum requirement, Table 6.8 shows there is a high probability that

Table 6.7. Probability of Success: Glide Path with 70% Target Income and a Decumulation Engine with a 10% Tolerance Level

			Age			
% Annuity	85	90	95	100	105	110
A. Social Security at 65						
0%	97%	94%	91%	87%	83%	73%
10%	97	94	91	88	84	75
20%	97	94	91	88	84	76
30%	96	93	91	88	85	77
40%	96	93	90	88	85	78
B. Social Security at 70						
0%	98%	98%	98%	98%	98%	98%
10%	98	98	98	98	98	98
20%	97	97	97	97	97	97
30%	96	96	96	96	96	96
40%	93	93	93	93	93	93

Table 6.8. Probability of Triggering the Decumulation Engine

	Social Security at 65			Social Security at 70		
% Annuity	70	85	100	70	85	100
0%	60%	76%	79%	66%	80%	80%
10%	57	75	79	63	80	80
20%	53	73	78	59	78	79
30%	50	72	78	56	77	78
40%	46	70	77	53	76	77

it may be triggered, even if temporarily. When an individual begins claiming Social Security at age 70, the probability of triggering the decumulation engine increases. This is to be expected because postponing Social Security will drain the asset portfolio more quickly unless retirement is also postponed to 70. This situation may be detrimental to the retiree if unfavorable return scenarios occur during this period. Furthermore, as will be shown in Chapter 8, postponing Social Security to age 70 may not always be risk/longevity optimal.

The probability of triggering the decumulation engine is concentrated in the first 5 to 10 years after retirement. As expected, however, it is significantly reduced by the presence of annuities. This result supports the view that nominal annuities are highly efficient at managing short-term market uncertainty. Annuities reduce the likelihood of triggering a decumulation engine and improve the retirement income of the individual in the event of a trigger.

When approaching retirement, an individual should evaluate if postponing retirement is advisable from both financial and non-financial perspectives. Also, whether or not retirement can be postponed, a decumulation engine should be considered within the limits of acceptable consumption adjustments.

Finally, to evaluate if a PT utility function is consistent with the safety processes and improvements proposed in this section, the utility function was tested within the parameters of the previous simulations. More specifically, we evaluated if the expected utility as of age 65 resulting from a 60/40 portfolio combined with 30% in annuities and Social Security at 70 is superior to that of a 40/60 portfolio with Social Security at 65. The level of utility, as defined earlier, was significantly greater.

6.5. Conclusion

At this point, we should realize that much can be done to improve the quality of life of individuals at retirement without even discussing active portfolio management. Much of this improvement comes from proper allocation policy and management of longevity risk. The concepts, principles, and financial knowledge are already available. What we need are proper tools that can integrate the complexity of real-life situations that encompass many dimensions (taxes, savings programs, insurance needs, housing and mortgages, children's education, and so on) within an integrated and well-designed user-friendly tool and process.

7. Completing the Financial Planning Framework

After the first six chapters, we now have a basic framework for managing accumulation and decumulation. To make this framework more realistic, however, we need to add details such as asset allocation and taxation and to recognize that retirement is more complex for a household than for a single individual. Other relevant features to consider are the appropriate income replacement ratio, housing and reverse mortgages, and other insurance products such as life insurance and variable annuities. These nuances often complicate the retirement-planning process and require the use of a retirement-planning tool to properly and more easily integrate all components.

7.1. Asset Allocation

This section covers three dimensions of the asset allocation process. One could write an entire book about the asset allocation decision, but our objectives are to emphasize the most important aspects: those that account for most of the benefits and risks to which investors are subjected. Furthermore, we are interested in the long-term strategic allocation that makes sense for most investors, not the allocation that could result from an adaptive dynamic process that would integrate forecasts of returns, volatility, and serial correlation. Nor are we interested in exotic asset classes, such as artwork and farmland, that are accessible to only a limited number of individuals. We can cover only so much material in *Secure Retirement*. Adapting our approach to the special needs of wealthy investors would add complexity but does not change the basic principles.

Therefore, we discuss three dimensions of asset allocation: which broad asset classes are incorporated, how to decide between domestic and non-domestic assets, and whether active management should be considered.

7.1.1. The Choices among Broad Asset Classes.
Broad traditional asset classes are equity, fixed income, and cash. Within equity, there are significant style and geography choices. Investors can allocate to investment-grade and below-investment-grade (high-yield) fixed income and to alternative investments such as commodities and hedge funds. Not all investment classes are easily accessible to small investors or accessible at a reasonable cost.

Equity and investment-grade fixed income/cash are part of any diversified portfolio. The allocation strategy applied to equity and within equity is discussed in Section 7.1.2. Here we focus on whether other asset classes should play a role. We have already discussed inflation-linked bonds, and municipal bonds are covered in the section on taxation. Therefore, the discussion here is limited to high-yield debt and commodities. Allocating to hedge funds is discussed as part of active management. The issue is not whether the "average" investor can appropriately time an entry and exit point for these assets but whether evidence suggests such assets should strategically receive a constant portfolio allocation. We tend to believe that the average investor's portfolio should usually avoid the more complex and/or costly asset classes, especially now that investors have access to "cheap" index products through ETFs and low-cost implementation processes.

High-yield bonds benefit from higher yields to maturity, but they are penalized by larger expected losses in bad economic environments and usually have higher management fees than other bonds. They are also highly correlated to equity and have less liquidity during difficult financial and economic periods. For example, **Table 7.1** compares an investment-grade corporate bond ETF with an ETF based on a known high-yield bond index as of 30 June 2018. The yield of the latter is 2.0% higher, but the expense ratio is also significantly greater, and the return differential achieved over the previous five years is less than 1% in what could be considered a good environment for risky assets. In a bad environment, the entire 1% advantage, or more, could be lost.

Some investment strategists advise incorporating high-yield bonds as a diversifier. Because these bonds are highly correlated with equity, however, we should ask whether a contemplated allocation to high-yield bonds could be replaced by a slightly larger allocation to equity.

We compared a 60/40 allocation to equity and investment-grade fixed income with a 58/5/37 allocation to equity and, respectively, high-yield and investment-grade fixed income over the period July 1983 to April 2018. Both portfolios had basically identical compounded returns (9.73% versus 9.72%), very similar volatility (9.25% versus 9.18%), and nearly identical worst

Table 7.1. Characteristics of Investment-Grade and High-Yield Bond Products

ETF	Yield	Duration	Fees	Five-Year Return (net of fees)
Investment grade	4.1%	6.4	0.07%	3.49%
High yield	6.0	3.8	0.49	4.24

drawdowns (–32.7% and –32.8%).[62] The correlation between the investment-grade fixed-income portfolio and equity was 14%, but that of the high-yield fixed income with equity was nearly 60%.

More interesting is the rolling annualized return differential of the two portfolios over periods of three years shown in **Figure 7.1**. The range of annualized excess return is usually +/–40 bps. Despite the high correlation to equity, the excess return of the 58/5/37 portfolio has a negative correlation to the return of the 60/40 portfolio itself, in the range of –0.30. Hence, high-yield bonds may not improve a portfolio's Sharpe ratio, but they do have some effect on the pattern of returns.

In the end, a long-term unsophisticated investor could do very well with a simpler asset allocation that does not incorporate high-yield bonds. A more sophisticated investor may appreciate the greater nuances that high-yield bonds can bring. Although they worsened the effects of the financial crisis in the 36-month period ending in late 2008, they stabilized the equity shock following the burst of the tech bubble. As a rule, however, it is not obvious that high-yield bonds bring great benefits to the average long-term investor,

Figure 7.1. Annualized 36-Month Return Spread against a 60/40 Allocation When a High-Yield Component Is Added

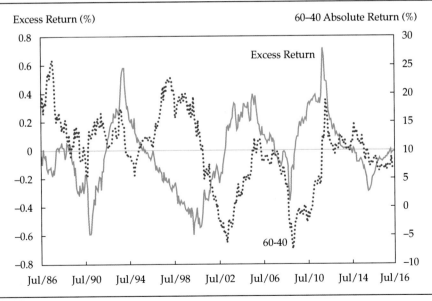

[62]Calculation are based on indexes. However, we attributed a 40-bp excess fee to the management of high-yield bonds.

considering their lower liquidity and the added anxiety and complexity they may bring.

Commodities are often presented as a strong diversifier and as an inflation hedge. As Lussier (2013) postulates, however, it is difficult to recommend a strategic and constant asset allocation to an asset class when we cannot confirm the existence of a risk premium for holding it. Unlike traditional asset classes, exposure to commodities is achieved through futures contracts, a market in which short and long positions always sum to zero, implying there are always as many buyers of futures contracts as there are sellers. The fact that commodity exposure is achieved through futures contracts implies that if a risk premium indeed exists, we cannot assume it is necessarily paid to the buyers of the contract or even that it may not change sign depending on the circumstances.

Although diversification is a valuable objective, it cannot be at the expense of a huge sacrifice of long-term returns. The annualized performance of equity has outperformed that of commodities (represented by the S&P Goldman Sachs Commodity Index) by a factor of 3 from December 1979 to April 2018 (11.6% versus 3.7%).[63] Furthermore, we must also realize that much of the performance in energy-related futures contracts in the 1980s and 1990s came from backwardation—that is, the fact that futures contracts were trading below the spot price. Finally, commodity returns are as volatile as equity, although the correlation to equity is only 18.7% over the period.

There is, however, the argument that commodities are an inflation hedge, although this does not appear to be the case for all commodities. For example, although Bhardwaj, Hamilton, and Ameriks (2011) find that commodities provide some protection against unexpected inflation, Attié and Roache (2009) conclude that short-term hedging benefits may be hurt by medium-term reversal, given that higher inflation may lead to higher interest rates that eventually hurt real prices.

Again, but for different reasons than for high-yield debt, commodities have a role to play in some portfolios but should likely be held solely in the context of a dynamic allocation process that would allow the investor to trade in and out of positions based on changing expectations.[64] Furthermore, they may be less appropriate for investors whose domestic equity market is strongly linked to commodities, such as those in Canada and Australia.

---

[63]Other indices have not materially performed better against equity.

[64]For example, the TOBAM Commodities Fund uses measures of price momentum to determine whether to adopt long or short positions in each commodity.

7.1.2. Allocation to Domestic vs. International Equity. Three dimensions most affect the size of the home bias in equity, excluding regulations: the economic diversity and stability that the home country equity market allows, the structural nature of the home country currency—that is, whether it is pro- or countercyclical—and the taxation rules as they apply to income from domestic versus non-domestic assets. Again, because this is not an exercise in dynamic asset allocation, we concentrate on the core structural aspects of asset allocation. To better understand the principles of this process, consider the situations of a US and a Canadian investor.

Investors in the United States live in a country where equity markets

- account for approximately 50% of global market capitalization,

- offer broad sector diversification,

- have relatively low concentration of companies within most sectors,

- offer exposure to a wide range of mid- and smaller-cap firms as well as greater liquidity than elsewhere, and

- offer exposure to non-domestic markets through the activities of the country's corporations (approximately 45% of sales of S&P 500 firms are non-US, 36% from outside the Americas).

In addition, the US dollar is countercyclical, because it appreciates in uncertain times and depreciates in good times.

This environment is very different from the one facing an investor in Canada, where equity markets

- account for approximately 3.0% of global market capitalization, and

- have greater sector and security concentration in traditional sectors such as financials, energy, basic materials, and industrials.

In contrast to the US currency, the Canadian dollar is pro-cyclical—it appreciates in good times and depreciates in uncertain times.

Table 7.2 compares the structure and sector exposure of the two markets and identifies their respective dominant components as of January 2019.

The US economy and its equity market provide significantly broad exposure in all sectors. Information technology and communication services represent a significant exposure, one unmatched in other countries except perhaps in emerging markets. Markets such as Canada are a bet on the financial, energy, and materials sectors. World markets also offer a more balanced exposure than Canada as well as exposure to globally important firms such as Nestlé, Toyota Motor Corporation, and Novartis International. But many of

Table 7.2. Structure of US, World ex-US, and Canadian Equity Indexes

	Russell 1000	MSCI World ex-USA	MSCI Emerging	MSCI Canada
Number of securities	982	1,012	1,123	91
Average market cap	24.7	22.6	4.4	18.7
Communication services	9.8	5.5	14.3	3.3
Consumer discretionary	10.4	10.7	10.6	4.2
Consumer staples	6.8	10.7	6.7	4.5
Energy	5.3	7.2	8.1	20.5
Financials	13.4	21.3	24.8	39.2
Health care	14.7	10.3	2.8	1.5
Industrials	9.7	13.8	5.5	9.3
Information technology	20.1	5.8	14.0	4.4
Materials	3.0	7.6	7.6	10.2
Real estate	3.7	3.5	3.0	0.7
Utilities	3.2	3.6	2.7	2.3
Security 1	Microsoft (3.2)	Nestle (1.8)	Tencent (4.9)	Royal Bank (8.2)
Security 2	Apple (3.0)	Novartis (1.3)	Alibaba (4.0)	TD Bank (7.4)
Security 3	Amazon (2.8)	Roche (1.3)	Taiwan Semi (3.5)	Enbridge (5.4)
Security 4	Alphabet (2.6)	HSBC (1.2)	Samsung (3.5)	BNS (5.2)
Security 5	Berkshire (1.6)	Toyota (1.0)	Naspers (1.9)	CN Rail (4.6)

the technology leaders are in the United States, although emerging markets, even if much smaller, are now dominated by technology firms. Hence, global markets offer diversification to all investors, but a US investor can justify a significant home bias because of the breadth and depth of the US domestic market and its firms' exposure to the global economy.

Currency behavior is another factor that can support a greater home bias from a US investor's perspective. Portfolio exposure to international equity measured from a US dollar viewpoint usually has more volatility than a similar exposure analyzed from the perspective of investors in other currencies.

Consider the following example. In October 2008, the Canadian equity index declined by 16.8% while the US index declined by 17.5%, each in their respective local currencies. The Canadian dollar declined by 12.2% against the US dollar, while the US dollar rose by 13.9% against the Canadian dollar.[65] Even the euro depreciated by 9.7% against the US dollar during that month. Hence, in terms of the investor's currency, in which liabilities are set, four returns were possible for that month:

- Canadian investor invested in Canada: −16.8%

- US investor invested in the United States: −17.5%

- Canadian investor invested in the United States: −6.6%

- US investor invested in Canada: −27.5%

As Lussier (2013) indicates, the optimal level of currency hedging on a long-term strategic basis (h) is determined by the following equation:

$$h = 1 + \rho(P, ER) \times \frac{\sigma(P)}{\sigma(ER)}, \qquad\qquad \text{Eq. 7.1}$$

where $\sigma(P)$ and $\sigma(ER)$ represent, respectively, the volatility of the asset in its local currency and the volatility of the exchange rate measured in units of the investor's currency per unit of the non-domestic currency; and $\rho(P, ER)$ is the correlation between them.

We first reconsider our discussion in the context of equity hedging. The US dollar is a countercyclical currency, and the correlation of the exchange rate (as defined) with equity is positive on average. Also, the ratio of equity volatility to exchange rate volatility is greater than 1, supporting a very high hedge ratio. The reverse would be true for a Canadian investor. An empirical analysis completed by Lussier and Langlois (2014) shows Canadian investors would benefit in the long run from *not* hedging currency risk, whereas US investors would benefit from significantly hedging this risk. For this reason, a number of large Canadian pension funds, which once believed that hedging 50% of their non-domestic equity exposure represented a neutral position, now have a strategic policy of not hedging their equity exposure.

Even though this section is devoted to equity allocation, consider now the same equation in the context of fixed income. The volatility of fixed income is relatively less relative to exchange rate volatility. Correlations are also weaker on average than with equity. Hence, for these reasons, the argument

---

[65]As we know, percentage of appreciation and depreciation are not symmetrical.

to fully—or close to fully—hedge non-domestic fixed income is even stronger whether the currency is pro- or countercyclical. Investment-grade fixed income is an asset characterized by low volatility. Currency risk will increase the volatility of this asset's returns if left unhedged.[66]

The last structural aspect of domestic versus international asset allocation is taxation. In many countries, non-domestic dividends may be taxed more highly than domestic dividends. There is also the issue of withholding taxes, to be discussed later in this chapter, and of taxes that may be imposed in specific countries when securities are bought and or sold by a non-domestic investor. For example, the United Kingdom imposes a 0.5% tax when securities are purchased. Taxes should have a lesser effect on the allocation decisions of US taxable investors because, as we will discuss in the section on taxation and asset location, dividends sourced in many countries are taxed at the same rate as dividends from US firms. It does not mean that all withholding and other taxes are avoided but rather that taxes on securities are, on average, less of an issue for US investors.

Overall, we could conclude the following: Representing more than 50% of global capitalization, the US market and its firms offer global exposure to US investors. Furthermore, unhedged US investors are penalized by market volatility when invested overseas because the US dollar is a countercyclical currency. Hence, on a structural basis, US investors can justify a significant home bias. Canadian investors cannot.

7.1.3. Active Management and Hedge Funds. The evidence on the success of active management supports what we should already know conceptually. If all securities are owned by investors, whether individual or institutional, the aggregate performance of all investors must equal the market's performance. It is a zero-sum game for all. In other words, if we ignore fees and other active management expenses, for each dollar of outperformance realized by an investor against the market, one or more investors must be losing that dollar. After fees, however, there must be more than one dollar of losses for each dollar of gains. The greater the fees, the greater the discrepancy between gains and losses and the smaller the likelihood of outperforming.

The argument could be made that specific groups of investors in the market have more expertise than others. For example, even if we accept the zero-sum game argument, could it be that a group of investors can systematically extract value at the expense of another group of investors because they have

---

[66]The conclusion could be different in the case of high-yield bonds because such bonds are much more correlated to equity and to the movement in exchange rates. Riskier credit tends to behave like equity in crisis situations.

superior expertise, or perhaps because some investors may not be value maximizers? Think of central banks and perhaps some governments as investors. It is conceptually possible, but this is a situation where we can look at the empirical evidence.

The S&P Indices Versus Active Funds (SPIVA) periodically publishes a scorecard of managers' performance in different countries (Soe and Poirier 2017). Their effort at quantifying the active–passive debate started 16 years ago. It is based on the CRSP Survivor-Bias-Free US Mutual Fund Database, the only complete database of both active and liquidated or merged mutual funds. It provides information related to performance, style consistency, and survivorship for equity and fixed-income managers in many categories. Some of the information from the 2017 scorecards is presented in **Table 7.3**, which shows the percentage of managers who have not outperformed their benchmark over periods of 5, 10, and 15 years.

On average, results are not encouraging, given that usually more than 80% of managers underperform their benchmark. Other groups have measured the consistency of managers' performance. The firm DiMeo Schneider & Associates regularly updates a study on the return profile and pattern of top-quartile managers (Novara, Long, and Rice 2015). The firm usually finds that approximately 90% of 10-year top-quartile mutual funds are unable to avoid at least one 3-year stretch in the bottom half of their peer groups, and 50% to 60% of managers cannot avoid a 5-year stretch. Consistent performance is a challenge, and investors could easily abandon what will become a top-quartile manager but has yet to outperform. For example, in an earlier study, the firm found that 97% of the top-quartile funds in the Morningstar large-cap blend peer group (over a 10-year period ending in 2006) were in the bottom half of the peer group after the 3-year period ending December 1999. (This is probably because of the market's shift from favoring growth over the earlier period to favoring value in the later period. Such shifts happen all the time and should be factored into investors' decisions.)

Table 7.3. SPIVA Scorecard for US Managers (2017): Percentage of Funds Outperformed by Their Benchmarks over Specific Horizons

	5 Years	10 Years	15 Years
Domestic funds	86.7	86.7	83.7
International funds	70.9	81.7	91.6
Emerging market funds	77.8	85.1	94.9
Investment-grade long funds	95.5	95.4	97.7
Emerging market debt funds	85.7	73.7	66.7

Much evidence supports skepticism about active management, although it certainly does not mean that active management, or investing differently from the market portfolio, should be ignored by all investors. Even though investing is a zero-sum game for all investors before fees, it is not a zero-sum game for individual investors having specific life goals. An investor approaching retirement may, for example, rationally prefer investing in a lower-volatility, higher-payout portfolio. Furthermore, strong evidence suggests that volatility and dependence (correlations) can be predicted with significantly more accuracy than returns. Therefore, a long-term investor can make use of this information. Finally, if we recognize the value of the literature on factor investing, whether through fundamental or systematic processes, long-term investors can potentially benefit from good processes.

But as the DiMeo Schneider & Associates research shows, even if a specific manager's investment process is comprehensive and theoretically sound, a long time horizon is required to increase the likelihood of outperforming the market. (Considerable literature is available on this aspect. See, for example, Ang 2014; Ilmanen 2011; Langlois and Lussier 2017; Lussier 2013.) But any investment process benefits from having a long horizon and discipline. Much can be done to improve financial planning before incorporating active management.[67]

This brings us to hedge funds as an investment. Although some people consider hedge funds to be an asset class, we have delayed discussion of hedge funds until covering the topic of active management because hedge funds cut across the entire universe of asset classes. Hedge fund managers may be allowed much greater flexibility in investment policy than traditional long-only investment managers, but the funds are still actively managed. A most important question in this case is the following: If it is challenging for traditional managers, who have a more restrictive investment policy, to outperform the market in a zero-sum game world, should we assume that less restricted alternative managers should do better? Further, hedge funds can

---

[67]We also studied the integration of factor-based methodologies in our financial-planning engine. Factors such as market, size, value, momentum, betting against beta, or quality are defined as rewarded factors that are either explained by a risk premium and/or a behavioral bias and/or a limit to arbitrage. It would be imprudent to assume that a factor-based portfolio/ strategy would necessarily lead to a higher expected return in the long run. We can reasonably assume, however, that properly calibrated factor-based methodologies could be used to modify an equity portfolio's return distribution. For example, portfolios having a lower expected volatility or drawdown risk can be created using a specific calibration of factors, but at the expense of a higher active risk against the benchmark. Although this is not a topic we explore in detail in *Secure Retirement*, we have found that allocating a portion of the equity portfolio to specific factor-based methodologies improves the likelihood of achieving a retirement income goal even if we assume no improvement in expected return.

sometimes be mostly long-only strategies, even though they usually have a short component. In this context, it is relevant to ask if a specific strategy is exposed to a net positive risk premium or if risk premiums are neutralized on average, leaving alpha as the primary or only source of return.

Lack (2012) estimated that the average investor in hedge funds would have performed better investing in T-bills. This was not the case in the early days of hedge funds, when there were more market inefficiencies to exploit, but the presence of trillions of dollars in hedge funds has eliminated many of these inefficiencies. As such, the industry has performed worst as its assets have grown, and much of the gross returns generated by hedge funds were absorbed by high fees.

The hedge fund industry generated 4.5% of annualized performance from 1998 to 2016, compared with 6.4% for both the S&P 500 Index and a 60/40 portfolio. As Lack (2012) indicated as well, however, the performance was 16.1% from 1998 to 2003 and only 0.6% from 2004 to 2016, whereas a 60/40 portfolio generated 6.9% and 6.7%, respectively, over the same subperiods (Carlson 2017). There are great organizations within the hedge fund industry, but the evidence is growing that their ability to arbitrage risks and extract returns from special situations has been reduced in the last decade by growing competition.

7.1.4. Conclusion. Asset allocation is complex, but the process and components should be kept simple for the average investor. High-yield bonds have a positive risk premium but should probably be held mostly by sophisticated investors. Commodities are a great diversifier, but do they have a risk premium? They could be a significant drag on long-term performance and may be more appropriate in the context of a dynamic strategy. Hedge funds must be analyzed case by case. No two managers or strategies are alike. Similarly, passive management should be the starting point for the average investor. Over time, non-market-cap strategies can be added when appropriate.

The issue of domestic versus international asset allocation is relevant to all investors, however. Without going into the complexity of the dynamic asset allocation process, it is important to consider the diversification and scope offered by one's particular domestic market, the nature of the home currency, and the tax implications, when relevant. We conclude from these factors that US investors can afford a significant allocation to their market and a home bias, whereas Canadian investors should look abroad.

7.2. Taxation and Asset Location

Until now, apart from including a small section on withholding taxes on dividends, we have ignored the effects of taxation on asset returns. Yet the extent of these effects on financial planning is significant. In *Secure Retirement*, we concentrate on two aspects of taxation. First, within taxable accounts, different tax rates may apply to different sources of investment income, such as interest, qualified and unqualified dividends (to be explained), and long- and short-term capital gains. Second, in many countries, investors have access to savings plans that are exempt from and/or defer taxation of investment income and capital gains, such as traditional IRAs or Roth IRAs.

Whereas the previous section dealt with the allocation to asset classes across the entire portfolio, this section is concerned with how asset allocation should be prioritized across taxable, tax-deferred, and fully tax-exempt accounts based on the way different sources of income are taxed and the terms that apply to different types of savings plans. Although the following discussion will describe the situation for a US investor, the conclusions apply to most industrialized countries.

Kinniry, Jaconetti, DiJoseph, Zilbering, and Bennyhoff (2016) estimate that the asset location decision can add as much as 75 bps of value annually to a portfolio. They believe the greatest value occurs when the taxable and tax-advantaged (deferred and exempt) accounts are approximately of similar size, the asset allocation is balanced, and the investor is in a high tax bracket. Investors who would have most of their assets in one type of account could not benefit proportionally as much from the asset location decision. This does not mean that investors should not invest all their retirement assets in tax-advantaged accounts if contribution limits to tax-advantaged plans allow, but rather that in situations where excess capital must be invested in a taxable account, the asset location decision itself will have a greater effect on expected final wealth. They advise allocating tax-efficient equity (i.e., low-turnover, "qualified" issuers, long-term capital gains) and municipal bonds in taxable accounts while holding active (i.e., high-turnover strategies, short-term capital gains) and taxable bonds in tax-advantaged accounts. Their advice extends to the decumulation strategy. They recommend against decumulating more than required from tax-advantaged accounts. The authors conclude that the ability to compound return tax-free is advantageous in both the accumulation and the decumulation period.

Shoven and Sialm (2004) reached similar conclusions. They find that tax-efficient equity assets should be held in the taxable account, whereas tax-inefficient equity assets should be held in the tax-advantaged account. Similarly, taxable bonds should be allocated to the tax-deferred account, whereas tax-exempt municipal bonds should be allocated to the taxable account for investors in high tax brackets.

Much of the literature arrives at similar conclusions. As discussed in the coming pages, however, some of our recommendations clash to some extent with the existing literature on specific aspects of the asset location decision.

7.2.1. Tax Rates across Sources of Income. In the United States, interest income, nonqualified dividend income, and short-term capital gains—those realized within one of year purchasing the asset—are taxed as ordinary income. Qualified dividend income is taxed at the long-term capital gains rate, which is lower than the rate applied to ordinary income. Income from municipal bonds is exempt from federal taxation. Consequently, the yield on such bonds is lower than would be paid on a risk-comparable taxable security. Also, residents of certain states are usually exempt from taxation on the income of municipal bonds issued within that state.

Qualified dividends are those paid by a typical US corporation and by a qualified foreign corporation (QFC). These QFCs include certain corporations from countries that (1) have a comprehensive income tax treaty with the United States, (2) have an information-sharing agreement, and (3) have been approved by the US Department of the Treasury. Nearly 60 countries are deemed "qualified," including Canada, China, France, Germany, India, Mexico, and the United Kingdom. This list implies, according to Malik (2016), that a significant portion of foreign dividends received by the average US investor is deemed "qualified." **Table 7.4** presents some of the 2018 tax rates that apply at the federal level for a single filer.

There are also other tax aspects of significance. First, capital gains taxes are recognized only when realized upon the disposition of assets, but not all investment vehicles may be efficient at limiting capital gains. Investors using

Table 7.4. Ordinary and Long-Term Capital Gains Tax Rate According to Income

Income	Ordinary Tax Rate	Long-Term Capital Gains Tax Rate	Income	Ordinary Tax Rate	Long-Term Capital Gains Tax Rate
Up to $9,525	10%	0%	Up to $157,500	24%	15%
Up to $38,600	12	0	Up to $200,000	32	15
Up to $38,700[a]	12	15	Up to $425,800	35	15
Up to $82,500	22	15	Up to $500,000	35	20
			$500,001 +	37	20

[a]This tranche of income is in fact only $100 more than the previous one.
Sources: www.taxpolicycenter.org/sites/default/files/briefing-book/how_do_federal_income_tax_rates_work.pdf and www.fool.com/taxes/2017/12/22/your-guide-to-capital-gains-taxes-in-2018.aspx.

ETFs may trigger fewer capital gains in general than those using mutual funds. Many ETFs are indexed or based on low-turnover strategies, allowing much of the capital gains to be postponed. Also, mutual fund managers may have to constantly rebalance their portfolio by selling securities to accommodate redemptions, whereas ETF managers are better able to manage secondary market transactions, minimizing in-fund capital gains events. Further, investment income of high-income earners is subject to a net investment income tax (NITT). This 3.8% tax applies on the lesser of investment income or the modified adjusted gross income (MAGI) above $200,000 for single filers and $250,000 for married couples filing jointly. Finally, specific states may also tax investment income. Although taxation rates and tax rules do change, we should focus on the general impact of different tax rate levels on the asset location decision.

7.2.2. Taxable, Tax-Exempt, and Tax-Deferred Plans.

A Roth IRA is an example of a tax-exempt plan, and traditional IRAs and 401(k)s are examples of tax-deferred plans. All retirement plans are subject to maximum contribution limits. Tax-exempt and tax-deferred plans bring identical after-tax wealth benefits to investors under certain conditions. Equations 7.2a and 7.2b illustrate the final after-tax value (FV) of an initial contribution of $\$C_{te}$ in a tax-exempt plan and $\$C_{td}$ in a tax-deferred plan over n periods, assuming ordinary tax rates of t_0 at the current time and t_n at horizon-end and identical investment policies/returns in both plans:

$$C_{te} \times \left[\prod_1^n (1 + R_i) \right] = FV_{te} \qquad \text{Eq. 7.2a}$$

$$C_{td} \times \left[\prod_1^n (1 + R_i) \times (1 - t_n) \right] = FV_{td} \qquad \text{Eq. 7.2b}$$

In both plans, the periodic return (R_i) compounds tax free. What differs are the tax consequences when the initial contribution is made and when the capital accumulated is eventually withdrawn. In a tax-exempt account, the contribution is not tax deductible and the capital accumulated after n periods remains tax free. There is no tax-related event. In a tax-deferred account, the individual receives an initial tax deduction at the current ordinary tax rate, but the accumulated capital is taxed at the prevailing ordinary tax rate at period n, assuming all capital is withdrawn in a single transaction (which rarely happens in practice). The two options will lead to identical final after-tax values if two assumptions hold:[68]

- $t_0 = t_n$, implying the initial and final tax rates are identical, and

- $C_{td} = \dfrac{C_{te}}{1 - t_0}$, implying the initial contributions must be identical on a tax-adjusted basis.

Therefore, all else being equal, if an individual expects the future tax rate to be higher than the current tax rate or if she is concerned about the uncertainty of future tax policy, a tax-exempt account (i.e., Roth IRA) appears preferable. If the individual expects to be in a lower tax bracket or move to a lower-tax state in retirement, a tax-deferred account may be preferable. Furthermore, although contributions to a traditional IRA must end by age 70.5 and withdrawals must start by the same age, contributions to a Roth IRA can extend for as long as the individual generates earned income. There is also no minimal withdrawal requirement. The IRS phases out the ability of higher-income individuals or households to contribute to a Roth IRA, however, and it also phases out the ability to take a full deduction of traditional IRA contributions when single filers or at least one of the joint filers benefits from a workplace retirement plan.

These rules do not imply that nondeductible IRA contributions are forbidden. Individuals could still benefit from the tax-free accumulation, but the returns generated (not the capital) would be taxed at the ordinary tax rate upon withdrawals. Furthermore, when individuals withdraw money from the traditional IRA, the IRS does not allow them to selectively choose between investments made through deductible and nondeductible contributions. Instead, they must take a proportionate amount of both. The question is whether investing tax free in a nondeductible IRA and being taxed at the ordinary tax rate upon withdrawals is preferable to making taxable contributions but being taxed at the lower investment rates (for qualified dividends and capital gains). According to Hoffman (2017), the former may not be optimal even if the horizon is 30 years.

We evaluated this situation and found that although Hoffman's conclusion holds in most circumstances, in some scenarios nondeductible contributions could be warranted. For example, such contributions could be warranted when the individual lives in a state with a high taxation rate but moves into

---

[68]The conclusion would still be that the two types of plans are equivalent if capital amounts were withdrawn over time if the amounts withdrawn at each period from both plans were identical on an after-tax basis.

a state with a low taxation rate, although a long horizon—usually more than 20 years—is still required. They could also be warranted if the investor's portfolio also holds fixed-income assets, because the taxes on interest income could thereby be postponed by many years.

Yet another aspect currently favors tax-exempt over tax-deferred accounts. As of 2018, the IRS allows an annual maximum combined contribution to IRA plans, both Roth and traditional, of $5,500 until age 50 and $6,500 after that.[69,70] This rule implies that a $5,500 contribution to a traditional IRA prevents any contribution to a Roth IRA and vice versa. We have explained, however, that a $1 after-tax contribution to a tax-exempt plan is not equivalent to a $1 before-tax contribution to a tax-deferred plan. As illustrated in Equations 7.2a and 7.2b, the contribution to a tax-deferred plan would have to be adjusted upward by the tax rate, and the tax rate itself must remain constant. Nonetheless, the maximum allowed contributions are the same in both programs.

To understand the significance of this aspect, consider three scenarios for an individual, assuming a 24% ordinary tax rate, an annual equity investment return of 7% before tax and 5.95% after tax (considering a 15% tax rate on dividends and on long-term capital gains beyond one year), and a horizon of 20 years:[71]

- Scenario 1 involves a contribution of $5,500 to a Roth IRA.

- Scenario 2 involves a contribution of $7,236.84 to a traditional IRA. This is not a feasible scenario because the limit is $5,500, but it corresponds to the amount that would be required to achieve the same after-tax contribution ($7,236.84 × [1 − 0.24] = $5,500). This scenario is useful for comparison purposes, however.

- Scenario 3 involves a contribution of $5,500 to a traditional IRA and of $1,320 to a taxable plan. The $5,500 contribution generates a $1,320 tax reduction that is reinvested. Because the individual has maxed out her

---

[69]The contribution limit of a traditional IRA is unaffected by the level of income if the individual does not benefit from a 401(k) plan. The contribution limit to a Roth IRA, however, is gradually reduced once the MAGI is above $120,000 for a single filing and eliminated once the MAGI is above $135,000 (in 2018). Consequently, a high-income earner may have no other choice than to use a traditional IRA.

[70]Limits are not adjusted on a regular basis. In 2002, contributions limits for age 49 and below and age 50 and above were, respectively, $3,000 and $500. They were $4,000 and $500 in 2005, $4,000 and $1,000 in 2006, and $5,000 and $1,000 in 2008, and they have been $5,000 and $1,000 since 2013.

[71]The effective capital gains tax rate may be less because the portfolio turnover is unlikely to be 100%. This fact does not change the logic of the argument that follows, however.

IRA contribution and cannot contribute to a Roth IRA, however, she must invest the amount she saved in taxes in taxable assets.

The final wealth in each scenario is calculated as follows:

- Scenario 1: $\$5,500 \times 1.07^{20} = \$21,283.26$

- Scenario 2: $\$7,236.84 \times 1.07^{20} \times (1 - 0.24) = \$21,283.26$

- Scenario 3: $\$5,500 \times 1.07^{20} \times (1 - 0.24) + \$1,320 \times 1.0595^{20} = \$20,368.94$

As expected, the final values of Scenarios 1 and 2 are identical. As specified previously, however, Scenario 2 is not feasible because it requires an IRA contribution above the allowed limit. Scenario 3 has a significantly lower final value because the added contribution of $1,320 is invested at an after-tax rate of 5.95% instead of 7%. Scenario 1 is preferable to Scenario 3.

Contribution limits in Roth and traditional IRAs are extremely low, considering what is allowed for individuals involved in 401(k) plans and what is needed to retire. The 401(k) contribution limit in 2018 was $18,500 for workers age 49 and below and $24,500 for workers age 50 and above. Employers may also contribute to a 401(k). Furthermore, the traditional IRA limit is further constrained if the individual is covered by a retirement plan at work. Recall, however, that our objective is to understand the mechanics of the asset location decision, not to cover all the specifics of the Internal Revenue Code.[72,73] Nevertheless, the benefit of maximizing the contributions allowed under tax-exempt and tax-deferred plans is obvious.

Although much of the previous discussion was about comparing tax-deferred versus tax-exempt accounts in the context of traditional and Roth IRAs, priority should be given to 401(k) contributions if a corporate plan is available, because many employers will offer a company contribution match. The most common policy is to match 50% or 100% of employees' contributions up to a maximum percentage of salary. For example, John's employer may offer to match 50% of John's contribution up to a maximum of 3%. Hence, if John contributes 6% of his salary in the 401(k) program, the employer will add another 3%.[74]

---

[72]In other countries, such as Canada, the allowed contribution limits are independent of whether an individual participates in a work plan. Any contribution through an employer plan, however, will reduce the contribution that could be made through an individual plan. This approach offers a more even playing field to all individuals.

[73]Nevertheless, the proper rules have been appropriately coded in simulations presented in Chapter 8.

[74]An important aspect to consider is whether the company contributions are subject to a vesting requirement, such as the obligation that the employee remain with the company a minimum number of years for the company match to be earned.

7.2.3. "Optimizing" the Asset Location Decision.

In the context of an asset location decision across tax-deferred, tax-exempt, and taxable accounts, two strategies are considered: (1) preferentially investing the tax-deferred and/or tax-exempt accounts in equities and (2) investing the accounts in fixed income. We must also determine if the answer depends on whether fixed-income assets are investment-grade bonds, high-yield bonds, or tax-exempt municipal bonds. Finally, we must determine if and how the answer varies according to the investment horizon, differential tax rates across instruments, and the level of portfolio turnover attributed to either the underlying asset classes or the portfolio rebalancing across asset classes. The choices can be very confusing.

This section presents several scenarios and Monte Carlo simulations. We start this discussion by confirming again that all scenarios and simulations presented in this section lead to the same final after-tax value for tax-deferred and tax-exempt plans, assuming (1) tax rates are the same across time, (2) contribution limits for tax-deferred and tax-exempt plans are identical on an after-tax basis, and (3) tax-adjusted asset allocation is identical across scenarios. Hence, we present the results of tax-deferred and tax-exempt plans jointly.

The implications of identical tax-adjusted asset allocation follow here. Assume Investor A has accumulated $100,000 of taxable assets and $100,000 of traditional IRA assets. Investor B has also accumulated $100,000 of taxable assets and has $72,000 of Roth IRA assets. Both investors target a 50/50 allocation between equity and fixed income, and both are subject to an average ordinary tax rate of 28%. **Table 7.5** indicates what the asset allocation of each investor across the different accounts must be to reach the targeted asset allocation, depending on whether the equity assets or the fixed-income assets are preferentially placed in the tax-deferred and/or tax-exempt plans. (By investing in an account "preferentially" in equity, we mean that a given account is filled up with equity until the investor's overall appetite for equity has been reached or the account has reached its maximum permitted size, whichever comes first. Same for fixed income.) Note also that both investors have an after-tax wealth of $172,000, because Investor A would receive only $72,000 after tax from his IRA assets if they were fully withdrawn: $100,000 × (1 − 0.28).

All four scenarios in Table 7.5 present a 50/50 after-tax asset allocation. In the case of Investor B, the allocation to fixed income and equity is $86,000, whether the investor allocated in priority to fixed income or equity. In the case of Investor A, the after-tax value of all fixed-income assets, assuming fixed income was allocated to the IRA in priority, is also $86,000, because this investor owns $72,000 of after-tax assets in fixed income in the IRA and $14,000 in taxable assets. The same logic applies when equity is allocated in

Table 7.5. Examples of 50/50 After-Tax Asset Allocation across Four Different Plan Structures

| | Investor A | | | | | | Investor B | | | | | |
| | Traditional IRA | | Taxable | | Roth IRA | | Taxable | |
Prioritization	Equity	Fixed Income	Equity	Fixed Income	Equity	Fixed Income	Equity	Fixed Income
Equity	100,000	—	14,000	86,000	72,000	—	14,000	86,000
Fixed income	—	100,000	86,000	14,000	—	72,000	86,000	14,000

priority to the IRA. A main conclusion of this example is that asset allocation must be managed on a tax-adjusted basis to be risk and wealth consistent.

Scenario analyses of asset location. We first analyze the asset location decision looking at specific scenarios, concentrating initially on the impact of asset location on portfolio return rather than risk. A Monte Carlo approach that integrates return uncertainty follows. **Table 7.6** presents several potential scenarios for John over an accumulation period of 35 years. In all scenarios, we assume that John has an after-tax savings budget of $10,000 annually that is allocated 50/50 across taxable and tax-exempt/tax-deferred accounts. For simplicity, we have set the contribution limit to a tax-exempt plan to $5,000, and John takes full advantage of this possibility. Alternatively, he could contribute a maximum of $5,000/(1 $-t_0$) to a tax-deferred plan (the same after-tax amount), and we assume, for simplicity, that this is also the contribution limit. John's after-tax savings budget increases by 2% every year, and it is assumed the IRS is adjusting the contribution limits of all plans at the same pace. Our objective is to evaluate the differential final wealth, prioritizing the allocation to either equity or fixed income in the tax-exempt/tax-deferred account. For reference purposes, Table 7.6 also presents the impact of an all tax-exempt/tax-deferred portfolio—if such a portfolio could be constructed—and of an all-taxable portfolio. The comparison between the two illustrates the full wealth benefits of tax-advantaged retirement plans. The scenarios vary according to the following parameters:

- A fixed-equity allocation of 60% or a glide path of 90% for 15 years. This allocation declines toward 60% over the following 15 years (90% to 60%) and remains at 60% thereafter.

- Equity returns of 7% (2% from dividends) and fixed-income returns of either 3%, 5%, or 7%. Annual portfolio turnover within equity is either 20% or 100% to test the effects of capital gains taxation. Portfolio turnover attributed to asset class rebalancing is implicitly 100%.

- Several federal tax rates for investment income, assuming, for example, an average-income-tax payer who is not subject to the NITT and lives in a tax-free state such as Florida and a high-income-tax payer in a state such as New Jersey. We also assume that all capital gains are long term and equity assets are "qualified." Finally, unrealized capital gains are taxed at the end of the assumed time horizon.

Some tax scenarios are theoretical; that is, they do not correspond to actual tax brackets but are used for reference purposes to support an argument. Other tax scenarios are closer to reality.

Table 7.6. Accumulated Wealth Assuming Four Asset Location Contexts and 12 Scenarios of Asset Allocation, Returns, and Taxation

Scenario	Glide Path	Equity Return	Fixed-Income Return	LT Capital Gains Tax Rate	Ordinary Tax Rate	Turnover	Exempt/Deferred Equity First	Exempt/Deferred Bonds First	All Exempt/Deferred	All Taxable	Ratio Equity First	Ratio Bonds First
1	60%	7%	3%	0%	0.0%	0%	$1,353,397	$1,353,397	$1,353,397	$1,353,397	67%	33%
2	60%	7	3	15.0	15.0	100	1,305,829	1,203,019	1,353,397	1,154,832	69%	37%
3	60%	7	5	15.0	15.0	100	1,487,849	1,424,629	1,590,341	1,318,939	63%	47%
4	60%	7	7	15.0	15.0	100	1,694,121	1,694,121	1,876,811	1,511,431	55%	55%
5	60%	7	3	15.0	35.0	100	1,253,897	1,202,585	1,353,397	1,102,844	71%	37%
6	60%	7	5	15.0	35.0	100	1,384,562	1,424,629	1,590,341	1,219,266	67%	47%
7	90%–60%	7	3	15.0	35.0	100	1,385,322	1,359,092	1,516,436	1,226,697	67%	44%
8	90%–60%	7	5	15.0	35.0	100	1,479,197	1,517,137	1,686,588	1,312,408	63%	50%
9	90%–60%	7	3	15.0	35.0	20	1,389,707	1,371,340	1,516,436	1,244,555	67%	43%
10	90%–60%	7	5	15.0	35.0	20	1,484,289	1,532,037	1,686,588	1,332,936	63%	49%
11	90%–60%	7	3	32.8	49.8	20	1,317,263	1,233,101	1,516,436	1,029,423	70%	49%
12	90%–60%	7	5	32.8	49.8	20	1,386,251	1,383,896	1,686,588	1,084,595	67%	54%

The first scenario assumes a fixed allocation of 60% equity, expected equity returns of 7% and fixed-income returns of 3%, no taxation, and no portfolio turnover. In this context, the final after-tax value remains the same under all four account allocation contexts:

- whether equity or fixed income is allocated first to a tax-exempt/tax-deferred portfolio in a 50/50 allocation of after-tax contributions across a taxable and a tax-exempt/tax-deferred portfolio, or

- whether all contributions are made either in a tax-exempt/tax-deferred portfolio or taxable portfolio.

The last two columns show the final ratio of after-tax value of the tax-exempt/tax-deferred plan to that of all plans, assuming either equity or fixed income has been allocated in priority to the tax-exempt/tax-deferred portfolio. It is not surprising that this ratio is greater when equity is allocated in priority, because the higher-yielding asset will compound faster in the tax-exempt/tax-deferred plan. The ratio is always greater than 50% when equity is allocated in priority to the tax-exempt/tax-deferred plan, implying that some fixed-income assets must be allocated to the tax-advantaged plan to maintain the 50/50 asset allocation target.

Scenarios 2, 3, and 4 illustrate the consequence of identical tax rates across all sources of income and assuming 100% portfolio turnover for three scenarios of fixed-income return: 3%, 5%, and finally 7%—implying no return premium over equity, a purely theoretical exercise. Unsurprisingly, the 0% return premium scenario leads to the same final wealth whether equity or fixed income is allocated in priority to the tax-exempt/tax-deferred portfolio. If the return on fixed income is lower, however, as in Scenarios 2 and 3, allocating equity first to the tax-exempt/tax-deferred portfolio leads to a larger final value. One of the reasons is that the nominal taxes paid on fixed income (15% of either 3% or 5%) are less than those paid on equity (15% of 7%).[75] This is not the only reason, however.

Scenarios 5 and 6 illustrate what happens if the tax rate applied to interest income is significantly greater than what is applied to long-term capital gains and dividend income. Assuming a 3% fixed-income return, and thus a 4% return premium of equity versus bonds, prioritizing equity still leads to a larger after-tax final value. Assuming a larger fixed-income return such as 5%, however—which means a 2% return premium of equity versus bonds—makes

---

[75]Although the tax rate is assumed to be identical, the nominal amount of taxes paid is greater in the equity case, implying that the impact of lower compounded returns attributed to taxation is more significant when equity is taxed.

it no longer preferable to prioritize the equity allocation. The reason is the combination of a higher tax rate on bond income and a lower equity premium.

The 3% fixed-income return case is particularly interesting because the taxes paid on equity and fixed income are both 1.05% of principal (15% × 7.0% versus 35% × 3.0%), yet prioritizing the allocation to equity is still preferable. The explanation lies in the effect of return compounding. When equity is prioritized (and therefore dividend and capital gains returns are exempt from taxation), a larger portion of the equity allocation is expected to compound at the before-tax return of 7% while a greater portion of the fixed-income allocation is expected to compound at 1.95% (3.0% − 1.05%).

If fixed income is prioritized, however, a larger portion of the fixed-income allocation is expected to compound at the before-tax return of 3% and a greater portion of the equity allocation is expected to compound at 5.95% (7.0% − 1.05%). On a total compounded basis, the first situation is superior to the second. Hence, the tax location decision is not only about the effective tax rate differential between two types of assets but also about the added compounding impact of the higher-yielding asset. The longer the horizon, the greater the compounding effect.

For example, assume the investor makes a $100 investment, split 50/50 between equity and fixed income without rebalancing (to simplify but without affecting the general conclusion). Under one scenario, the investor holds the equity investment within a tax-exempt/tax-deferred account (receiving the full 7% untaxed equity return) and has fixed income within a taxable account (receiving the 1.95% after-tax fixed-income return). The alternate scenario assumes the reverse account allocation. The investor receives a 5.95% after-tax equity return and a 3% untaxed fixed-income return. The final value of a portfolio after 10, 20, or 30 years is shown in **Table 7.7**.

The power of higher return compounding is such that to neutralize the advantage of prioritizing equity into the tax-exempt account, the tax rate on interest income would have to rise from 35% to 50% if the horizon were

Table 7.7. Accumulated Wealth Assuming Alternative After-Tax Asset Location

Horizon (years)	Equity in Tax-Exempt/Tax-Deferred Account and Fixed Income in Taxable Account (equity at 7% and fixed income at 1.95%)	Equity in Taxable Account and Fixed Income in Tax-Exempt/Tax-Deferred Account (equity at 5.95% and fixed income at 3.00%)	Difference
10	318.0	312.6	+1.7%
20	534.1	498.3	+7.2
30	939.7	761.2	+16.2

10 years, 82% if it were 20 years, and more than 100% if it were 30 years. The results are less dramatic when a portfolio-rebalancing policy is implemented, but the basic principle remains the same.

Scenarios 7 and 8 lead to similar conclusions in the context of a 90–60 glide path, although the wealth differential between the two strategies is less, especially when equity is prioritized in the tax-exempt/tax-deferred portfolio. This result is to be expected because the allocation to equity dominates the portfolio for many years. The same can be said of reducing the turnover. The effect will be less significant if much of the equity allocation has been put in the tax-exempt/tax-deferred plan, as seen in Scenarios 9 and 10.

Finally, Scenarios 11 and 12 present the same information for a high-income investor living in a high-tax state such as New Jersey.[76] Assuming a 3% fixed-income return, the advantage of prioritizing equity is even greater. Assuming a 5% fixed-income return, the two strategies lead to similar final values even though annual taxes paid on fixed income are now greater than those paid on equity. It is even more important to shield high-return assets from higher taxes.

Therefore, if an argument can be made to prioritize the allocation to equity issuers that pay qualified dividends, the argument would be even stronger for (1) nonqualified issuers, assuming expected before-tax returns are similar and are *not* significantly affected by withholding taxes, and (2) high-turnover strategies that generate short-term capital gains. Similarly, there may be an argument for prioritizing high-yield debt securities, assuming their expected return, net of losses, is higher than that on investment-grade bonds. The larger the tax rate that applies to high-yielding assets, the greater the incentive to locate these assets in the tax-deferred/tax-exempt account.

The last issue is that of tax-exempt municipal bonds. Compared with traditional corporate bond indices, municipal bonds have lower (i.e., before-tax) yields and lesser liquidity but higher average credit ratings. They have experienced lower default rates than corporates, however. Two-thirds of municipal bonds are in the AA and AAA Moody's rating categories, compared with fewer than 15% in the Bloomberg Barclays US Corporate Bond Index (see Martin and Howard 2017). Our objective is to determine in what circumstances it may be appropriate to invest in municipal securities instead of traditional (taxable) bonds on an after-tax basis, assuming similar duration and relative risk.

---

[76]This investor has a federal tax rate on investment income of 40.8%—if the NIIT is added—and pays 8.97% in state tax. Long-term capital gains and "qualified" dividends are taxed at 23.8%, including the NIIT.

Table 7.8. Characteristics of Corporate and Tax-Exempt Fixed-Income Products (30 June 2018)

ETF	Yield to Worst after Fees	Duration	Percentage Rated A and Above
Tax exempt	2.53%	5.7	90.7%
Corporate	4.03	6.4	45.5

Table 7.8 presents information on two products offered by a low-cost ETF provider. The first is a tax-exempt bond ETF and the second a corporate bond ETF as of 30 June 2018.

The corporate bond's duration is slightly longer. The average quality of the municipal is more than that of the corporate. The yields after fees are, respectively, 2.53% and 4.03%. There is little relevant literature on how much to allocate to municipal bonds, but considering the lower liquidity, smaller size, and narrowness of the market relative to corporate bonds, the allocation should probably be less than 50% in combination with an aggregate-bond product.

For example, consider the after-tax return of the two products for high-income earners living in New Jersey. We assume state taxes will not be significantly avoided because the investor would likely want to own a diversified portfolio of bonds issued by many municipalities across the country. Assuming a state tax rate of t_s and a federal tax rate combined with the NITT of t_{fn}, the before-tax yield equivalent of a municipal bond is

$$R_m \times \frac{(1-t_s)}{(1-t_{fn}-t_s)}. \qquad \text{Eq. 7.3}$$

Table 7.9 presents the before-tax municipal bond yield equivalent of individuals in the highest federal tax bracket (37% + 3.8% NITT) and living

Table 7.9. Before- and After-Tax Yields (30 June 2018)

	Municipal Bond		Corporate Bond	
State Tax	0%	8.97%	0%	8.97%
Before-tax equivalent yield	4.27	4.59	**4.03**	**4.03**
Before-tax spread	—	—	−0.24	−0.56
After-tax equivalent yield	**2.53**	2.30	2.39	2.02
After-tax spread	—	—	−0.14	−0.28

in states with a 0% income tax rate, such as Florida, or in an environment with a higher state income tax, such as New Jersey (8.97%). The benefits of tax-exempt bonds can be relatively significant, more so for residents of high-income-tax states. The benefit when compared to a corporate bond ETF for investors in a low tax bracket, however, would be small to negative.

The question for municipal securities is not whether they have any role to play in a tax-advantaged account—they do not—but for which type of investors an allocation is justifiable in a taxable account. For investors in a 32% tax bracket, some allocation could be justified from a diversification perspective. For others, in a higher tax bracket, they can be justified from the standpoint of both return and diversification.

Overall, these observations lead us to the following recommendations thus far:

- Tax-inefficient equity and high-yield debt should be allocated to the tax-advantaged account in priority. As discussed in the previous section, however, it is questionable whether for most investors, high-yield debt could not be substituted for a slightly higher allocation to equity in the long run.

- Tax-efficient equity could be prioritized next into tax-advantaged accounts over even taxable investment-grade bonds if the long-term return equity premium appears reasonable.

- Municipal bonds belong to the taxable account but make sense only for investors in a high tax bracket.

Obviously, all these observations would have to be reconfirmed periodically as changes occur to gross yields, relative yields, expected return premiums, and tax rules.

Monte Carlo analyses of asset location. The simulations are based on two tax profiles. First is a high-income New Jersey investor paying 40.8% federal tax including the NITT, 8.97% state income tax, and 32.8% combined capital gains tax rate (state, federal, and NITT). Second is a lower-income Florida investor with tax rates of 25% and 15% for income and capital gains, respectively. In all cases, the glide path has a 90–60 declining equity allocation and the equity has a low 20% turnover. We assume an equity return with a long-term average of 7% and volatility of 16%. Returns are i.i.d.[77] To help with the comparisons, we assume a savings budget that allows a 50/50

---

[77]We did evaluate returns having a slight negative autocorrelation, but the effect was insignificant.

allocation between tax-advantaged and taxable accounts. For each scenario, **Table 7.10** presents

- the after-tax difference in final wealth between allocating to equity first in the tax-advantaged account and doing the reverse,

- the after-tax difference in volatility of final wealth, and

- the likelihood that the after-tax wealth is lower by prioritizing equity over fixed income in the tax-advantaged account and the scope of this advantage, looking at the best (5th percentile) and worst (95th percentile) scenarios.

If we are to assume that the long-run average fixed-income yield is 3%, implying that the expected equity return premium relative to fixed income is 4%, a strong argument can be made for allocating equity to the tax-advantaged account first. The reason is not only that the likelihoods of achieving lower wealth are only 28.2% and 35.2%, respectively, but also that a strong asymmetry exists between the best and worst scenarios. In fact, the increased volatility of wealth that occurs when equity allocation is prioritized is largely explained by the distribution's positive wealth skew. The argument is not as strong when we assume that the yield on fixed income is 4%, implying a return premium of 3%; but in the case of a wealthy individual, it can probably still be supported, because unlike the example shown, much of the savings budget would have to go to the taxable account because of contribution limits.

Hence, we could conclude that for wealthy, highly taxed individuals, prioritizing equity in the tax-deferred accounts makes sense, whereas for less wealthy, lower-taxed individuals, whether to prioritize the tax-deferred

Table 7.10. Impact of Tax on Asset Location under Different Yield Environments

	New Jersey		Florida	
Fixed-Income Yield of:	3%	4%	3%	4%
Difference in final wealth	+7.5%	+3.9%	+3.1%	+1.4%
Difference in volatility of final wealth	32.7	26.6	13.6	11.5
Percentage of scenarios with lower final wealth	28.2	45.6	35.2	55.6
Best scenario	44.3	31.8	16.9	14.7
Worst scenario	−4.6	−7.2	−2.6	−3.9
5th Percentile	19.1	14.5	8.3	6.5
95th Percentile	−3.7	−6.2	−2.1	−3.4

account depends on our views of the long-term risk premium of equity versus bonds, although the significant excess return asymmetry favors equity first.[78]

7.3. Life Insurance, Variable Annuities, and Taxation of Insurance Products

7.3.1. Life Insurance Contracts.
Chapter 4 explained that an investor can purchase an annuity contract promising the annuitant an income for the rest of his life. This income can also be guaranteed for a minimum period (to the annuitant's heirs) in the event of an early death. It can start immediately (as a SPIA) or be deferred to a later date (as a SPDA). As described in Equation 4.1, the cost of an annuity depends on the size of the income payout, the survival probabilities associated with each payout, the discount or interest rates, and insurers' overhead costs: upfront sale and ongoing administration and profit charges.

Unlike an annuity that provides an income for as long as the annuitant is alive, a life insurance policy will pay a death benefit to the beneficiary only once the insured dies. There are several reasons to buy life insurance, however. The most important is protecting family members (i.e., children, spouse) from the death of a parent when the family has little wealth accumulated and/or is responsible for a significant mortgage or other expenses. It is often recommended that the coverage (such as 10 times the annual work income) extend at least until the children are expected to leave the household, in 20 years or more. In business, life insurance may also be required to cover the risk related to the loss of a key partner. Finally, life insurance may be required to cover capital gains taxes upon a succession or to finance some legacy need. Some advisers believe life insurance should be used as an investment vehicle, but we disagree; this strategy is not appropriate for most individuals.

---

[78]Some authors argue that a reason for holding equity in the taxable account first is that securities in taxable accounts receive a step-up in basis at death, eliminating the remaining capital gains taxes. Even were we to assume the portfolio is infrequently rebalanced or is invested in indices having very low security turnover, however, the allocation to equity could be gradually transferred from the tax-efficient accounts to the taxable accounts in the last few decades of the investor's life. Before this, a diversified portfolio of securities invested in a taxable account would have gone through many rebalancings that would have triggered capital gains. Furthermore, as Lussier (2013) illustrates in Chapter 9 of *Successful Investing Is a Process*, investors whose strategy is to fully minimize capital gains and who avoid even a reasonable rebalancing policy often pay the price in terms of long-term compounded returns, in part because their portfolio suffers from higher return volatility attributed to poor diversification. The decision to avoid rebalancing in order to limit taxation at death should be evaluated case by case.

Many types of life insurance products are available, making it very difficult to fairly assess each type because of their complexities and specific terms. Some products strictly offer life insurance (a benefit paid at death if it occurs while the policy is active); other products combine the life insurance component with an investment component, implying that the life insurance contract eventually builds cash value. Example of life insurance policies of both types are term life insurance and permanent life insurance:

- Life Insurance Only—term life insurance, which provides life insurance for a limited period such as 10, 20, or 30 years. The policy will lapse (i.e., will no longer be in force), however, if premiums are no longer paid.

- Life Insurance and Investment Vehicle—permanent life insurance, such as whole life and universal life, builds some cash value but is expensive because of the need to fund the investment component. Whole life is the simplest policy in this category. A permanent life insurance policy can also lapse if payments are no longer being made and the built-up cash value, which can be used to satisfy the periodic payment requirement, is depleted.

Let us first understand the complexities of these products, starting with term life policies. Equation 7.4 illustrates a simplified pricing mechanism for a term life insurance of T years, assuming level annual premium payments of P and nominal death benefit of B.

$$\sum_{t=0}^{T-1} SP_t \times DP_{t,t+1} \times \frac{B}{(1+k)^{t+1}} = \sum_{t=0}^{T-1} SP_t \times \frac{P}{(1+k)^t}, \qquad \text{Eq. 7.4}$$

where SP_t is the survival probability of the insured for a given current age at t years in the future (such as survival probabilities at age 41, 42, and so on) for an individual age 40. This probability is 100% when the policy is purchased and then gradually declines as t increases. $DP_{t,t+1}$ is the probability that the insured is deceased at time $t + 1$, knowing that he was alive at time t. The discount rate is k, which is assumed to be constant for the sake of simplicity. The left side of the equation is the present value associated with the expected death benefit, and the right side is the present value of the expected premium payments. In this formula, we assume that the premiums would be paid at the beginning of each year and the benefit would be paid at the end of the year, assuming death has occurred. Premium payments would end as soon as death occurs.

For example, assume a 50-year-old individual has a 0.20% chance of dying in the coming year. Therefore, she has a 99.8% chance of being alive at year end. If she is alive then, she has a 0.22% chance of dying the second year. Assuming a $500,000 two-year term policy and a 3% discount rate—and to simplify, assuming death can occur only at year-end—the market price of that protection would be as shown in **Table 7.11**.

In other words, the nominal cost of this policy over two years ($2,005.65 = $907.87 + $1,034.78) is determined by the likelihood that it would be triggered in Year 1 (0.20%) and, if it is not, by the likelihood that it would be triggered in Year 2 (0.2196%), assuming the insured has survived the first year (99.8%). This corresponds to a premium amount (paid yearly in advance) of approximately $1,006.

This example illustrates the basic principles of term life insurance pricing. The reality, however, is far more complex. The premium size would be affected upward by sales, administrative, and profit charges, but two factors could make term life significantly less expensive. First, the insurance company is likely to use a mortality table that factors in the insured's specific level of health, not a generic mortality table such as the one used for Social Security (as we did here). An individual who never smoked, is not overweight, and has no known health conditions would benefit from significantly lower mortality assumptions, thereby significantly reducing the annual premium. For example, a study by Albert, Bragg, and Brooks (2010) indicates healthy males and females age 75 have an almost four-year longer life expectancy than smokers of the same age.

Lapses constitute the other factor. It is estimated that approximately 6% of individuals stop paying, or abandon, their term life policies every year. Such a high rate may imply that few individuals buying a 20-year term life policy keep the policy until maturity. This represents a significant financial gain for insurance companies, especially when policies have level premiums (i.e., the same premium amount every period), while the likelihood of death increases with each passing year. It means that the premium paid on a level

Table 7.11. Pricing Methodology of a Two-Year Term Life Policy

	Year 1	Year 2
Probability of being alive at $t-1$	100%	99.8%
Probability of dying between $t-1$ and t	0.20%	0.22%
Probability of benefit being paid	100% × 0.20%	99.8% × 0.22%
Dollar value of expected benefit	$1,000 ($500,000 × 0.20%)	$1,097.80 ($500,000 × 0.2196%)
Present value of expected benefit	$907.87	$1,034.78

premium policy is larger than it should be in the initial years and less than it should be in the latter years. Thus, lapses are a financial gain to insurers; part of the expected financial impact of lapses may be incorporated into the premium pricing, thereby reducing it. As a result, the cost of term life insurance for a healthy individual is much less than what would be estimated from a generic mortality table.

The debate concerning whether to buy term or permanent life policies is ongoing. It is easy to find as many experts who favor term life policies as those who favor permanent life policies. Both groups will say that mathematics does not lie, implying each has a mathematical proof that one product is better than the other! The analysis consists generally of a comparison between buying a more expensive permanent policy that builds cash value against buying a cheaper term policy and investing the difference in the market (i.e., BTID, or buy term and invest the difference). Proponents of permanent policies will sell the fact that the cash value buildup accumulates tax free while providing lifetime insurance coverage, whereas proponents of term policies point to the high premiums and fees of permanent policies, low returns within these products, high lapse rates among buyers (40% to 50% within 10 years), and slow accrual values because insurance companies take the early premiums to offset the costs of issuing the policies. Each group of experts implies that the other has a flawed understanding of insurance products. The significant lapse rate, however, signals that inappropriate products, whatever the reasons, are sold to many investors.

Before we express an opinion on this issue, consider the overall principle of a whole life policy. A traditional whole life policy is a blend of a pure life insurance and an investment cash account. The cash account is funded from the higher premium amount of the whole life policy, above the amount required to pay for the life insurance portion. It is receiving a dividend related to a formula, and the policy may offer a guaranteed minimum return. According to Rockford (2014), the size of the dividend is believed to be influenced by the

- cash value of the policy, net of loans;

- actual mortality and expense rates that the company experienced over the course of the year;

- company's financial performance;

- amount of profit the company decides to retain in cash reserves for the year; and

- prevailing interest rates, which influence the insurer's portfolio returns.

Initially much of the premium is used to cover the insurer's upfront costs. Hence, the cash value builds very slowly in the first 10 years.[79] Also important to understand is that the cash value is a component of the death benefit. Because there is little or no cash value in the beginning, the entire life insurance cost is funded from a portion of the premium paid, and the death benefit is covered from the pure (term) life insurance portion of the policy. As the policy's cash value grows over time, however, this value covers an increasing portion of the death benefit. For example, if John buys a whole life policy of $100,000 and dies when the cash value is $40,000, the beneficiaries will receive $100,000, not $140,000. If the annual returns on the policy are significant, the death benefit could eventually be larger than the initial life insurance coverage amount. In other words, with a whole life policy *you are gradually self-insuring with your own savings*. Whole life policies are usually designed so that the cash benefit will reach the value of the death benefit at an advanced age such as 100.

Because a whole life policy combines life insurance and investment, it is substantially more expensive than a term life policy. For example, a 30-year-old male could pay $2,500 a year for a $250,000 whole life policy but $150 and $230, respectively, for 20- and 30-year term policies, according to different insurance-related websites. The two products have different features. The term life policy covers the insured for a predetermined period only, but the lower premium leaves the buyer with money that can be invested elsewhere. The whole life policy covers the individual's entire life and builds cash value, but the insured must not allow the policy to lapse. Can we determine which option is preferable for a given investor, strictly using logic and without doing a single calculation?

First, lower-income investors likely cannot afford to pay the significant premium on a permanent life policy and at the same time invest fully in their 401(k) and/or their IRAs and Roth IRAs. For many lower-income investors, the alternative is not choosing between tax-free return compounding in a whole life insurance plan versus taxable return compounding in a private investment account but rather choosing between two tax-exempt return compounding alternatives. Second, in the case of a whole life policy, a withdrawal from the cash value beyond the total amount of premiums paid is taxable. Hence, the tax-exempt argument put forward by permanent life proponents does not apply to lower-income households. The "lower incomes" facing this situation extend well into what we conventionally call middle-income brackets.

---

[79]www.policygenius.com/life-insurance/is-whole-life-insurance-worth-it/

Third, as explained, a whole life policy is a combination of a life insurance policy and an investment vehicle, with the insurance portion gradually being covered through the cash value account. Although high returns could even lead to an increase in death benefit, the increase simply means the cash value account has performed well. Hence, if a product can be decomposed into its components, it should be feasible to build a similar payoff expectation from the underlying components.

Obviously, this assumes that the investor benefits from effective financial planning. But this assumption is not necessarily sound: Many proponents of permanent policies point to the reporting by Dalbar QAIB (Quantitative Analysis of Investor Behavior) that investor performance significantly lags market performance. Improving investor behavior while providing efficient financial planning at a reasonable cost, however, is the main agenda of *Secure Retirement*. Furthermore, the commitment to higher premiums in whole life policies occurs early in life when investors can benefit most from the smoothing effect of the accumulation process in their investment portfolio.

There is no magic solution. Hedging a downside risk has a cost, and the same management and hedging principles apply across industries. Because the sales, administrative, and profit charges of insurance company products can be significant, we doubt that the certainty equivalent of a whole life policy is greater than the certainty equivalent of the combination of a cheaper term life policy and a comparable investment portfolio managed at a much lower cost.[80]

Finally, and perhaps most importantly, there is the issue of lapses. Allowing a term life policy to lapse after 10 years does not have the same sunk-cost impact on investors as lapsing a whole life policy that accumulated barely any cash value. As the evidence shows, assuming average investors will remain disciplined and never allow their permanent policy to lapse is imprudent. Reasons for lapsing vary: The coverage is no longer needed, the family can no longer afford the premiums, investors believe they have found a better alternative, the returns are disappointing, and so on (Mincer 2011).

Furthermore, as investors become better informed and gain access in coming years to more comprehensive financial planning tools and advisory support, is it likely that insurance policies will eventually be purchased by more informed investors and that the lapse rates will fall substantially? How would this scenario affect the profitability of insurers and the policy dividend? As analyzed by Zians, Miller, and Ducuroir (2016), "From our recent survey,

---

[80]This agrees with the conclusion reached earlier that an immediate annuity guaranteed 10 years is likely more expensive than the sum of a deferred annuity starting in 10 years and a portfolio of zero-coupon bonds purchased at a low cost.

we observed the issue is still widely underestimated by Belgian insurers, while basis interest rate mathematics show it could easily mean the difference between profitable and unprofitable business overall." A whole life contract can be in place for decades. No one can see that far into the future, especially in a financial industry currently challenged by new business models.

Making a significant financial decision that cannot easily be reversed at a reasonable cost is difficult to integrate into a financial planning exercise. Therefore, we advise investors to separate the investment decision from the life insurance decision to avoid this debate. For lower- to middle-income investors, we advise use of term insurance to protect loved ones and avoid potential regret. Some 40% of investors express regret within 10 years of buying a permanent policy. Of the remaining 60%, some may also have regrets but have not necessarily taken any action because the decision to act is difficult once a policy is already in place. Finally, as mentioned previously, a 40% lapse rate on a potentially significant financial commitment indicates a failure to properly evaluate the policy's appropriateness for investors.

For wealthier investors, who otherwise would be taxed on their savings, the approach could be different. The role of permanent life policies should be evaluated case by case if the following conditions are met:

- It is very likely that the insured will be able to keep the policy active.

- A product has been identified that has a reasonable chance of providing a tax-exempt return compounding high enough to compensate for the higher fees associated with the product and to outperform a taxable portfolio.

- The investor has access to an adviser who truly understands all the specific terms of the insurance contract.

Unfortunately, we cannot assume that all conditions are necessarily met in most cases. A commitment to a multidecade life insurance product requires serious analysis.

7.3.2. Variable Annuity Products.
As investors became more concerned with outliving their retirement savings, new products, such as variable annuities, have been engineered in the past two decades to tackle this issue. The guaranteed lifetime withdrawal benefit (GLWB) products are a rider to a variable annuity contract. A GLWB product is an insurance contract. In its most basic form, it guarantees the investor a lifetime minimum stream of periodic withdrawals, either starting immediately or deferred to a later date. Should the asset portfolio be exhausted because of weak market conditions and permitted minimum withdrawals, the insurance company would cover

the remaining withdrawals. GLWBs differ from regular life annuities in that they offer upside potential. Instead of investing in low-risk fixed-income securities, the investor chooses a balanced portfolio of funds, and guaranteed income can increase if the portfolio value goes up. The annual "lifetime" retirement income is determined by the combination of two variables—namely, the benefit base and the withdrawal percentage.

- Benefit Base: This value is based on the amounts contributed to the contract and can increase if there is no cash withdrawal during any year. In the absence of withdrawals, the participant may benefit from a bonus added to the benefit base, such as 5% a year. It may also increase if, at specific intervals, the market value of all units attributed to the contract (which of course is affected by all regular withdrawals) is greater than the current benefit base. For example, if the current GLWB benefit base is $100,000 and the units' market value (adjusted for market returns, fees, and scheduled withdrawals) is more than this amount at the anniversary of the contract three years from now, this market value will become the new GLWB benefit base. This value can be adjusted downward only if excess withdrawals are made.

- Withdrawal Percentage: This amount is the percentage of the benefit base the investor can withdraw each year. For example, a participant will be guaranteed the right to withdraw annually 5% of the benefit base at age 65.

These GLWB contracts can have significant fees. The documentation explaining these products often provides several examples of how the benefits could evolve in very specific circumstances. Rarely, however, does it provide potential participants with information about the cumulative impact of fees on their financial well-being over horizons of 20 years or more. Understandably, participants are usually not told how well they would have done in the same market circumstances had they not invested in this product but instead selected a cheaper alternative without all the bells and whistles. In other words, GLWBs offer guarantees, but investors have little understanding of the costs and benefits of these guarantees.[81]

Lussier, Langlois, and Grantier (2015) completed an analysis comparing the performance of Canadian and US GLWB contracts from different insurance providers. Annual fees ranged from 1.77% (from a lower-cost US provider with fees of 0.57% during accumulation) to 3.95%! Guarantees also

---

[81]The guarantees offered are expensive to hedge. In a prior role, we were involved in the management of the guaranty of such products.

differed among products. Using a Monte Carlo analysis, the researchers compared the performance of a GLWB approach with simply investing in a low-cost 60/40 portfolio of ETFs. The analysis compared a scenario in which a GLWB contract is purchased at age 55 and withdrawals start at age 65 with a scenario in which the capital remains in a 60/40 portfolio and the same dollar withdrawals are made from that portfolio at age 65. Assuming the cheapest contracts, the results indicate an 8% probability that the investor would be better off with the GLWB approach at age 85, 21% at age 90, 34% at age 95, and 45% at age 100. For a male age 65, the probability of reaching age 95 is between 7% and 12% and of reaching age 100 is 1% to 3%. Probabilities of ruin at or before the specified ages were higher for the more expensive products. Thus a GLWB is basically an expensive longevity product.

As demonstrated in the first chapters, the objective of *Secure Retirement* is implicitly to integrate risk management processes within the financial strategy of the individual. This is accomplished through the purchase of low-cost annuities, the management of income withdrawals and asset allocation, and support from technology at the lowest cost possible. Therefore, some of the risk management benefits a GLWB contract could bring will be achieved through the management process allowing investors to keep the excess wealth that can be achieved in more-favorable management environments.

For example, we compared the performance of a lower-cost GLWB retirement strategy promoted by a well-known asset management firm with that of a simpler approach. The GLWB strategy is gradually implemented between ages 50 and 65, at which point all the retiree's assets are invested in GLWB contracts. The simpler approach assumes the following:

- Capital is invested in the same asset classes used in the GLWB but using low-cost ETFs.

- Assets are allocated according to the 90–60 glide path used previously.

- Fully 30% of assets are converted to 10-year certain annuities between ages 61 and 65.

- Periodic withdrawals under the simpler approach are identical to those of the GLWB contracts for each of 50,000 individual scenarios of performance from age 50 until 100.[82] A portion of these withdrawals is funded by the annuity payout, and the balance is extracted from the investment portfolio.

---

[82]Stochastic return scenarios were generated using the same block bootstrapping methodology used in prior chapters.

Table 7.12. Probability the GLWB Approach Leads to Greater Wealth at Death

Age	65	70	75	80	85	90	95	100
Probability	75.3%	41.7%	16.4%	1.1%	1.8%	6.1%	12.2%	19.0%

The objective was to identify the number of scenarios resulting in greater wealth at death for different ages ranging from 65 to 100. Results are presented in **Table 7.12**.

The higher probabilities at age 65 and 70 occur because of the losses resulting from the initial investment in annuity contracts in the event of early death. If 30% of the wealth is invested in an annuity, the market value loss is still relatively important even if the annuity has a 10-year certain guaranty if death occurs very quickly. This effect dissipates over time, however, so a retiree expecting to live to at least age 75 is unlikely to benefit from the GLWB approach. Even for annuitants at an advanced age of 100, we could identify only 19% of scenarios for which the GLWB strategy would be preferable.

7.3.3. Taxation Aspects of Insurance, Annuity Contracts, and Social Security. Annuities can be acquired with before-tax (IRA/401(k)) money, subject to limits, or with after-tax money. If the annuity is purchased with before-tax money, income will be fully taxable when realized. In the case of annuities purchased with after-tax money, only the income in excess of return of principal will be taxed. Even then, income is apportioned into taxable versus nontaxable components based on the annuitant's remaining life expectancy according to the IRS mortality tables. Hence, a portion of the periodic income is excluded from taxation until the principal has been fully returned. Furthermore, withdrawals before age 59.5 may be subject to a 10% additional penalty tax.

Dobler (2013) provides two examples of annuity taxation. A 65-year-old individual invests $100,000 in a SPIA five-year certain. The annual income to be received is $7,020 with a life expectancy of 21.9 years according to the IRS Uniform Lifetime Table. The individual will be exempt from taxation on $4,566 of yearly income, implying an exclusion ratio of 65% ($4,566/$7,020) until all capital is repaid. This implies that after 21.9 years, all annuity income will become taxable.

In the case of a SPDA with a deferral period of 10 years, the expected income would be much greater—$14,796 in our example—but the life expectancy at the point when the annuity becomes effective is much shorter at 13.9 years. The yearly amount excluded from taxation is thus $7,194, and the exclusion ratio is 48.6%. Also, buying an annuity with before- or after-tax income does not represent the same after-tax capital investment, because $100 in an IRA does not have the same after-tax value as $100 invested with after-tax money.

It is not easy to find literature discussing which approach is preferable. A practitioner concluded that buying an annuity with after-tax money may be a poor decision because the retiree would be swapping lower capital gains tax rates for higher ordinary income tax rates on annuity gains (Kapan 2015). We have already indicated, however, that annuities should preferably be used as a substitute for a portion of the fixed-income assets. In this context, the differential tax rate argument is irrelevant.

Two sets of strategies were considered in a context where the retiree has $100 in before-tax money (in an IRA) and $100 in after-tax money. In the first set, the retiree has a choice between two options:

- Option A: allocating the after-tax money ($100) to annuities and the before-tax money ($100) to fixed income

- Option B: allocating the after-tax money ($100) to fixed income and the before-tax money ($100) to annuities

The first set of strategies assumes a 65-year-old individual, a 30% tax rate, a life expectancy of approximately 22 years, and an annual income payout rate of $8 after tax per $100 invested. In this context, Option A is preferable if the retiree has a life expectancy of more than approximately 20 years. If the income payout rate is lower, the breakeven point occurs earlier because the portfolio benefits more from the reinvestment of the lower-taxed high-annuity payout and vice versa. Under most scenarios of interest rates and taxes, however, individuals should consider Option A only if they expect to live beyond age 80.

Options A and B, however, do not have the same capital at risk. In the event of an early death, the money available to heirs would be lower under Option A. The second set of strategies compares the following Option C with Option B. Option C consists of allocating 70% (i.e., 1 minus the tax rate) of the after-tax money ($70) to annuities, the balance of the after-tax money to fixed income, and the before-tax money ($100) to fixed income. Assuming again a 30% tax rate, Option B is always preferable and becomes increasingly so as time passes. Using a lower tax rate such as 20% and an 80% allocation of the after-tax money to an annuity, the two options lead to similar results, but Option B is still slightly preferable, especially if expected longevity is beyond 85 years of age. Therefore, when allocating to an annuity, we advise the investor to prioritize allocating to an annuity, if it is required, from before-tax (IRA) money or from the 401(k) plan.

Social Security income is not fully taxed. The portfolio of Social Security income that is taxable is mostly a function of the combined income defined as gross adjusted income plus nontaxable interest plus 50% of Social Security income. It can be fully exempted in the case of individuals and joint filers with income below $25,000 and $32,000, respectively, but up to 50% of Social Security income generated above these amounts can be taxed if income is less than $34,000 and $44,000, respectively. Above these income levels, up to 85% can be taxed. Income generated from annuities, dividends, and most other investments, however, does not affect the entitled benefits.[83]

Finally, there are two main taxation rules to remember in the case of life insurance. First, payout to beneficiaries is not taxable, unless it becomes part of the estate for household estates larger than the allowed estate and gift tax exemption. Also, profits realized from surrendering a cash value policy are taxable if the cash value exceeds what was paid in.

7.4. Income Replacement Ratio and Other Income Factors

Financial planners often recommend a before-tax income replacement ratio of 70% to 80% in retirement, where the replacement ratio is defined as gross income after retirement divided by gross income before retirement. In general, many possible reasons explain why a replacement ratio less than 100% can be justified:

- No Social Security payment contributions are required once an individual is no longer employed.

- Social Security is not fully taxed.

- Private savings are no longer required, assuming the retirement objectives have been met.

- The mortgage is likely paid, and children may have become financially independent.

- Work-related expenses, such as transportation and clothing, decline, as does, potentially, spending on restaurants.

On the other hand, a potential issue for US retirees is the rising cost of medical care and the higher cost of Medicare benefits and of insurance policies. Also, some individuals may have costlier leisure goals, such as extensive travel. This section addresses two issues. First, what are the replacement ratios usually observed among retirees, especially across different levels of income?

---

[83]www.retirementhq.com/immediate-annuity-exclusion-ratio-can-impact-retirement-tax-burden/

183

Second, what ratio is appropriate for planning purposes, and how should it be estimated?

Purcell (2012) analyzed how the household income replacement ratio evolves after retirement and differs according to various criteria, such as the income level. **Table 7.13** presents the median before-tax replacement ratios for the all-household category as well as for households from the lowest to the highest quartile of income for Years 1 and 2, Years 3 and 4, and Years 9 and 10 after retirement.[84]

An important aspect of these results is how the observed replacement ratios decline, especially by Years 3 and 4. A possible explanation is that the data available on cohorts of retirees do not appropriately capture the transition from work to retirement. In other words, some of the employment income of the last work year may be inappropriately attributed to the first retirement year. Also, income from part-time employment may be affecting the ratio. It may also be that as presented in Chapter 4, Section 4.5.3, a downward consumption adjustment occurs in the first few years of retirement, thereby reducing income requirements.

Therefore, we cannot be sure that income replacement ratios estimated for the initial years of retirement reflect the longer-term reality. Furthermore, according to a study by Smith (2003), measuring the median replacement ratio on an after-tax basis would raise the ratio by 20%. In other words, the 63.5% income replacement ratio measured for Years 3 and 4 for all retirees would be 76.2% on an after-tax basis.

Another important aspect is the decline of the replacement ratio that persists even beyond the initial years. This decline is observed in all income quartile groups, but it is more significant for retirees belonging to the highest

Table 7.13. Replacement Ratios of Households after Retirement on a Before-Tax Basis

	Years 1 and 2	Years 3 and 4	Years 9 and 10
All	73.5%	63.5%	53.7%
Lowest quartile	73.8	69.5	60.1
Second quartile	73.0	65.3	59.8
Third quartile	75.1	66.4	61.0
Highest quartile	**71.8**	**59.3**	**50.6**

[84]Within each quartile of income, however, the income replacement ratio for the 75th percentile of individuals can be as much as above 100% for all income quartiles in Years 1 and 2 and from 80% to 90% in Years 9 and 10. The 90% level is specific to the lowest quartile of income.

income quartile. This trend may indicate that wealthier individuals change their lifestyle more significantly as they age, whereas less affluent retirees do not indulge as much early in retirement.

Are retirees satisfied with their consumption levels, however? As Banerjee (2016) reports, less than 48.6% of retirees declared themselves very satisfied with their retirement situation as of 2012, compared with 60.5% in 1998. These two ratios were 66.7% and 75.6%, respectively, as of the same years among the retirees in the highest asset quartile. They were 28.9% and 41.1%, respectively, for retirees in the lowest asset quartile. More informative are the results of a survey concluding that among retirees who are very satisfied or somewhat satisfied with their situation, the median income before-tax replacement ratio was 72%, whereas it was 60% among those not at all satisfied.

Other studies look at the income required to maintain the same purchasing power post retirement once adjustments are made for (lower) taxes, (less) savings, and change in age- and work-related expenditure. A study by Aon Consulting (2008) concludes that mid- to high-income individuals need to target replacement ratios of 77% to 81%, whereas lower-income individuals—those earning less than $40,000 annually—need 85% to 94% to maintain their previous standard of living. As of the date of this specific study, according to the Congressional Budget Office report by Harris, Sammartino, and Weiner (2012), approximately 40% of households had an income below $40,000. Therefore, it would be sensible to use an initial target income replacement ratio of approximately 75% for households with income among the top 60% of households and gradually increasing this target toward 90% for the bottom 40% of households. It may also be sensible to assume that the required income replacement ratio may decline over time, especially for individuals in higher-income groups, given that people in this group may have achieved many of their retirement goals in the initial decade after retirement.

Even if we have a general idea of what income replacement ratio to target as of retirement, however, we also need to understand how the income of an individual/household will evolve from a younger age to a retirement age such as 65. Guvenen, Karahan, Ozkan, and Song (2015) did an extensive study of the life cycle of earnings in the US population using the Master Earnings File (MEF) of the US Social Security Administration records. Two major observations are noted:

- Earnings growth is highly skewed. For example, the median individual has observed an overall real earnings growth of 38% from age 25 to 55, or about 1.07% per year. An individual at the 5th percentile (from the top), however, has experienced growth of 230%, or 4.06% yearly.

- Much of the earning gains occur in the first 10 years. For example, if we look at the gains of the median individual starting at age 35, instead of 25, overall real growth is close to zero. After age 45, fewer than 2% of individuals experience real growth.

Earnings growth potential will reveal itself in the first 10 to 20 years of an individual's work life. When plotting a retirement plan for a young individual, how do we determine if the expected income growth is likely to be stronger or weaker than the median? This is a question that the adviser and the individual/household must answer together, but indications are that individuals with a higher level of education experience stronger income growth. **Table 7.14** shows the average income growth for cohorts of males and females born in either 1949, 1959, or 1969 according to the level of education: less than college, college, and postgraduate. The data appear to indicate that higher education leads to stronger income growth, although the female college-educated cohort of 1969 does not support this assertion.

From an economic standpoint, education enhances human capital. But according to Spence (1973), a worker's schooling is largely just "signaling," implying that a college degree does not materially add to a worker's productive capability but merely signals the existence of such intrinsic ability. Carneiro and Lee (2011) find that increasing college enrollment has led to a decrease in the average quality of graduates, reducing their income premium. Another study (Arum and Roksa 2011) shows that 45% of college students made no significant improvements in their critical thinking, reasoning, and writing skills during the first two years of college. Finally, perhaps as an expression of these observations, the billionaire entrepreneur Peter Thiel has offered fellowships for certain students to postpone college and work at technology companies.

Table 7.14. Income Growth from 1988 to 2012 According to Education

Cohorts	1949	1959	1969
Male < College	−0.63%	0.06%	0.48%
Male = College	1.59	2.20	2.35
Male > College	3.9	2.23	5.05
Female < College	−0.23%	0.25%	1.28%
Female = College	1.67	1.15	0.56
Female > College	2.02	1.05	5.65

Source: Penn Wharton Budget Model (2016).

Although income growth for the median individual age 25 may be concentrated in the first 10 years, college-educated workers may see growth that extends longer. In most cases, however, whatever real growth in income is observed is largely completed by age 45 to 50. It may make sense to recognize some potential growth in early income as we plan in the initial years of savings, but by age 35, individuals (and their advisers) should have a better idea of what can be expected.

Despite the previous comments, to believe we can accurately forecast the income needs (or resources) at age 65 of an individual who is currently 30 years old would be presumptuous. Therefore, assuming that a growth income pattern has been established, the following process is recommended:

- In the initial stage of savings, target retirement income ranging from 75% (for higher-income household) to 90% (for lower-income household) of the projected income in the years before retirement and adjusting for a reasonable decline in income needs post retirement.

- Revisit the issue as soon as it becomes possible to compute a better estimate, such as in the last 5 to 10 years before retirement. At this point in life, the individual's household situation and life goals are likely better understood and realizing a proper retirement budget more feasible. For very wealthy investors, it may be preferable to specify the income needs in real dollar terms than as a proportion of gross income. Furthermore, retirees and their advisers must remain realistic. We have already cautioned that the retirement situation of an individual or household cannot be improved by assuming unreasonably high future asset returns. Similarly, it cannot be improved by assuming unreasonably low and declining future consumption.

This aspect is reinforced by MacDonald, Osberg, and Moore (2016), who conclude that for several reasons, the traditional measure of earnings replacement based on final employment earnings is a poor indicator of income needs in retirement. First, the last year of employment earnings may not be representative of working-life living standards. Second, it fails to consider several important specificities, such as other sources of income and the size of households. Third, it ignores how individuals actually consume while working. The researchers introduce a measure called the living standard replacement rate (LSRR), which is the ratio of the money available to spend on consumption in retirement to the money available to spend on consumption while working.

    187

Both low-income and higher-income households present challenges for the retirement-planning process. Low-income households are more heavily dependent on Social Security benefits. As noted by Munnell (2003), however, the proportion of income needs provided by the Social Security program has been declining and is expected to decline further for several reasons:

- The full retirement age is rising from 65 in 2000 to 67 in 2022.

- Although Social Security benefits can be exempt from taxation or partially taxed depending on specific income triggers, these triggers are not indexed and occur at quite modest income levels.

- Premiums associated with Medicare Part B are directly deducted from the Social Security benefits. Although the Hold Harmless Act prevents the Social Security benefits of a retiree from declining because of an increase in Medicare premium, it also means that significant increases in these premiums may prevent a retiree from benefiting from COLA. For example, many retirees did not see their Social Security benefits increasing in 2016 and 2017 because Medicare premiums increased significantly while the COLA was flat in 2016 and up 0.3% in 2017.

- As previously mentioned, the Social Security funding gap increased significantly. According to the 2018 Social Security Trustees Report, the funding deficit rose from 1.7% of employee payroll in 2008 to 2.84% in 2018. This means that payroll taxes would currently have to increase by 2.84% to keep the Social Security system solvent. The Congressional Budget Office has even more unfavorable estimates.

Assuming the funding gap will be resolved half through a reduction in benefits and half from new revenues, the average worker's replacement income ratio will decline from 41.2% in 2000 to approximately 26.9% in 2030. This decline does not change the income needs of lower-income households, but it does mean that they face even greater savings challenges. It is prudent to account for the funding gap and other aspects such as the absence of indexation in a financial planning exercise, because many current and future retirees will likely be affected by these factors.

Finally, another issue for average and higher-income earners is the treatment of housing assets. First, households currently living in an expensive metropolitan area may have the option and desire to move to a less costly area in retirement, further contributing to their financial wealth. This aspect can be significant and should be integrated into the financial plan whenever appropriate. The potential gain must be significant, however, given friction costs such as moving expenses, closing costs, and broker fees. Nonetheless, moving 50 to 60 miles from an expensive large city will considerably reduce housing investment while maintaining access to major airports and hospitals (Miller 2011).

A more comprehensive issue is how to integrate the fact that many households have significant home equity as they enter retirement (Polyak 2017).[85] Housing is usually the largest nonpension asset. According to Sass, Munnell, and Eschtruth (2014) of the Center for Retirement Research at Boston College, two-person households of ages ranging from 65 to 74 have 20% more in home equity than in financial assets. Munnell and Soto (2005) argue that a home is an asset that offers potential consumption—for example, its value can be accessed through a reverse mortgage—but most retirees hold onto their homes well into retirement. The authors report that 90% of couples and 62% of singles enter retirement owning their homes and that in the absence of a significant event, such as the death of a spouse, most households keep their own homes well into their 80s. "Thus," Munnell and Soto say, "people do not appear interested in tapping their home equity for non-housing consumption" (p. 24). But should they?

7.5. Role of Reverse Mortgages

For households with significant financial assets, extracting value from a house is not a pressing issue. For others, there are two options that are not mutually exclusive. First, households that enter retirement with a mortgage should consider downsizing and/or moving to a cheaper location. Higher-income mortgage-free households may even want to consider this possibility, because moving to a different location in retirement may have been part of their plan all along. The financial gains resulting from downsizing could help fund an annuity purchase.

A house is a source of independence for retirees, however. They may have no mortgage, although they still face property taxes and maintenance costs. Also, many consider their home equity as a reserve asset for health-related eventualities and as an asset to leave to children and/or charity. Even if all these concerns are considered, it is still financially beneficial to integrate the potential benefits of home equity into the planning process in order to optimize the pattern of consumption during retirement. For example, we indicated in Chapters 3 and 4 that the accumulation process smooths portfolio performance during equity shocks but that this effect is negated or reversed during decumulation. A thoughtful use of home equity can help smooth

---

[85]Nevertheless, the percentage of households entering retirement with a mortgage rose from 23.9% to 35% between 1998 and 2012.

financial volatility during decumulation without necessarily reducing legacy wealth.

A reverse mortgage is a loan that allows the homeowner to get money from the home's equity without having to sell or move out of the house. The amount that can be borrowed will depend on the homeowner's age, the home's appraised value, and current interest rate conditions. A reverse mortgage does not require any payments until the homeowner moves out of the house, sells it, or, as the last borrower, dies.

The proceeds of a reverse mortgage can be obtained in a combination of any of the following four possibilities:

- lump-sum payment, although not necessarily the full amount

- tenure payment: much like a life annuity, a fixed monthly payment for as longs as the borrower lives and remains in the home

- term payment: a fixed monthly payment for a fixed amount of time

- line of credit: borrowing capacity that does not have to be fully spent or even ever be used (A consumption/investment strategy could be designed using the flexibility that a line of credit offers. This option is the most appropriate for financial planning.)

Appendix III explains the working principles of reverse mortgages.

Since 2012, many articles have discussed the strategies leading to the most efficient use of reverse mortgages. The work initially started with Sacks and Sacks (2012) and Pfeiffer, Salter, and Evensky (2013), who looked at reverse mortgages not as a last resort option but as a decumulation and wealth management tool. Sacks and Sacks were drawing on the line of credit of the reverse mortgage only in years when the investment portfolio generated negative performance, whereas Pfeiffer et al. were covering spending from the line of credit only when the portfolio balance was below 80% of the wealth level estimated to be needed to maintain consumption on a sustainable path. Unlike the Sacks and Sacks strategy, the reverse mortgage is repaid when the portfolio is again above the threshold.

Pfau (2016) evaluated six different reverse mortgage strategies, including that of Sacks and Sacks and a variation of the Pfeiffer et al. approach called Texas Tech Coordination. The author compared the results with a no–reverse mortgage approach as well as the following four strategies:

- home equity as a last resort—delaying securing the reverse mortgage until the investment portfolio is depleted

- home equity first—drawing from the reverse mortgage first

- home equity last—securing the reverse mortgage now but waiting for the investment portfolio to be depleted

- tenure payments—securing the reverse mortgage now and receiving an annuity-type payment

Pfau (2016) looked at the probability of success in terms of maintaining a 4% after-tax (about 5.33% before-tax) initial withdrawal rate adjusted for inflation. Unsurprisingly, all strategies had significantly better probability of success than the status quo, but the most effective were home equity last, Sacks and Sacks, and Texas Tech Coordination. Home equity first was not as successful, considering the after-tax cost of borrowing using a reverse mortgage. Home equity as a last resort was also not as successful because waiting to initiate a reverse mortgage reduced the size of the line of credit. In other words, it is preferable to open a line of credit early but delay its use or use it strategically.

If the objective is greater legacy wealth, however, the conclusions differed according to the relative evolution of portfolio wealth versus net real estate wealth. For example, in situations where investment returns are favorable, it is preferable to preserve the assets within the portfolio and draw down the home equity first. Hence, using home equity first or tenure payments leads to greater legacy values. In scenarios of bad market returns leading to poor or even negative legacy wealth, however, home equity last does better. Keep in mind, of course, that the main objective of *Secure Retirement* is improving the life of retirees, not maximizing legacy wealth.

More recently, Neuwirth, Sacks, and Sacks (2017) introduced the Rule of 30 in the context of using a reverse mortgage credit line to improve the management of retirement income. Their analysis is based on the combination of liquid asset portfolio and home equity wealth. The Rule of 30 was designed to sustain initial inflation-adjusted income with a 90% probability level. It also happens that the initial income that allowed this objective to be met was approximately 1/30 of total wealth as defined. They also tested a Rule of 34 (1/34) when using more conservative expected return assumptions. The approach is applied to households having similar levels of wealth but a different distribution between portfolio and home equity. Two strategies are compared. Strategy 1 is Sacks and Sacks coordination, and Strategy 2 is home equity as a last resort. As expected, Strategy 1 had a 90% success ratio at a 30-year horizon, whereas Strategy 2 had much lower success rates, especially in cases where home equity is a relatively more important component of wealth.

Obviously, other financing options, such as a home equity line of credit (HELOC), are available to households seeking to extract value from their home. A HELOC requires monthly interest payments, however; the loan can be called in if the borrower's credit is deteriorating, and it does not allow for the borrowing capacity to potentially increase beyond the home's appraised value for individuals or households that have a very long life. A HELOC adds a different type of uncertainty and is not an efficient tool for retirement-planning purposes. With a reverse mortgage, the borrower retains ownership of the house, does not make monthly payments, cannot be removed from the house, and can never owe more than 95% of the home's value.

Reverse mortgages add one more tool to the retirement management toolbox. Individuals already face a compromise between the initial level of retirement income, the adjustments to retirement income that may be necessary if unfavorable financial circumstances occur—which would be amplified by a higher initial income target—and the legacy they may wish to leave their heirs or a charity. Reverse mortgages can be used as an instrument to stabilize retirement income and reduce the likelihood of not achieving a specific income target and/or as an instrument to increase expected retirement income.

The discussion in Chapters 4 and 6 about a decumulation engine is consistent with some aspects of the reverse mortgage literature. For example, some of the dynamic strategies proposed for reverse mortgages require drawing from the line of credit when the portfolio balance is below X% (such as 80%) of the level required to maintain a sustainable consumption, or using a coordination strategy with a Y% (such as 90%) likelihood of sustaining the required income level. Although we need to define a tolerance level for reducing consumption in the event of unfavorable financial returns, a reverse mortgage could help support that threshold level.

Hence, reverse mortgages can improve the total utility that households can derive from their consumption. Given that a house remains the last source of potential income for many households, integrating the housing assets as a component of retirement planning should lead to requiring a high probability of income sustainability. To believe we can precisely represent all of an investor's preferences through a utility function, however, would be naive. We may need to clarify specific issues with each household. When facing a difficult financial environment, for example, would household members prefer first to adjust consumption or to draw on their line of credit? To avoid simply replicating analyses performed by other authors, we postpone further analysis of reverse mortgages to Chapter 8 as we consider the use of reverse mortgages within an integrated retirement strategy.

7.6. Mortality Tables

We have used the Social Security mortality table in several sections of this book. Although they reflect the anticipated life expectancy of the general population, they are not necessarily appropriate to the issue of retirement planning for a specific individual. The discussion around mortality tables in Chapter 4 shows that numerous socioeconomic aspects can justify significant differences in life expectancy among different individuals. There are in fact three contexts in which mortality tables must be discussed in the context of retirement planning: products for which the tables are not required, mortality tables required to price annuities, and necessary mortality assumptions.

7.6.1. Products That Do Not Require Mortality Tables for Retirement Planning. Although from a public policy point of view the Social Security mortality table is useful to evaluate the program's sustainability, only two aspects matter from the point of view of retirement planning for a specific individual:

1. Under the current Social Security rules, what level of benefits can an individual expect? This income is based on the history of wages and on the timing of when Social Security income is first claimed (between ages 62 and 70).

2. What is the appropriate assumption for Social Security income post-2034, when the Social Security Trust Fund is expected to be depleted if no action is taken before then? The worst-case scenario is a reduction of Social Security benefits of approximately 23%. The reduction is likely to be applied unevenly—that is, a larger reduction for higher-income beneficiaries and perhaps no reduction for the lowest. It is likely that a future political compromise will affect the outcome.

Similarly, when evaluating the income to be expected from a defined benefit plan, the beneficiary does not have to know the mortality assumptions used by the plan's actuaries. The income will be based on specific rules related to number of work years, age of retirement, and potentially other aspects such as the wage measure as of retirement and whether the benefits are fully, partially, or not indexed.

7.6.2. Mortality Tables Required to Price Annuities. Pricing insurance products, whether a life insurance or an annuity, is difficult because small changes in parameters can significantly affect the pricing. It requires using an appropriate yield curve and accurate estimates of distribution and administration costs as well as profit margins, lapse rates (for life insurance products), and mortality tables.

Insurance companies often have two sets of internal mortality tables—one for life insurance and another for annuities—and will make further adjustments for an individual's sex, reason for product purchase (compulsory or voluntary), and even income and occupation. Actuaries may also devise cohort mortality tables to account for future trends in mortality (McCarthy and Mitchell 2002). Some of these adjustments are meant to address adverse selection risk—that is, the fact that purchasers of annuities tend to have lower mortality rates than the general population. Because we advise the use of term life insurance that does not affect the savings budget significantly, the balance of this section concentrates on annuity pricing.

In addition to the Social Security mortality table are tables provided by the Society of Actuaries (SOA).[86] For example, the RP-2014 table provides mortality estimates for employees and for healthy annuitants—both males and females (starting at age 50)—for categories of employees such as blue- and white-collar employees and for the total dataset of employees. **Figure 7.2** presents the survival probabilities until age 110 for males and females currently age 60 according to the general Social Security tables and according to

Figure 7.2. Probability of Survival at Age 60 According to Social Security and SOA Mortality Tables

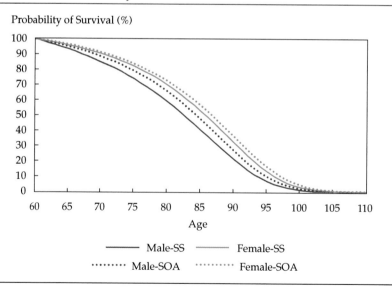

---

[86]www.soa.org/experience-studies/2014/research-2014-rp/

the SOA tables for healthy annuitants. Figure 7.2 clearly shows higher probabilities of survival for healthy annuitants versus the population in general for both males and females.

From a retirement-planning point of view, it is important to use the most appropriate mortality table available. In Table 4.5, we compared the value to men and women of different annuities against their current market price using two sets of mortality assumptions, Social Security and SOA for healthy annuitants. The choice of mortality tables had a nonnegligible effect on this ratio.

Considering the nuances in annuity pricing, there is no better estimate of what an annuity would cost in the near future than the annuity pricing quotes that can be obtained from an online pricing source or directly obtained from several insurers or insurance brokers. Hence, a retirement tool should be supplied with information related to current annuity pricing. Such a tool, however, also requires estimating the cost of purchasing annuities in the future in different yield environments for individuals who are still years from considering this transaction; this estimation is more difficult.

In Chapter 8 of *Secure Retirement*, the pricing of annuities is based on the SOA tables for healthy annuitants because an adviser would be unlikely to recommend an annuity to an unhealthy beneficiary. Furthermore, to achieve reasonable pricing estimates, the annuity model is calibrated using current pricing for immediate and deferred annuities for males and females, with the objective of finding the spread against the appropriate yield curve that leads to the most accurate pricing for the average of all annuities. This is similar to the internal rate of return (IRR) method explained by Mitchell and McCarthy (2002), which seeks to solve for the IRR that equates the price of an annuity as determined by the present value of its payouts with a specific mortality table. This process is highly effective. For example, when we applied the pricing optimization to nine annuities (four for males, four for females, one joint) having different terms (immediate, deferred by five years, guaranteed 120 months, not guaranteed), the largest annual payout difference between the model and outside sources was 12 bps.

7.6.3. Mortality Assumptions Required for Retirement Planning.
Information about mortality assumptions is not required by the retirees to estimate their benefits from either Social Security or from a DB plan. Those benefits can usually be estimated from one's work income history. Current annuity pricing is available from online sources, but estimating the future price of annuities requires the use of generic mortality tables. Calibrating the retirement income of an individual like John and evaluating the sustainability

of this income, however, would preferably require us to use mortality assumptions that are most representative of John's specific situation. For example, if a retirement plan is designed to target a 90% probability of success, it implicitly assumes that this probability is applied to a mortality table that applies to John. There is evidence in the literature (e.g., Siddiqi and Mervyn 2017) that, other factors being equal, mortality rates are greater on average for

- former blue-collar workers than former white-collar workers,
- former private-sector workers than former public-sector workers, and
- pensioners receiving small pensions.

As an illustration, **Figure 7.3** presents the probability of survival for blue- and white-collar workers according to SOA.

The calibration of a mortality table to an individual's specific characteristics can go even further. Life sciences, sensory analytics, and dynamic questioning can be used to provide real-time insight into an individual's health status and longevity. This work is grounded in algorithms using state-of-the-art machine-learning techniques capable of examining an individual's physical features from a digital image to determine longevity, health status, and disease susceptibility (Olshansky 2017). In principle, this technology has the potential to improve estimates of longevity for everyone. Although we are not yet ready to apply such technology here, it is likely that personalized

Figure 7.3. Probability of Survival at Age 60 for Blue- and White-Collar Workers

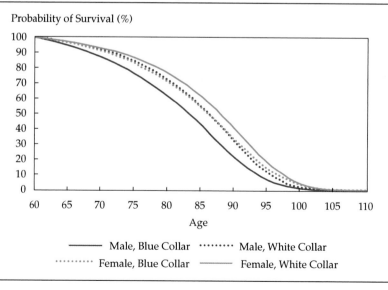

mortality tables will eventually become more easily available, albeit the prospect of evaluating our personal longevity more precisely could be emotionally troubling.

7.7. Complexities of a Household

Research on retirement timing concludes that many couples retire at about the same time, suggesting that retirement is a joint decision. Evidence is mixed, however, about whether the retirement-planning exercise is coordinated between the two spouses (see Carman and Hung 2017). The issue of spouses adds further complexity to the financial planning process; fortunately, the same concepts apply. At least five categories of aspects require scrutiny:

- savings, asset allocation, and asset location decisions
- strategically timing Social Security
- single or joint annuities
- consumption adjustments upon death of a spouse
- use of joint survival probabilities to evaluate consumption utility

7.7.1. Savings, Asset Allocation, and Asset Location Decisions.
When only one spouse has access to a work retirement plan with matching corporate contributions, the household should, in principle, attempt to prioritize maximizing contributions to this plan. When only one of the spouses is receiving an income, the earning spouse should contribute to a spousal IRA.[87] When the household's savings rate is significant, it is financially profitable to maximize the use of all tax-exempt and tax-deferred accounts. The gains that can be generated from the asset location decision discussed in Section 7.2 in the context of a single individual apply to the context of a household as well. The operationalization of the appropriate investment principles is simply made more complicated by the optimization of savings, asset allocation, and asset location across two spouses to coordinate the appropriate risk level and maximize the tax benefits. **Table 7.15** presents the yearly IRA contribution and deduction rules that applied to 2018 returns for single and joint filers.

Optimizing allocation, location, and contributions does usually not lead to an even split of all accounts between spouses. The main circumstance in which it is theoretically optimal to achieve an even split between spouses is when they are of similar age and income, have a corporate plan with similar features (or have no corporate plan), and intend to retire at approximately the same time.

---

[87]A spousal IRA requires a joint tax return.

Table 7.15.   IRA Contribution and Deduction Limits for 2018 Returns

			Before 50	After 50
Contribution	Traditional IRA		$5,500	$6,500
Size limit	Roth IRA		5,500	6,500
	Both		5,500	6,500
			MAGI	**Deduction**
Traditional IRA	Workplace plan	Single	<63,000	Full
Deduction limit[a]			In between	Partial
			>73,000	None
		Joint	<101,000	Full
			In between	Partial
			>121,000	None
	No workplace plan	Single	Any Amount	Full
		Joint	Any Amount	Full
		Joint & Spouse covered	<189,000	Full
			In between	Partial
			>199,000	None
			MAGI	**Contribution**
Roth IRA		Single	<120,000	Full
Contribution limit			In between	Partial
			>135,000	None
		Joint	<189,000	Full
			In between	Partial
			>199,000	None

[a]As discussed previously, although deductible IRA contributions are limited by the level of income, it is possible to make nondeductible IRA contributions up to the normally allowed limit. Although the contribution is not deductible from income, the money will accumulate tax free and only the return portion is taxed when withdrawn.

Source: Publication 590-A, Internal Revenue Service.

Next, understanding what can happen in cases of divorce is important. Splitting an IRA plan is not like splitting a home. There are rules to follow to avoid triggering penalties and taxes. First, it is often recommended to avoid taking any action until a divorce decree is issued. Second, in the case of a 401(k), a Qualified Domestic Relation Order (QDRO) is required to legally start a split process.[88] We touch only briefly on this subject, because addressing the specifics of these issues and the complexity of appropriately navigating the legal process is not within the scope of this book.

7.7.2. Strategically Timing Social Security.

In Section 4.6, we supported the argument for postponing the start of Social Security payments in retirement. We reached similar conclusions in our simulations in Chapter 6, although postponing Social Security to age 70 is not always the optimal solution. Implicit in this conclusion is the assumption that the beneficiary has a reasonably long life, between 85 and 90 years of age depending on how many years Social Security is postponed. We could conclude that spouses of similar income and in good health would both have an incentive to postpone receiving Social Security benefits as long as they have other sources of income or can reasonably draw down assets. Similarly, we could conclude that if a spouse has a shorter life expectancy, perhaps because of some illness, it may be preferable not to postpone Social Security. In Chapter 8, the optimal timing of Social Security benefits is determined according to the maximization of the investor's utility.

There is a strategy that should be considered during the financial planning process, however, because of a specific rule. When one spouse dies, the other spouse can claim the higher monthly benefit. In this case, it makes further sense to postpone the claim/benefit of the higher-income earner to the potential benefit of both spouses, even more so if one spouse is healthier and/ or has the lower income.[89]

7.7.3. Single or Joint Annuities.

Whether to invest in single or joint annuities is a serious decision to make, one involving a compromise between a greater payout in the short term versus lesser probabilities of maintaining a higher payout in the long run. Consider the case of John and Jane, who are each 65 years old. John and Jane have a choice between investing $250,000 each in a life annuity 10-year certain or $500,000 in

---

[88]Ed Slott, "Can Inherited IRAs Be Split in a Divorce?" (2018) www.investmentnews.com/article/20180716/FREE/180719949/can-inherited-iras-be-split-in-a-divorce.

[89]There is another possible strategy, but in 2023 it will no longer be available, because it is now available only for spouses who reached the age of 62 in 2015. Working spouses can opt to claim benefits based on their own work record but can also opt to claim 50% of their spouse's benefit, although only when this spouse has reached full retirement age. On a standalone basis, one of the spouses still has an interest in postponing Social Security. However, postponement also means that there are circumstances in which postponing the Social Security for the other spouse is no longer as favorable because the opportunity cost of postponing Social Security is greater. We ignore this option in our analyses because it is being phased out.

a joint annuity 10-year certain. The payout rates as of 20 July 2018 were, respectively, 6.56% (John) and 6.24% (Jane) for single annuities (6.40% on average) and 5.66% for a joint annuity (100% payment to the surviving spouse), which obviously pays less (0.74% less) because it will fully pay until both annuitants are deceased.

Because all these annuities have a 10-year certain feature, the single annuities would be preferable if both John and Jane were to die within the first 10 years. Beyond those 10 years, however, if one spouse were to die before the other, one of the single annuities would stop paying, whereas the joint annuity would still fully pay until the second spouse has died. The worst scenario in the case of single annuities would occur if one of the two spouses died right after the payout guarantee ends.

One way to understand the potential effect of choosing single over joint annuities is to assume that the excess cash flows of the single annuities versus the joint annuity are invested in the taxable portfolio (assuming, for example, a 60/40 allocation)[90] and to measure the number of months this excess cash flow would cover the loss of one of the two annuities, assuming the death of a spouse, such as John. Results indicate that if John were to die at age 75, when the 10-year certain guaranty has ended, the excess cash flow would cover the loss until approximately age 79. Unsurprisingly, we conclude that it would have been preferable to acquire the joint annuity. If John were to die at age 80 or 85, however, assuming Jane is still alive, the breakeven ages would be approximately 87.1 and 96.75 years of age. We can conclude that in the context of John and Jane, the single annuities are likely preferable if they both expect to live beyond 80 to 85 years of age.

Without a full context, concluding which decision is better is difficult. Nominal annuities offer a higher initial payout than can be expected from a financial portfolio on average and act as a safety buffer in a financial crisis. A joint annuity still offers an interesting payout amount, but it is lower. The risk related to this choice will manifest itself only later in life. Furthermore, the risk of this decision is likely not independent of several factors, including the following:

- the portion of total income generated from the single annuity,

- the amount of Social Security benefits John was receiving,

- whether Jane can claim a higher benefit upon John's death,

---

[90]We could also assume that the annuity with the lower payout drains the taxable portfolio further.

- whether John has a work pension plan and if it is partially inheritable by Jane, and

- the impact of John's death on Jane's total income needs.

7.7.4. Consumption Adjustments upon Death of a Spouse. Upon the death of a spouse, a household's total income is likely to decline unless a life insurance policy is in place—and it might decline even in that case, depending on the policy's size. Although income needs are also likely to decline, the effect on the surviving spouse can be significant if the reduction in expenses is far less than the decline in income. The aspects related to the evolution of income upon the death of one spouse have already been covered. Still, we must better understand the expected normal decline in expenses.

A widow's expenses are not reduced by half of the previous household expense. Unless the death results in a downsizing of the home and a significant lifestyle change (e.g., frequency of restaurant meals, travel, number and types of cars), retirement planners usually project a reduction of no more than 20% related to food, clothing, and some change in lifestyle (Rodgers 2018). McClements (1977) and the OECD (2009)[91] have developed equivalence scales that show the income needs of a single individual relative to the income needs of a couple, but the scales are not necessarily limited to retired individuals, and the ratios appear too low in the context of retirement, such as, respectively, 61% and 67% (Corden, Hirst, and Nice 2008; Anyaegbu 2010).

As indicated in Section 7.4, we advise one to assume a target retirement income need of 75% to 90% during the financial planning of the accumulation period but refine this estimate as the couple nears retirement, in the last 5 to 10 years after analyzing the household's budget and expected lifestyle.

7.7.5. Use of Joint Survival Probabilities to Evaluate Consumption Utility. If we consider retirement planning in the context of a household, we cannot avoid using joint/conditional survival probabilities. We have just established in Chapter 7 that retirement income and expenses are affected by the death of a spouse. Therefore, the process must consider what the appropriate retirement income and expenses are when both spouses are alive and what happens when either spouse dies early. Such a process requires us to consider, at each period in the future, the probability that both spouses are alive and the conditional probabilities that each spouse is alive, considering the death of a first spouse.

---

[91]OECD (2009) "What Are Equivalence Scales?" Available at http://www.oecd.org/els/soc/OECD-Note-EquivalenceScales.pdf.

7.8. Conclusion

Retirement planning is not solely about work income, savings rate, asset allocation and returns, longevity, and the uncertainty inherent in all these variables. Nuances abound, such as whether a household should plan jointly or separately, incorporating the complex effect of taxes and optimizing the tax location, timing Social Security, determining if annuities are appropriate, whether to consider a reverse mortgage program, which income replacement ratio is appropriate and how it could evolve as we age, and what mortality tables are most appropriate.

How do we integrate these choices without losing track of the final goal? The purpose of *Secure Retirement* is to improve the quality of retirement. How do we ensure, however, that the added financial science is not used simply to reduce the savings effort required, leaving retirees no better off in retirement? Our goal must remain not only to ensure an adequate income but also to reduce the likelihood it will not be achieved. For some individuals, a secure retirement may be possible with their current savings effort; but for others, we may still conclude that more effort is required. It will be very important to properly frame the objective and the process.

8. Designing a Financial Plan for John

8.1. A Comprehensive Model of Retirement Planning

Chapter 7 introduced many of the real-life details that make retirement planning a complex task if attempted without the support of a comprehensive software tool. There are simply too many dimensions that must be incorporated. **Figure 8.1** organizes the components integrated into the financial tool we have designed for *Secure Retirement*. They are grouped into four categories: input data, submodules, multiportfolio framework, and core engine.

Chapter 8 analyzes John's situation as of January 2019 using this framework in a more detailed context than before. John's basic context follows:

- John is 30 years old and has a college education. The education information is used to support the pattern of expected growth of his real income.

- John currently earns a work income of $120,000 a year. He also intends to work part time after retirement for at least five years. His in-retirement work income would be approximately 20% of his prior work income.[92]

- He lives in the suburb of a large city in a low-tax state. Although John has little savings, he owns a home currently valued at $400,000. John renegotiated a $300,000 mortgage with a 20-year amortization in June 2016. He expects to commit 75% of his mortgage payments to retirement savings once the mortgage is repaid.

- John's target retirement age is 65. Based on our understanding of individuals of similar income levels, John could live comfortably on 85% of the after-tax income he expects to earn before retirement (called PIO for preferred income objective). His income need post retirement is expected to evolve in accordance with a traditional consumption curve, such as a reduction of 0.5% per year for the first 15 years. Although not a desirable scenario, it is believed that John could live on 85% of the PIO (called the EIO for essential income objective) curve. This corresponds to 72.2% (85% × 85%) of the after-tax income he expects to earn before retirement. This information will be used to calibrate recommendations to the pattern of income during decumulation in the event of poor financial

---

[92]It is impossible to properly evaluate circumstances 20 to 40 years in the future, such as health, marriage, funding of children's education, and job prospects. Adjustments will have to be made as John ages. Some assumptions, however, are made simply for the purpose of isolating the effects of specific actions.

Figure 8.1. The Structure of the Retirement Puzzle

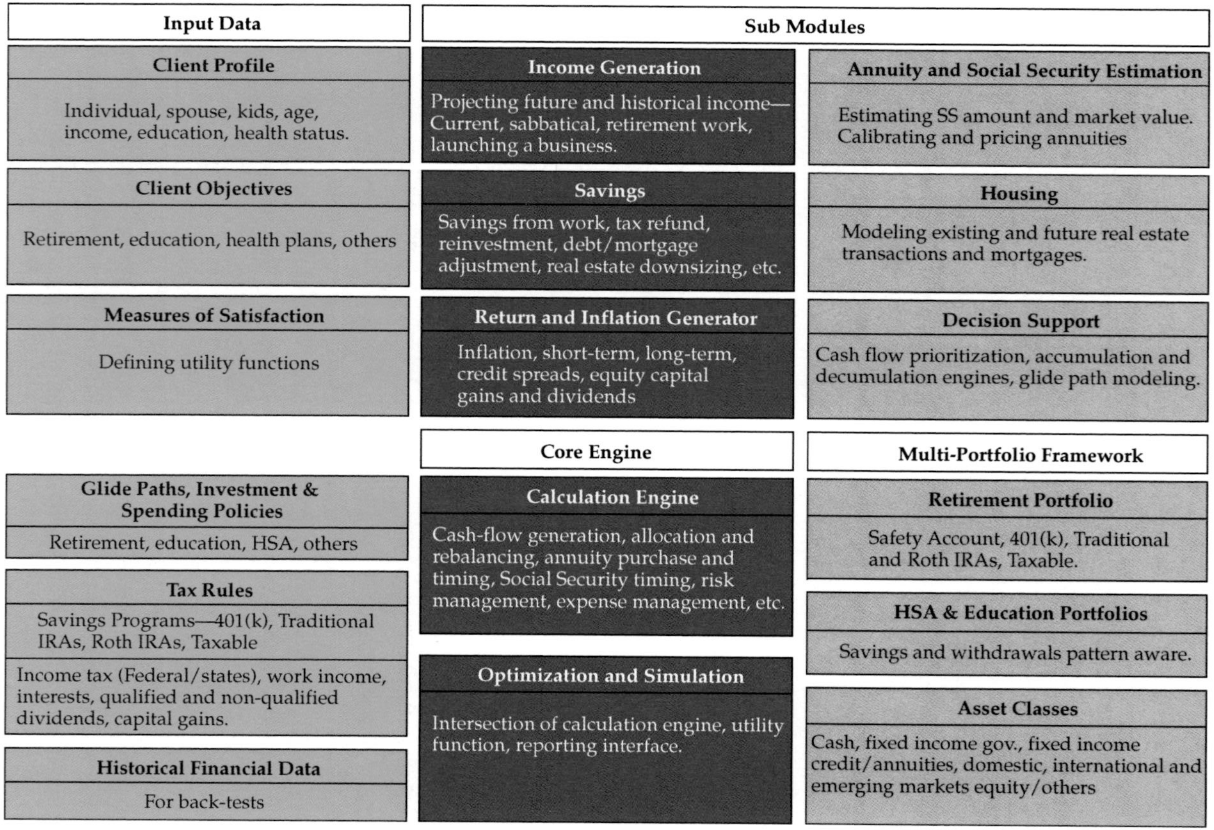

Input Data

Client Profile	Individual, spouse, kids, age, income, education, health status.
Client Objectives	Retirement, education, health plans, others
Measures of Satisfaction	Defining utility functions
Glide Paths, Investment & Spending Policies	Retirement, education, HSA, others
Tax Rules	Savings Programs—401(k), Traditional IRAs, Roth IRAs, Taxable. Income tax (Federal/states), work income, interests, qualified and non-qualified dividends, capital gains.
Historical Financial Data	For back-tests

Income Generation

Box	Description
Income Generation	Projecting future and historical income—Current, sabbatical, retirement work, launching a business.
Savings	Savings from work, tax refund, reinvestment, debt/mortgage adjustment, real estate downsizing, etc.
Return and Inflation Generator	Inflation, short-term, long-term, credit spreads, equity capital gains and dividends

Core Engine

Calculation Engine	Cash-flow generation, allocation and rebalancing, annuity purchase and timing, Social Security timing, risk management, expense management, etc.
Optimization and Simulation	Intersection of calculation engine, utility function, reporting interface.

Sub Modules

Annuity and Social Security Estimation	Estimating SS amount and market value. Calibrating and pricing annuities
Housing	Modeling existing and future real estate transactions and mortgages.
Decision Support	Cash flow prioritization, accumulation and decumulation engines, glide path modeling.

Multi-Portfolio Framework

Retirement Portfolio	Safety Account, 401(k), Traditional and Roth IRAs, Taxable.
HSA & Education Portfolios	Savings and withdrawals pattern aware.
Asset Classes	Cash, fixed income gov, fixed income credit/annuities, domestic, international and emerging markets equity/others

performance and to evaluate the utility resulting from generating income below and above the minimum target.

- John will have a glide path starting with a 90% equity allocation in the initial years, transitioning toward 60% over a period starting 20 years and ending 6 years before retirement, then finally shrinking to 40% as of retirement. Annuities are not considered initially. The overall management fees paid by John are 0.3%, although the effect of higher fees is evaluated.

- His yearly personal savings is equal to 9.0% of before-tax income.

Figure 8.2 summarizes the basic assumptions for real after-tax work income, savings, and retirement income.

Other events could have been considered, such as funding the education of children, buying a second home, downsizing the primary home in retirement and moving to a different state, taking a sabbatical, or specifying a more complex savings pattern. Although such aspects should normally be considered if pertinent, doing so would add further complexity to the example; our goal, in contrast, is simply to illustrate how we can more efficiently improve the quality of John's life under a given set of lifestyle assumptions and circumstances using the processes described in *Secure Retirement*. These

Figure 8.2. Evolution of John's Work Income, Savings, and Retirement Income

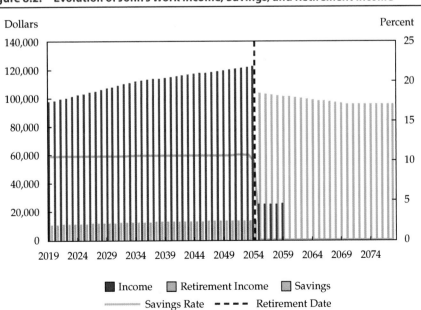

other considerations could be added without affecting the general conclusions reached in this chapter.

The simulations required a scenario generator to provide a comprehensive and coherent set of monthly financial and inflation scenarios. More specifically, inflation, short-term real rate, 10-year real rate, credit spread, equity dividend, and equity capital gains are allowed to vary. The generator allowed for regime switching between a calm and a volatile financial environment.

8.2. The Canadian Approach to Retirement

Another objective of Chapter 8 is to compare how the same individual would fare under the plan policies offered in the United States and Canada for the management of tax-deferred and tax-exempt accounts. Fortunately, Canadian policies can be summarized in two paragraphs.

Tax-deferred plans (akin to 401(k) and traditional IRAs): Canadians are allowed tax-deferred contribution up to 18% of their income, subject to a yearly limit of $26,230 in 2018. This limit, however, covers both corporate retirement programs—DC as well as DB plans—and traditional IRA-like accounts (called RRSPs). Any allowed contribution not used in a corporate plan can be used for a personal plan. This creates a level playing field for retirees not benefiting from a corporate DC or DB plan, although these individuals will not have access to corporate matching of personal savings contributions. Furthermore, there is no need for a catch-up provision in Canada (such as increasing allowed contributions at age 50 or above), because unused contribution allowances can be carried forward fully until age 71. Although the contribution limits are less than those allowed in the United States for 401(k) plans, they are more than enough for individuals earning as much as $250,000 a year.

Tax-exempt plans (akin to Roth IRAs): Canadians are currently allowed a tax-exempt contribution of $6,000 per year in a tax-free savings account (TFSA). This contribution is not subject to any salary limit and can continue for as long as the investor is alive. Unused amounts are carried forward indefinitely. Hence, Canadians not currently taking full advantage of allowed tax-deferred contributions would benefit from using as much of the cumulative unused contributions made before age 71 (or before retirement) and then maximizing the use of their tax-exempt cumulative unused contributions. For example, Canadians having a significant amount of unused TFSA contributions who are downsizing their home before retirement could reinvest the capital extracted from the transaction in a TFSA and benefit from a significant amount of tax-free income.

8.3.   Analyzing the Situation of John: Basic Scenarios

The first analyses are based on a deterministic return environment. This allows us to calibrate the overall financial strategy before evaluating the efficiency of different investment processes. We also want to avoid running Monte Carlo simulations using a set of assumptions for accumulation and decumulation that will very likely fail even if financial returns were stable and met expectations. **Table 8.1** compares two possible situations:

- access to a DC plan matching 100% of the first 3% of savings and 50% of the next 3%, for a maximum employer contribution of 4.5% of work income

- no DC plan

For each situation, we assume the tax-deferred and tax-exempt plans are either those currently in place in the United States or those in place in Canada. The benefits received from Social Security have also been incorporated. Because the objective is solely to compare the efficiency of policies in both countries, however, we use the tax rates on work income, investment income, and Social Security benefits that apply in the United States.

We use three measures of utility or satisfaction. They are consistent with the material covered in Chapter 6. The first measure is intuitive. The other two measures are more comprehensive and may be more useful in the context of simulations, optimizations, and model calibrations.

- Percentage of PIO target: A weighted average measure of the percentage of PIO being met over John's lifetime. All years prior to a 25% survival probability have a weighting of 100%, whereas years beyond a 25% probability have a weighting determined according to a mortality table for healthy annuitants.[93] We seek a percentage of PIO target as close as possible to 100%.[94]

- Utility score 1, consumption only: As described in Section 6.3, using the same survival probability structure as before but using a function that penalizes a realized income below the EIO twice as much as it rewards a score above the EIO.

- Utility score 2, consumption and wealth: As before, but where all the utility of consumption beyond the 25% survival probability level is replaced by a measure of the utility of total wealth available at this age, including housing and mortgage (if a reverse mortgage strategy is implemented).

---

[93]The age corresponding to a 25% survival probability level implies that 75% of males in the same age cohort as John would have died.
[94]The simulations in Chapter 8 account for the fact that the age corresponding to a 25% probability of survival changes as John ages. A different probability level could be specified.

Table 8.1. Various Measures of Satisfaction

Measures of Utility	US Retirement Policies		Canadian Retirement Policies	
	DC Plan	No DC Plan	DC Plan	No DC Plan
Failure age (years)	87.8	82.6	89.2	85.6
Percentage of PIO target	88.1%	71.8%	92.4%	81.7%
Utility score 1	−2.8	−12.1	−0.37	−6.5
Utility score 2	4.6	−4.7	7.0	0.8

The second measure of utility is more relevant when consumption is the primary concern, whereas the third is more appropriate when there is a considerable amount of excess wealth or if a legacy objective is incorporated. We also report in some cases the failure age—that is, the age at which the desired retirement income is not fully met for the first time. This measure in not always a good indicator, because a decumulation engine to be implemented later in this chapter may recommend a small but early reduction of consumption to increase the long-term sustainability of retirement income, rendering the idea of failure fuzzy or incompletely defined.

Access to a DC plan has a significant effect on retirement income sustainability. It adds approximately five years of full retirement income sustainability and raises the percentage of PIO target achieved by approximately 16%. Canadian retirement policies would add another 4%. Much of the differential in this case can be attributed to what happens post retirement. The difference is even greater when a DC plan is unavailable (because of the low traditional IRA contribution limit in the United States). It also becomes more significant at a higher level of work income, such as $200,000.[95]

Investment and savings decisions can have a significant effect on expected retirement income. For example, if we concentrate on the first scenario (DC plan and US policies), not allocating the 75% of the mortgage payments to savings once the mortgage is paid would lower the failure age and percentage of PIO target to 83.6 years and 74.7%, respectively. Similarly, paying 1% in management fees instead of 30 bps would lower these two measures to 82.9 years and 72.7%, respectively. Finally, although not under the control of US retirees, if the Social Security Trust

---

[95]Because contributions to a tax-deferred plan are made on a before-tax basis, whereas contributions to a taxable plan are made on an after-tax basis, the analysis assumes that any tax refund associated with an IRA plan, in the no-DC-plan scenario, is reinvested to allow for a fair after-tax savings comparison.

Fund is fully depleted in 2034, as currently expected, and no adjustments are made by Congress, the two measures would decline to 86.5 years and 82.9%.

Two actions can easily improve John's situation. First, postponing his first Social Security claim to age 68 (the age that maximizes the consumption utility measure in the current context) would raise the percentage of PIO target slightly to 88.4%.[96] Although this postponement does not change the failure age, John's Social Security payments will be greater for all remaining years. This result assumes, however, that Social Security benefits will not be reduced in 2034.

Second, if we also change the glide path from 90–40 to a riskier 90–60 but neutralize the added risk by allocating 30% to a series of life annuities 10-year certain purchased in the last four years before retirement, the percentage of PIO target increases by more than 4% to 92.7% and the failure age by nearly one year to 88.7.[97,98] The annuities significantly improve the percentage of PIO target because they provide a higher income for all remaining years even if the full target is not being met.

Despite these adjustments, the current financial plan does not meet the standard of achieving success at the 25% probability of mortality level. For example, at age 65, John has a 25% probability of living past age 91.7. To sustain the expected full income to age 91.7 or more, the model derives the trade-offs John faces:

- raising the average savings rate from 9.0% to 10.0%,

- postponing retirement by approximately 12 months (Assuming John retires as of age 66 instead of 65, the age that corresponds to a 25% probability level of dying increases slightly from 91.7 to 91.8.), and

- lowering the initial level of consumption by 5%, from 85% of after-tax income to 80%.

---

[96]Although the optimal age for Social Security is 68 in this case, it could be different under other circumstances, such as if John owned annuities. The optimal age is not only a function of expected mortality assumptions but also very much dependent on other circumstances.

[97]Five annuities are purchased. The first annuity is purchased four years before retirement and the last one, as of retirement. The amount of annuity purchased each year is calculated to allow the annuity portfolio to represent 6% of all financial assets (including the annuity itself) four years before retirement and subsequently target 12%, 18%, 24%, and finally 30% as of retirement.

[98]The average glide path differs from the conservative glide path by maintaining an equity allocation of 60% once it is reached.

All these scenarios would lead to a percentage of PIO target of 100%. This is not a decision that can be optimized or easily isolated from a utility function. In this case, a software tool can provide John with options, but it is up to him to choose. It is interesting that adding one year to the retirement date has approximately the same effect as increasing the savings rate by 1% for many years. Without a comprehensive model, it would be impossible for most advisers and investors to accurately identify these trade-offs.

Assume John decided to postpone his retirement to age 66. Postponing retirement implies one more year of return and savings before retirement and one year less of retirement income withdrawal. A single year of retirement income equals several years of savings. **Figure 8.3** illustrates the expected evolution of John's after-tax wealth in real dollars of 2019.

Most of John's assets are held in the DC plan. The downward jagged blue line illustrates the impact of purchasing annuities from the DC plan,[99] in this case over a period of five years. The black line represents the market value of these annuities. Their total value declines as the 10-year guaranty ends and as John ages. John does not contribute to a traditional IRA (the tax deduction

Figure 8.3. Sources and Evolution of John's Wealth after Tax and in Real Dollars

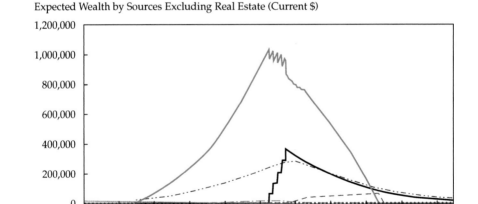

Expected Wealth by Sources Excluding Real Estate (Current $)

---

[99]The annuities could be purchased within the DC plan if possible or externally using assets available in the DC plan.

would not be allowed) or to a Roth IRA for many years (his income level eventually exceeds the threshold). When John retires but earns income working part time, however, he can accumulate a small amount of wealth in a Roth IRA. Finally, Social Security accounts for a reasonable proportion of John's wealth. It eventually becomes a more important source of wealth than the portfolio of nominal annuities because of the COLA.

8.4. Analyzing John's Situation: Monte Carlo Analyses

Retirement planning is not a simple task. Returns are neither stable nor known in advance. This uncertainty and the numerous changes that occur in a lifetime (e.g., children, marriage, health situations, careers, buying a second home) require that the process of evaluating John's situation be repeated and recalibrated regularly, perhaps once a year as well as whenever a significant change in circumstances occurs.[100]

Section 8.3 considers two sets of strategies. The first set evaluates aspects that are relevant mostly to the accumulation period (i.e., the choice among several glide paths and the implementation of an accumulation engine to limit calendar year drawdowns) and to both the accumulation and the decumulation period (i.e., the level of fees). We also evaluate the benefits of introducing annuities, even if their effect is felt only during the decumulation period, in order to have a better logical transition to the second set of strategies.

As indicated previously, we also assume John has already decided to plan for a retirement age of 66 and to trigger his Social Security benefits at the same time. As John ages, and as the reality of financial market returns is observed and life events unfold, he may have to or may be better able to evaluate several elements of his financial plan, such as his target retirement age or even his income objective. For now, however, these are the parameters that will be used. We could also evaluate the benefits from optimizing the asset location, but unfortunately, John is not expected to generate enough savings to allocate significantly to a taxable account. This option would have no effect on the efficiency of the investment process.

Figure 8.4, Panel A presents the distribution of the percentage of PIO target for 1,000 scenarios in ascending order. Four strategies are presented:

- 90–40 glide path with average fees of 100 bps

- 90–40 glide path with average fees of 30 bps

---

[100]This exercise is not time consuming when the proper software tool is available. In most uneventful years when circumstances have not changed significantly, reviewing an individual's situation can take less than half an hour.

- 60–40 glide path with average fees of 30 bps

- 90–40 glide path with the accumulation engine (AE) described in Chapter 3.

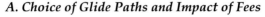

Figure 8.4. Distribution of Percentage of PIO Target

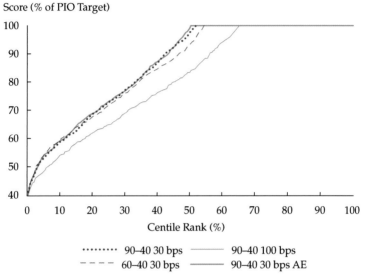

A. *Choice of Glide Paths and Impact of Fees*

Score (% of PIO Target)

Centile Rank (%)

········· 90–40 30 bps   ──── 90–40 100 bps
─ ─ ─ ─ 60–40 30 bps   ───── 90–40 30 bps AE

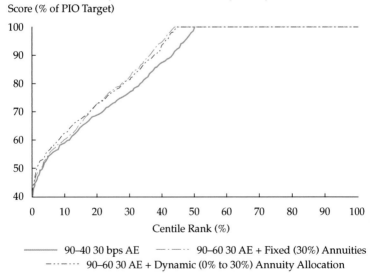

B. *Choice of Glide Paths and Impact of Annuities*

Score (% of PIO Target)

Centile Rank (%)

───── 90–40 30 bps AE   ─·─·· 90–60 30 AE + Fixed (30%) Annuities
─··─··· 90–60 30 AE + Dynamic (0% to 30%) Annuity Allocation

All other strategies incorporate the accumulation engine. Panel B presents three strategies:

- previous 90–40 glide path with the accumulation engine (as a reference)

- 90–60 glide path with average fees of 30 bps but in which 30% of the portfolio is allocated to annuities purchased annually over a five-year period prior to retirement

- 90–60 glide path with average fees of 30 bps but in which the allocation to annuities is determined using an algorithm that accounts for the level of John's surplus wealth as he nears retirement with an allocation range of 0% to 30%

All glide paths transition from the higher to the lower allocation in the last 20 years before retirement. **Table 8.2**, Panel A also presents a number of

Table 8.2. Measures of Satisfaction

Average Measures for All Scenarios	Percentage of PIO All/Bottom Half	Consumption and Wealth Utility	Average Wealth at 25% Probability for Top Half	Worst Calendar Return
A. At 30 years old				
90–40 100 bps	81.2%/64.9%	2.36	$736,061	−24.3%
90–40 30 bps	86.3%/72.6%	7.27	1,623,918	−24.2
60–40 30 bps	85.7%/71.7%	5.66	1,077,638	−18.0
90–40 30 bps AE	86.5%/73.0%	7.19	1,548,816	−18.2
90–60 AE + 30% Annuities	88.6%/77.1%	9.97	2,184,216	−18.0
90–60 AE + Dynamic annuity allocation	88.6%/77.1%	10.90	2,470,300	−18.0
B. At 60 years old				
90–40 30 bps	92.9%/85.7%	9.58	$877,773	−6.4%
90–60 AE + Dynamic annuity allocation	93.3%/86.6%	10.51	1,177,793	−6.0
Above + Optimized Social Security	93.9%/87.9%	11.35	1,212,723	−6.0
Above + Reverse mortgage (with refund)	93.9%/87.8%	11.05	1,148,826	−6.3
Or reverse mortgage (with no refund)	95.0%/90.0%	11.65	1,125,889	−5.9
Above + Decumulation engine	94.9%/90.1%	12.54	1,314,139	−6.3

relevant characteristics for all strategies evaluated, such as the average PIO target achieved for all scenarios and for the bottom half of the scenarios; the measure of consumption and final wealth utility; the average remaining financial wealth in real dollars (net of mortgage debt) for the top 50% of scenarios as of the age corresponding to a 25% survival probability;[101] and the average worst yearly calendar portfolio performance over the entire accumulation period.

90–40 100 bps vs. 90–40 30 bps: The impact of higher fees considerably reduces John's likelihood of achieving his retirement income goal. Only 34.8% of scenarios meet the target at 100 bps of fees versus 48.2% at 30 bps of fees. Furthermore, the level of remaining real wealth for the top 50% of scenarios as of approximately age 91.8 is considerably lower at $736,061 versus $1,623,918.

If we concentrate solely on the lower-fee case, the worst scenario scores only 36%, and 25% of scenarios score below 72.5%. This information indicates the considerable uncertainty when planning for an objective that is several decades away. The financial planning process must seek to reduce the range of possible results as John ages and achieve greater certainty of meeting his retirement consumption needs for the rest of his life. One goal in this chapter is to determine how these results can be improved even if the individual is still far from retirement and much uncertainty remains.

90–40 30 bps vs. 60–40 30 bps: As noted in Chapter 3, the results of this comparison illustrate that adopting a very conservative asset allocation in accumulation has few long-term benefits, unless limiting short-term drawdowns is the main objective. The low-risk approach does not improve the percentage of PIO target for the bottom half of scenarios and leads to a lower level of average wealth at age 91.8.

90–40 30 bps vs. 90–40 30 bps AE: The accumulation strategy is highly efficient. It was calibrated to avoid any adjustment to the equity portfolio amounting to more than 50% of the recommended allocation according to the glide path. For example, if the recommended equity allocation at a specific point in time is 90% or 60%, the actual allocation could never be less than 45% and 30%, respectively. It led to performance on par with the non-AE strategy while limiting the average of the worst calendar-year returns to those obtained with a 60–40 glide path.

We also tested for a dynamic accumulation strategy with no constraint on the equity allocation. These results are not shown but were only slightly better than the constrained approach. It is also possible to limit an equity

---

[101]The value of the primary house is not included, but its expected value is identical in all simulations.

adjustment to another level, such as 60% instead of 50%, resulting in a small loss of efficiency. In this case, if the recommended equity allocation is 90%, the actual allocation could never be less than 54%. Finally, we considered modifying the transition point at which the glide path lowers the allocation below 90% according to the ratio of human capital wealth to portfolio wealth in each scenario. The dynamic accumulation strategy makes such a process unnecessary, however.

90–40 30 bps AE vs. 90–60 bps AE with 30% Annuities: Using a riskier glide path in combination with a fixed-annuity component significantly improves all satisfaction and risk measures as well as legacy wealth.

90–40 30 bps AE vs. 90–60 bps AE with Dynamic (0% to 30%) Annuity Allocation: The dynamic annuity strategy is designed to determine the level of annuity required (ranging from 0% to 30%) as a function of the level of excess wealth.[102] The strategy is particularly efficient at increasing residual wealth. It has little effect at lower levels of wealth when approaching retirement because the algorithm would advise a similar allocation to annuities as the fixed option in these cases. This is the approach that will be favored from now on.

Despite the improvements in worst calendar-year returns achieved by the accumulation strategy (and to residual wealth achieved by a riskier glide path combined with an annuity strategy), we must recognize that it is unlikely a significant asset deficiency close to retirement can be resolved fully by an after-retirement strategy if the level of wealth achieved as John nears retirement is well below what is expected. Approximately 44% of all scenarios fail to meet the PIO target, many by a wide margin. As specified before, John may have to reevaluate his goals as he ages. One hopes that by repeating a financial planning exercise yearly, John will be able to make some adjustments. This adjustment to changing circumstances is a key element of retirement planning, and its importance cannot be emphasized enough.

Therefore, the second set of strategies looks more precisely at the decumulation phase and requires that we transition John to a later time in his life. Postponing Social Security benefits, implementing an annuity strategy, applying a decumulation engine, or implementing a reverse mortgage income stabilization strategy cannot perform miracles. These tools will not resolve the financial issues caused by insufficient savings or poor asset returns, resulting in insufficient wealth after the accumulation phase is nearly completed. When John reevaluates his situation over time, he may find that he must plan for a later retirement (beyond 66) and/or accept a lower retirement income and/or downsize his home, among other options—or he may be pleasantly surprised

---

[102]For example, assuming financial returns have been extremely favorable and John did not increase his PIO target, John may no longer need to purchase the same amount of annuity.

and find he could retire earlier because real asset returns were higher than expected. To reduce the uncertainty about retirement that John faces when he is 30 years old, it is obvious that some adjustments will have to be made in coming decades. This retirement planning is a living, dynamic process. Hence, the benefits of implementing specific decumulation strategies before and during retirement will be more evident if we have a better understanding of John's situation as he nears retirement.

Thus we now assume that John is 60 years old. For simplicity, we also assume that John accumulated a level of wealth in line with his earlier expectations. He therefore maintains the same retirement date and retirement income targets. Because John is 60, the glide path now recommends an equity allocation of 60% (six years before retirement). Assuming a 90–40 glide path, the accumulated wealth is just enough to reach a percentage of PIO target of 99.6%. This means that John faces only the uncertainty of the next six years of accumulation and of the entire decumulation period. It also implies we should expect a narrower range of financial outcomes than when John was 30. This allows for a more precise evaluation of the benefits of each of the decumulation strategies that John could adopt. The 90–40 glide path will still be used as a reference for all other strategies, listed below:

- 90–60 AE with dynamic (0% to 30%) annuity allocation (although the recommended annuity allocation likely will be approximately 30% in most scenarios, because John has reached a percentage of PIO target slightly below 100% at age 60. It would require large positive asset returns over a very short period for the annuity recommendation to be significantly less than 30%.[103])

- + optimizing the Social Security timing

- + implementing a reverse mortgage strategy with refund[104]

- + implementing a reverse mortgage strategy with no refund

- + implementing a decumulation engine

---

[103]Although allocating 30% to annuities may seem like too much to some investors, we must remember that the 10-year certain annuity contracts could be replaced by a combination of zero-coupon bonds covering the first 10 years after retirement and by a lesser amount in 10-year deferred annuities at a cost even lower than assumed in this example. In this situation, approximately 16% of that 30% would be allocated to the bond portfolios, while the remaining 14% would be allocated to the deferred annuities. The zero coupons could also be replaced by a dynamically managed portfolio of two bond funds (of shorter and longer durations).

[104]The reverse mortgage strategy with refund implies that if John borrows against the property, the mortgage would be repaid if market returns on the financial assets are favorable.

The simulation results are presented in **Figure 8.5** as well as in Table 8.2, Panel B.

90–40 with 30 bps Fees at 30 Years Old vs. 90–40 with 30 bps Fees at 60 Years Old: The decline in uncertainty is significant, assuming we have approximately the same expected percentage of PIO target at both ages (in this case, both are close to 100%). The percentage of scenarios expected to fully meet the target rises from 48.2% to 56.5%. The average percentage of PIO target observed for the bottom 50% of scenarios rises from 72.6% to 85.7%. The average expected worst calendar-year drawdown declines from −24.2% to only −6.4%, not only because the portfolio is now more conservative but also because we have fewer years ahead before retirement for an unfavorable environment to occur.

90–60 AE with Dynamic (0% to 30%) Annuity Allocation vs. 90–40: The accumulation engine is less likely to have a significant effect because the equity allocation is lower at this age but also because the risk management process is implemented only until retirement. Also, the 90–60 and 90–40 glide paths have the same equity allocation as of age 60. Six years before retirement, the 90–60 glide path has a 60% allocation that will be maintained; the 90–40 glide path also has a 60% allocation, but it will gradually be reduced toward 40% in the next six years. Therefore, we have identical starting points for the comparison.

The annuity component option improves not only the percentage of PIO target but also the level of remaining wealth at the age corresponding to a 25% probability level of mortality. These improvements occur for two reasons. First, the annuity portfolio's IRR is relatively high if John lives to age 92 or older. Second, although the remaining security portfolio is smaller after retirement, it remains invested with a greater equity allocation for several decades.

The worst calendar-year return is computed on the liquid assets only (excluding the effect of potential annuities that may have been purchased). Despite the greater average exposure to equity, the 90–60 glide path with AE does not present a greater downside risk than the 90–40.

Optimizing for Social Security: As of age 60, the age of claiming Social Security benefits that maximizes the consumption utility measure is 69. It was expected to be 68 when John was 30 years old. This estimate should be reevaluated yearly as John approaches and engages in retirement. The strategy improves the percentage of PIO target as well as the consumption and wealth utility measure not because it leads to significantly greater legacy wealth but because it improves the worst-case scenarios. The combination of annuities and Social Security optimization means that if John lives to be very old (e.g.,

Figure 8.5.   Distribution of Percentage of PIO Target

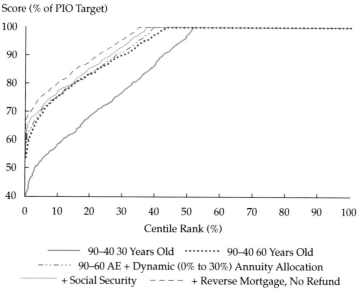

A. Choice of Glide Paths, Impact of Annuities and Social Security Optimization

Score (% of PIO Target)

Centile Rank (%)

———— 90–40 30 Years Old   ·········· 90–40 60 Years Old
–·–·–· 90–60 AE + Dynamic (0% to 30%) Annuity Allocation
———— + Social Security   – – – – + Reverse Mortgage, No Refund

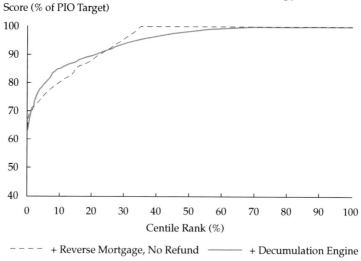

B. Integrating a Decumulation Strategy

Score (% of PIO Target)

Centile Rank (%)

– – – – + Reverse Mortgage, No Refund   ———— + Decumulation Engine

age 95 or older) and market returns are unfavorable, he could at least count on receiving nearly 45% of his PIO target and 55% of his EIO target instead of 28% and 33%, respectively. He still has access to his home equity as a last resort.

Implementing a Reverse Mortgage Strategy with Refund: The results of this strategy are not presented in Figure 8.5, Panel A but are reported in Table 8.2, Panel B. The strategy consists of borrowing against the primary property whenever calendar-year returns are below a specific threshold (such as −5%) and paying off the mortgage fully or partially whenever the calendar-year returns are above another threshold (such as +10%). The amount of borrowing allowed is limited to 30% of the estimated borrowing capacity at any time. Any residual debt amount is subtracted from legacy wealth.

The strategy is designed to stabilize the size of the liquid investment portfolio but does not contribute to improving any measure of satisfaction or risk.

Implementing a Reverse Mortgage Strategy with No Refund: This strategy is identical to the one just described; however, whenever John borrows against his property, the amount is never paid back. Instead, the debt is removed from the legacy wealth measure.

As Figure 8.5, Panel A and Table 8.2, Panel B illustrate, the mortgage strategy with no refund is effective and preferable to the strategy with a refund. It significantly improves the percentage of PIO target from the bottom-half scenarios without penalizing the legacy wealth. There is no doubt that this strategy could be refined further.

Implementing a Decumulation Engine: Figure 8.5, Panel B presents the outcome of implementing a decumulation engine. First, it is important to understand the nuance between the effect of the probability level used to estimate the different utility measures and this probability level's effect on the decumulation engine's implementation. When John reaches age 66, we estimate the mortality age at a 25% probability level to be 91.7 years. Once he reaches ages 67, 68, and later, we reevaluate the age that corresponds to a 25% probability; this number, of course, increases over time. Hence this estimate changes in our model only when John ages—although to calibrate the utility functions, we never use an estimate based on an age below the retirement age.

The probability level used to implement the decumulation engine, however, has a more dynamic impact on the process. As we project different scenarios for John at any given age, we continuously reevaluate, for each projected month and for each projected scenario of the Monte Carlo simulation, the sustainable level of income withdrawal. For example, when John retires at age 66, we evaluate how much he can withdraw at 66 years and 1 month, at 66 years and 2 months, and so on. Three factors will affect these estimates:

(1) how much wealth is available, (2) the estimated portfolio volatility at the end of each month, and (3) John's expected longevity at the end of each month as he ages in each scenario of the simulation. We already know that when John is 66 years old, the answer at a 25% probability level is 91.8 years. If John lives to age 85, however, the estimates for that month and that scenario will be based on an expected (25th percentile) longevity of nearly 95 years. Hence, as we age John within a specific scenario, the challenge of meeting the expected income requirement within the model increases. Thus the decumulation engine adapts to changing circumstances. It is designed to add, within the decumulation process, a hint of prudence that adapts to John's aging.

The results presented in Table 8.2 indicate that the percentage of PIO target did not improve. Figure 8.5, Panel B shows, however, that the decumulation engine worked exactly as expected. The distribution of the percentage of PIO target is compared with the previous strategy that incorporated the reverse mortgage approach with no refund. It improved the percentage of PIO target of the lowest quartile of scenarios, but it decreased this measure for the second quartile of scenarios. The decumulation engine adds prudence that is reflected in the amount of legacy wealth remaining, which is more than four times greater for the scenarios in the 25th to 37.5th percentiles. We end this process with 90.7% of scenarios having a percentage of PIO target above 85%.

8.5. Conclusion

Because we have looked at several strategy adjustments in this chapter, it is useful to consider the overall improvements achieved. We started this effort when John was 30 years old. Assuming a 90–40 glide path and 100 bps of fees, we estimated a 51.6% probability that the percentage of PIO target would remain below 85% (our EIO minimum target). Assuming fees of 30 bps, this probability falls to 38.2%. Even though retirement is far away still, if we use a 90–60 glide path but allow for the possibility of introducing a set of annuities as we approach retirement (using an algorithm that considers excess wealth in each scenario), the probability is further reduced to 32.9%.

As John ages, his financial position is reevaluated and his life goals may, more than likely, need to be adjusted. The only thing we know for sure is that when John turns 60, our assessment faces less uncertainty because we now have confirmation of what has happened over the last 30 years. Assuming the necessary adjustments are made (if required) to achieve a 100% PIO target using a deterministic return scenario, we can evaluate further improvements to the decumulation process. Evaluating John as of age 60, we could reduce the probability of not meeting 85% of the PIO target to less than 10%.

This discussion also ignores the fact that we achieved these results while reducing the average of worst calendar-year drawdowns by approximately 30%. The overall process helps manage many of investors' concerns. Although a high level of equity exposure is tolerated early in the accumulation process, the dynamic accumulation strategy reduces the size of the drawdowns. As they approach retirement, investors who do not have substantial excess wealth will benefit from incorporating an annuity component that not only reduces income risk but also allows for substantial wealth growth compared with a conservative glide path with no annuity. An annuity also effectively mitigates the impact of a significant market correction and provides greater comfort in rebalancing in the event of a crisis, which is emotionally difficult for most investors. The effective management of retirement income through a decumulation engine and possibly a reverse mortgage strategy helps navigate the uncertainty related to longevity. Representing these many moving parts to investors in a clear, well-designed visual interface would significantly help build confidence in the financial planning process.

9. Looking to the Future

An effective retirement strategy is not solely about implementing investment and risk management processes. It starts with the ability to provide a clear financial picture to investors. Is the investor's retirement ambition realistic? What trade-offs are available that increase the likelihood of reaching the investor's goals? This kind of information and feedback constitute the first step in educating investors. Although the number of aspects to be integrated in the process is substantial and creates complexity, every piece is essential to build a user interface that simplifies the data input and presents the results to investors in an intuitive way. It is especially important to express the many dimensions that must be considered and the likelihood of achieving each goal. Effective financial planning is not only about the mathematics, which most investors will never fully understand, but also about the effectiveness of the communication tools.

The interface built for researching Chapter 8 of *Secure Retirement* goes beyond what we have presented here. It can consider complex patterns of work income, savings, and retirement income. The interface also allows us to define several objectives (retirement, education of children, home purchases and home trading, sabbaticals, and more) and measures the utility derived from achieving these objectives in different ways. It allows for both DB and DC plans. It integrates and prioritizes asset allocation both across a larger selection of asset classes than equity and fixed income and across different types of accounts (e.g., IRA, education, health savings, and taxable). This interface can incorporate existing annuities and new annuities, whether immediate or deferred, as well as Social Security. It can estimate the trade-offs available to investors for improving their chances of achieving their desired goals. It can optimize Social Security timing and annuity allocation and manage financial risks in accumulation and decumulation. Yet, more remains to be done.

First, the algorithms designed to achieve these functionalities are a significant improvement over the tools available to most investors, but they can be further improved. The current interface was not designed to provide quick feedback, especially on measures of risk. Traditional mathematical models cannot provide, in a reasonable amount of computing time, comprehensive, single-step optimized solutions that are continuously evaluated when so many dimensions must be considered over so long a timeframe, given the uncertainty surrounding the many relevant variables. These include work income, financial market returns, health and longevity, and special situations.

As we were completing *Secure Retirement*, we approached a world-class firm specializing in machine learning to determine whether it is currently possible to tackle this issue and provide more effective optimized solutions with a fast response time, especially when dealing with risk estimates and probabilities of achieving specific goals. The recent work of Gordon Irlam, based on deep reinforcement learning, shows that achieving optimized solutions in a reasonable amount of computing time is feasible. It can and it will be done.

Furthermore, upcoming applications will be able to tackle the issue of health and longevity more effectively. Currently it is possible to use data related to fitness, education, and life habits to identify and adjust mortality tables appropriate to a specific individual or a household. The combination of decades of longevity research with the recent evolution in life sciences and machine learning, however, allows us to design predictive algorithms that can more effectively calibrate assumptions about a specific individual's longevity. This technology already exists. Such expertise should be integrated into financial planning platforms. It would help determine, for each individual or household, whether annuities are appropriate, what level of portfolio risk is acceptable, and what level of payout is statistically sustainable.

One of the main conclusions we should draw from *Secure Retirement* is that active management should not be the primary concern of investors planning for retirement—in fact, it should be their last concern. The first consideration is to design a portfolio around a set of low-cost investment assets. The second is that skillful financial planning can significantly increase investors' certainty-equivalent financial gains through proper asset allocation and risk management. The net return achieved by investors can be significantly enhanced without active management, and drawdowns significantly reduced, at no explicit cost. Diversification is a free lunch. A properly diversified portfolio is the base case for any investor. Risk management does not add explicit insurance costs, unless we impose strict floor limits (such as by using put options). Optimizing asset allocation and maximizing the use of government-sponsored programs are also free lunches.

Beyond the mathematics of financial planning is the communication challenge. Our experience in dealing with many investors, along with evidence from many surveys and questionnaires, shows that financial education at age 50 or older is difficult. If 50% of individuals cannot divide 2 million by 5 (see Chapter 1), how can we hope to appropriately advise investors and keep them on the right path? There are still many investors who chose a financial product simply because it performed well in the last two or three years. Education about principles such as return compounding, debt management (e.g., of credit cards, mortgages, and personal loans), and benefits of tax-exempt or tax-deferred savings could easily be taught in mathematics courses in high school. Such education is a generational project.

For those already in their 40s or 50s who have yet to commit seriously to the savings effort, however, the quality of the communication tools is of paramount importance. There are so many aspects to consider that it is easy, even for an adviser, to overlook a specific life dimension or an implicit assumption. It is essential in any application to have a dashboard or checklist that summarizes all the decision components. Also important is the ability to quickly represent to the investor how each decision significantly improves their expected quality of life in retirement. What is the effect of saving another 1% of income? What is the effect of not buying a second home that is not really needed? How can small sacrifices allow one to retire two years earlier or increase the expected retirement income by 15%? A good interface would motivate individuals and households to consider retirement planning not as something that is too far away to think about but as something to aspire to—and to begin quickly if one has not already done so.

Whether individuals are middle income, high net worth, or super-high net worth, they all face the same investment principles. All types of investors would be well served by the insights of *Secure Retirement*. Investors who have accumulated a few millions in financial wealth can immediately use the current functionalities as presented. For those with less wealth, the interface and process can be simplified. For super–high net worth individuals, the issue is allowing for more-complex investment portfolios that could include single securities, commercial real estate, artwork, exotic cars, and other alternative assets. Advisers to the super-wealthy must consider more-complex tax situations related to owning a business, family trusts, or successions, and they must possibly urge clients to make greater use of specific insurance products.

A last issue to discuss is public policies. Numerous government programs, such as 401(k) accounts, traditional IRAs, Roth IRAs, and health savings accounts, currently support the retirement effort. As we tried to illustrate in Chapter 8, it may be worthwhile to consider whether a better integration of these programs could make them more effective and create a fairer, level playing field for most investors.

In the introduction to *Secure Retirement*, we cited Robert Merton (2017), who said: "The retirement problem is a global problem. The good news is, finance science can be used to solve it. Design things on finance principles, rather than institutionally…. If you design on financial principles, it will work everywhere in the world." We can add to this statement that we now have the information technology capabilities and advances in machine learning that will enable us to build integrated financial frameworks to solve this retirement problem for most investors everywhere.

Appendix I. Factors Affecting the Decision to Acquire Annuities and the Type of Annuities (Immediate vs. Deferred)

Immediate vs. (Far) Deferred Annuities

Figure I.1 compares the internal rate of return (IRR) month by month of two different annuities purchased by men age 65 (the data start 120 months after both annuity contracts would have been acquired). The first contract is an immediate life annuity with a 10-year payment guarantee. The second is a deferred life annuity that will start paying in 15 years and guarantees a full cash refund to the beneficiaries in the event of death before age 80 and a cash refund of the remaining unpaid premium amount afterward.[105]

Even after 10 years (120 months), the immediate annuity has a negative IRR because the cumulative payments made to the annuitant are still nominally less than the premium paid for the contract. The immediate annuity reaches a 0% IRR at age 80.75 (65 years and 183 months). On the other hand,

Figure I.1. Comparing Immediate and Deferred Annuities

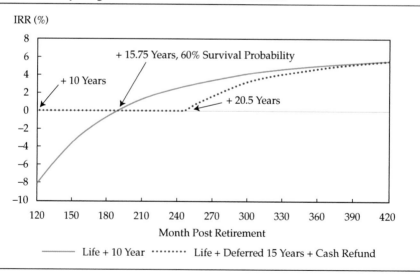

[105]For the purpose of these examples, we have used the annuity prices provided by immediateannuities.com.

the deferred annuity has a 0% IRR until age 85.5. This occurs because the annuity premium will be reimbursed to the successors if the annuitant dies before reaching age 80 and because if the annuitant dies after 80, the annuity will pay until the premium is nominally refunded.

The trade-off between the two annuities seems clear when there is no other consideration. If the annuitant dies before age 80.75, the deferred annuity was preferable. An average annuitant has a 60% probability of living beyond that age. If the annuitant lives beyond that date, the IRR of the deferred annuity does not catch up until age 120! We should also consider, however, that a deferred annuity has a higher payout ratio than the immediate annuity. Therefore, although the deferred annuity will contribute to a faster depletion of the liquid asset portfolio in the initial years of retirement, the same nominal payout in dollars can be purchased for a lower amount.

Lower- vs. Higher-Rate Environments

Figure I.2 answers the following question: Do we prefer fixed income to annuities relatively more or relatively less in a higher interest rate environment? The full and dotted blue lines on the left axis measure how fast a fixed-income portfolio with a consistent average maturity of about 8 years—such as a US aggregate portfolio—would be depleted if this portfolio were to provide the payout of an immediate annuity with a 10-year payout guarantee priced either under the yield curve as of 13 February 2018, or as the same yield curve moved

Figure I.2. Comparing Immediate Annuities Assuming Two Yield Curve Environments

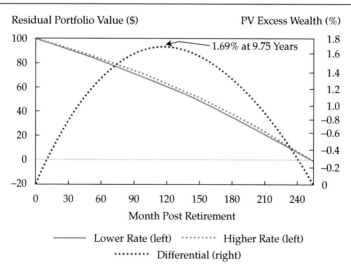

upward by 1%. In both scenarios, the fixed-income portfolio will be depleted after 255 months (21.3 years). Therefore, after 21.3 years, a retiree who purchased an annuity instead of a fixed-income portfolio should be clearly satisfied in both situations. We are interested in what happens earlier, before 21.3 years.

The red dotted line shows the evolution of the present value of the differential or excess wealth (PVEW) under both interest rate scenarios as a percentage of the initial fixed-income investment. Prior to capital exhaustion, the higher-return environment leads to a greater PVEW, reaching a maximum of about 1.69% of the initial investment after 9.75 years. The PVEW then declines toward zero. The reasoning is as follows: A higher-yield environment leads to a larger annuity payout. Because the annuity is priced under a higher yield curve, the wealth differential initially benefits from the higher reinvestment rate on fixed income. The higher annuity payout rate depletes the capital at an increasing rate, however, as the fixed-income balance is reduced.

Although we can conclude that a maximum PVEW spread of 1.69% is not to be ignored, the figure shows a specific time window in which this spread is more significant. Even if rates were to be higher by 2% at each point on the curve, the maximum PVEW would still be only 2.67%. Furthermore, it remains to be seen if this is significant in a context where only a portion of the retiree's assets are invested in an annuity and after considering that the presence of the annuity may affect the recommended asset allocation, the portfolio rebalancing, and the retiree's overall financial risk. This question will be answered in Chapters 4 and 8 by completing comprehensive simulations under stochastic interest rate scenarios.

Rising Rate Environment

The previous example compared a fixed-income investment with an annuity contract in either a lower or higher fixed-income yield environment. A greater concern for retirees, however, is the possibility that interest rates may increase after the annuity has been purchased. In such a case, the fixed-income portfolio will be affected by the rise in rates, which will cause capital losses initially and gradually raise the reinvestment rate, but the annuity contract's payout terms will already be set. Because the fixed-income portfolio's duration is likely shorter than that of the annuity, the long-term impact of having bought an annuity "too early" is almost certainly unfavorable.

Figure I.3 shows the present value of the wealth differential between a scenario in which interest rates gradually rise by either 1% or 2% over a period of five years and a scenario in which they remain stable. As in the previous example, we are assuming the fixed-income portfolio is used to fund the equivalent of the payout that an immediate annuity with a 10-year guarantee

Figure I.3. Comparing Immediate Annuities and Fixed Income under Rising Rate Environments

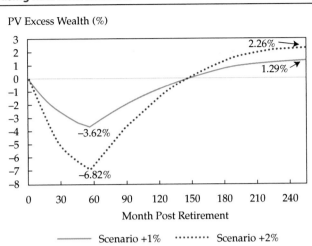

would have offered. We are also assuming again that the average maturity of the fixed-income portfolio resembles that of a US fixed-income aggregate mandate—about eight years.

The differential wealth is initially negative, because the scenario of rising rates leads to capital losses in the fixed-income portfolio. The annuity equivalent payments are the same in both scenarios, so the rising rate scenario eventually becomes more favorable as inflows are reinvested at higher interest rates. In this instance, the maximum present value of excess wealth is reached when the capital of the fixed-income portfolio under the stable rate scenario is depleted, after 21.3 years, whereas the alternative portfolio, under the rising rate scenario, still has some remaining wealth. The same question remains, however: Is this significant in a context where only a portion of the retiree's assets are invested in an annuity and where the presence of the annuity may affect both the recommended asset allocation and the retiree's overall financial risk? Furthermore, the participant selecting the annuity option would still benefit from an annuity payout after 21.3 years.

Lower vs. Higher Real-Rate Environments

A 3% yield can consist of 2% inflation and a 1% real rate or 1% inflation and a 2% real rate. We evaluate the effect on wealth of decumulating a specific spending amount in retirement, adjusted for inflation, assuming the retiree invests either in a fixed-income portfolio or acquires a life annuity with a 10-year guarantee. In this case, the annuitant's spending amount can differ from the annuity payout—an initial spending rate of 5% adjusted for inflation is considered, while the nominal annuity payout available as of the time of this analysis was 6.37%. We assume a 3% nominal interest rate with either a 1% or a 2% inflation rate.

For example, **Figure I.4**, Panel A is based on the 2% inflation rate scenario, implying a 1% real rate. The solid blue line represents the residual value

Figure I.4. Comparing Immediate Annuities and Fixed Income

A. 3% Rate Environment, 2% Inflation, and 5% Initial Spending Rate

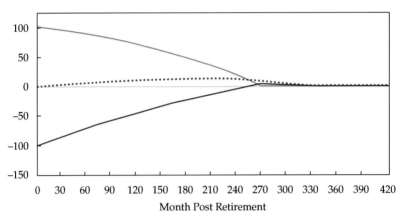

B. 3% Rate Environment, 1% Inflation, and 5% Income Payout

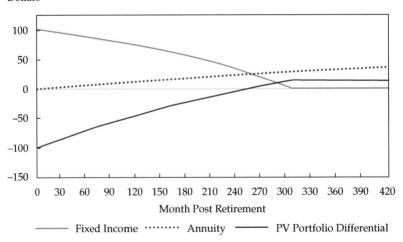

(Continued)

Figure I.4.   Comparing Immediate Annuities and Fixed Income (Continued)

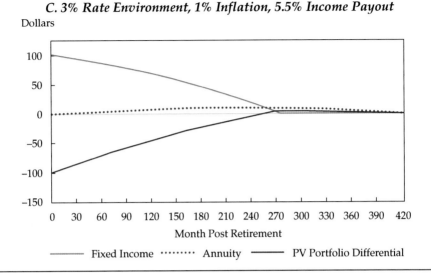

C. 3% Rate Environment, 1% Inflation, 5.5% Income Payout

of the fixed-income portfolio adjusted for the nominal spending amounts. The dotted blue line assumes the annuity has been purchased instead and shows portfolio wealth, assuming all excess wealth resulting from the difference between the annuity payout and the spending amount, if any, is reinvested in fixed income. The red line shows the present value of the difference in portfolio wealth between the two approaches.[106] The comparison is unfair because we ignore the effect of the 10-year certain payout guaranty on the annuity. The purpose of this example and of others presented later, however, is to concentrate on the cash flow differential between the two approaches in the long run.

The fixed-income portfolio's value declines over time because the spending rate is greater than the portfolio's nominal return. The decline accelerates because the spending amount increases with inflation. The portfolio is fully exhausted after 22.5 years.

The annuity approach initially builds some positive portfolio wealth when the annuity payout is greater than the spending amount but eventually falls as the spending amount surpasses the annuity payout. The portfolio wealth in the annuity approach is exhausted after 27.8 years, but the annuity will still provide an income after this period if the retiree is alive. This annuity

---

[106]The wealth under the annuity approach should also include the value of the guaranteed payout amounts, but our interest lies in the ability of both approaches to cover the income payout amount under the assumption the retiree lives a long life.

payout is not enough to meet the desired level of consumption, however, which explains why the portfolio wealth is nil. From a wealth perspective, the annuity approach becomes slightly preferable to the fixed-income approach after 21.2 years.

Figure I.4, Panel B illustrates what happens if we change the inflation rate assumption from 2% to 1%, implying a higher real rate. In this case, the fixed-income portfolio will not be exhausted until 25.6 years and the annuity approach can sustain the desired spending amount for as long as the retiree lives. From a wealth perspective, the annuity approach still becomes preferable to the fixed-income approach after the same 21.2 years. What determines this breakeven horizon is not our inflation or payout assumption but rather the annuity's pricing for a given yield environment—which is dependent on the mortality assumption.

We conclude that a higher real-rate environment is advantageous in both approaches but provides an even greater advantage for retirees who are concerned about living a very long life. It could also support a higher income payout. For example, Figure I.4, Panel C presents the same scenarios as Panel B but assumes a 5.5% income payout. Although the fixed-income approach has exhausted its capital after 22.6 years, the annuity approach can still support the full income payout.[107]

This result indirectly illustrates the importance of the assumptions made about the expected increases in income needs. A higher real rate has the same effect on wealth as consumption expenses that do not rise as quickly as the inflation rate. It will be important to know more about how retirees' consumption baskets evolve as they age.

Although many scenarios of varying levels of fixed-income yield and income payout rate were tested, the message is basically the same. Whether we approach the retirement issue using a fixed-income approach or an annuity approach, a higher real-return environment implies that we can afford a higher income payout. It does not change the fact that the annuity approach is less favorable if the retiree dies before the breakeven horizon or that the annuity is more favorable if the retiree lives longer.

Furthermore, the annuity approach does have another advantage in that it creates an accumulation process, as discussed in Chapter 3, that can support a higher level of risk. The cash flow surplus generated through the annuity approach could be invested according to the glide path allocation. This approach (not illustrated) reduces the breakeven horizon of 21.2 years shown in Figure I.4, Panel B by approximately 1.4 years.

---

[107]Milevsky and Huang (2011) also conclude that higher real rates can support a higher optimal rate of income withdrawals.

Appendix II. Quantitative Studies of the Life-Cycle Approach

Blake, Wright, and Zhang (2011)

Unlike Sheikh et al. (2015), Blake, Wright, and Zhang (2011) concentrate on the accumulation period and emphasize loss aversion (LA) in reference to a predefined objective. They explain that the concept of loss aversion, initially proposed by Kahneman and Tversky (1979) within the framework of prospect theory (PT) (Tversky and Kahneman 1992), can also be used to explain the equity premium puzzle—that is, the observation that the historical risk premium of equity far exceeds what could be expected from standard macroeconomic risk aversion models—and is better suited than standard utility models to explain observed attitudes toward risk.

Their process assumes the individual is risk averse with respect to a target retirement pension—as defined by the purchase of an annuity—and to a series of interim wealth targets. With this approach, allocation to equity increases if wealth is below the relevant target and decreases otherwise. If wealth is significantly above the target, the allocation to risky assets increases again as the ability to meet the target is secured. The process is based on a PT utility function relating investor utility to fund value. **Figure II.1** presents the shape of a typical PT utility function.[108]

Their participant, currently age 20, plans to retire at age 65 with two-thirds of his before-retirement income, assuming the purchase of a real income life annuity.[109] He saves 15% of his income. Using a recursive process, they determine the interim target wealth levels required to achieve the desired income level. As the portfolio wealth fluctuates in future years, it may lag or eventually lead the interim targets, leading to less- or more-aggressive asset allocation. The objective is to maximize the value function over time, given that deviations with respect to interim targets occur, while putting more emphasis on the last target. The return generation process is i.i.d.

---

[108] A PT function can be expressed as the following: $U_x(F_x) = \dfrac{[F_x - f_x(x)]^{v1}}{v1}$ if $F_x \geq f_x(x)$ and $-\lambda \dfrac{[f_x(x) - F_x]^{v2}}{v2}$ if $F_x < f_x(x)$, where F_x is the actual fund level, $f_x(x)$ the interim target, λ the loss aversion parameter, and $v1$ and $v2$ are the curvature parameters for gains and losses.

[109] The analysis does not incorporate the effect of Social Security.

Figure II.1.   The PT Utility Function

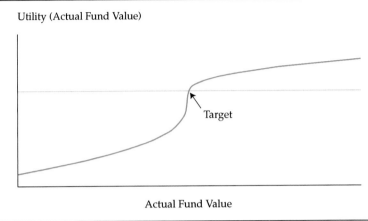

Table II.1 presents some results from their base case scenario as well as several sensitivity analyses. The process leads to a mean replacement ratio of 75.6% versus a target of 66.7% and to replacement ratios of 35.2% and 66.8%, respectively, at the 5th and 50th percentiles of scenarios of market return. Finally, the process leads to a 75.2% likelihood of achieving the target and to a 4.3% expected shortfall.[110]

Sensitivity analyses were completed on four parameters:

- loss aversion when wealth is below the target

- curvature parameter specifying how risk seeking the individual is when wealth is below the target

- weight attributed to meeting the interim targets versus the final target

- subjective discount rate

The authors also compared the base case scenario with a model in which utility is represented by a standard constant relative risk aversion (CRRA) function applied to final wealth.[111] We can observe that the choice of utility function (PT versus CRRA) has a far greater effect than the specification of the parameters within the PT function. The PT function offers better income

---

[110]Expected shortfall is defined as the mean of the difference between the target replacement ratio (of 66.7%) and the actual replacement ratio achieved, conditional on the actual replacement ratio being less than the target.

[111]This is a case in which, in the equation described in Footnote 107, there is no interim target and $v1 = 1 - \eta$ (which is the CRRA coefficient). In other words, $U_{65}(F_{65}) = \dfrac{(F_{65})^{1-\eta}}{1-\eta}$.

Table II.1.   Results under Alternative Scenarios of Loss Aversion and Other Parameters

	Mean Replacement Ratio	5th Percentile	25th Percentile	Prob. Achieving Target	Expected Shortfall
Base case	75.6%	35.2%	66.8%	75.2%	4.3%
Loss aversion					
Lower	79.0	33.6	66.9	75.3	4.7
Higher	73.0	36.5	66.4	74.3	4.0
Curve parameter					
Lower	77.8	33.3	68.9	77.4	4.8
Higher	71.9	39.1	65.0	71.1	3.8
Interim target weight					
Higher	75.6	35.2	66.8	75.1	4.2
Lower	76.1	35.0	66.7	75.1	4.3
Discount rate					
Lower	77.7	33.2	66.5	74.8	4.7
Higher	73.7	37.6	66.0	73.3	4.3
CRRA utility function	91.2	35.0	55.8	62.7	6.6

protection at lower percentile levels such as the 25th but at the expense of a significantly lower mean replacement ratio. Also, it does not substantially improve wealth at lower percentile levels.

Asher, Butt, Kayande, and Khemka (2015)

Asher et al. consider individuals working full time for a constant real salary until age 65, then retiring permanently. Longevity is uncertain but in accordance with Australian life tables (2005–2007), and individuals are expected to have died as of age 110. The distributions of asset class return (equity and cash) are generated from a nonparametric approach using past data. Decisions are centered on withdrawal amounts and asset allocation. The objective is to maximize lifetime utility of withdrawals, imposing a utility penalty when current consumption is less then prior consumption in real terms.[112]

---

[112]The utility for a single observation at x is

$$U_x = \left[\frac{(C)^{1-\eta}}{1-\eta} + \beta \times \min\left(0, \frac{(C)^{1-\eta}}{1-\eta} - \frac{(C_p)^{1-\eta}}{1-\eta} \right) \right] \left[1 - \frac{q(x)}{2} \right],$$

where C is the current consumption, C_p the previous consumption, β the penalty coefficient for decreased consumption, and $q(x)$ the mortality rate at age x.

The main conclusions are these:

- There is a clear decline in equity allocation starting 15 to 25 years before retirement, attributed to the increasing ratio of portfolio wealth over the remaining human capital wealth. After retirement, however, the allocation to equity is not very sensitive to the wealth level.

- Median consumption tends to trend upward until age 80, then decline to protect the remaining wealth because the retiree is entering a zone of greater longevity than would have been expected in earlier years.

The authors also point out that there is little discussion in the literature about whether survival probabilities should be integrated into the value function—they reduce the utility of later-in-life consumption. In addition, Asher et al. warn to be careful when designing a value function to avoid applying such probabilities when annuities are used, because doing so would constitute a double counting of the probability of not being alive.

Irlam (2017)/(2015)

Irlam (2017) assumes that an individual starts saving at age 20 and retires at age 65. Labor income and asset returns are uncertain. His objective is to determine the paths of asset allocation (cash and equity) and consumption, as a function of age and wealth, that maximize lifetime CRRA utility in the presence of a guaranteed income-producing but nontradable asset such as Social Security. To provide some perspective, his base case assumes a median income of approximately $35,000 and a retirement income from the nontradable asset of $7,000 in real terms (today's money) plus 25% of final employment income with a real cap at $31,000. Irlam interprets human capital as a nontradable before-retirement asset and Social Security as a nontradable after-retirement asset.

Assuming i.i.d. returns and ignoring Social Security income, he confirms that his numerical solution, using dynamic programming, leads to the same asset allocation recommendation as obtained with the Merton model (see Equation 6.2). For example, without Social Security, the recommended equity allocation for a CRRA coefficient of 6, an equity excess return of 5.3%, and a volatility of 16.2% is approximately a constant 34%.

In the presence of retirement income such as Social Security, however, the median equity allocation scenario assuming a CRRA coefficient of 6 is 100% until approximately 20 years before retirement, declining to about 70% as of retirement but staying at this high level and even increasing as the individual approaches 80. This scenario is like some of the scenarios tested in Chapter 4. The presence of nontradable assets increases the equity allocation.

First, Social Security income reduces risk and allows for a more aggressive allocation in the remaining portfolio. Second, at age 65, the value attributed to an individual's Social Security benefits after, say, age 85 and beyond are small in relation to the benefits expected to be received earlier. Once a person reaches age 85 or older, however, the value of the benefits beyond age 85 is significantly greater because the years from 65 to 85 have passed: that is, life expectancy has increased simply because the person has already survived 20 more years. Third, these higher survival probabilities apply to greater nominal payments, because Social Security benefits are indexed for inflation. For example, in John's case, presented in Figure 4.7, Panel A, the expected value of Social Security benefits as of age 65 did not represent more than 14.9% of total benefits for benefits to be received past age 85. In real dollar terms, those benefits are worth 60% more to John once he is 85.

Irlam also observes that in this context, consumption rises but eventually declines as individuals reach approximately age 90 because their "unexpected" longevity is depleting the asset portfolio. These conclusions do not apply to super-wealthy individuals, because Social Security will represent only a small proportion of their overall income needs and will therefore have little effect on asset allocation. In this case, allocation would revert to the Merton solution (assuming the restrictive assumptions still apply).

Irlam (2015) looks at the effects of Social Security but considers a situation in which an individual would target a core retirement income of $30,000 in real terms and a desired excess income of $10,000 (for a total of $40,000). He applies a more risk averse CRRA coefficient to the core income (a coefficient of 4) than to the desired excess income (a coefficient of 1). He also assumes that Social Security will account for 50% of core income. The recommended equity allocation according to the Merton model, excluding Social Security and assuming a CRRA coefficient of 4, is 36%. Using dynamic programming, Irlam analyzes the recommended asset allocation at different portfolio wealth levels. He finds the following:

- At low levels of wealth, equity allocation remains high (80%+) at any age, whereas at high levels of wealth, it is also high but tends to increase with age. The latter occurs because expected longevity is considerably reduced as we age, allowing one to take greater risk if wealth levels are still significant.

- When the individual is young, high equity allocation is observed at high and low wealth levels but is lower at median wealth levels; as we age, high allocations are increasingly observed at median levels of wealth. Again, this is consistent with declining life expectancy as we age but is contrary to what many glide paths advise.

Milevsky and Huang (2011)

Milevsky and Huang focus exclusively on the effect of longevity uncertainty on the optimal retirement withdrawal policy, making the argument that the 4% rule or any other fixed-spending policy has no basis in economics. They assume that the expected length of life obeys a unisex law of mortality whereby longevity risk increases exponentially over time (the Gompertz law). The authors calibrated this model using common mortality tables. Most of their examples assume an 86.6% likelihood that a 65-year-old individual will live to age 75, 57.3% to age 85, 17.6% to age 90, and 5% to age 100. They assume CRRA utility.

When length of life is stochastic, the optimal withdrawal rate declines with age and is positively correlated with the real rate of return. Although the initial results appear consistent with the 4% rule as of retirement, the recommended withdrawal rate differs at older ages, such as 90 or above. In other words, individuals who live longer than expected should eventually plan to spend less. Consumption is reduced in accordance with survival probabilities. Like Irlam (2015 and 2017), Milevsky and Huang consider the consequences of adding an income annuity component. They look at an individual receiving $25,000 per year in Social Security income, assuming different wealth levels.

Table II.2 presents the recommended withdrawal rates at ages 65 (first number) and 80 (second number) for different coefficients of longevity risk aversion (2, 4, and 8) and different allocations of initial wealth, where wealth is defined as portfolio wealth plus pension wealth such as Social Security. Pension wealth is priced like any asset using actuarial concepts. The withdrawal rates are those that apply to the portfolio components. The withdrawal rates do not include the pension income.

The presence of a stable pension component allows the retiree to increase the withdrawal rate on the financial asset portfolio. The withdrawal rate declines with age, however, unless full annuitization is implemented.

Table II.2. Impact of Risk Aversion and Pension Component on Withdrawal Rates

Percentage of Portfolio vs. Pension	Low Longevity Risk Aversion = 2	Medium Longevity Risk Aversion = 4	High Longevity Risk Aversion = 8
100–0	5.30%/4.57%	4.60%/4.28%	4.11%/3.97%
60–40	6.70%/5.77%	6.22%/5.78%	5.89%/5.68%
0–100	6.33%/6.33%	6.33%/6.33%	6.33%/6.33%

Irlam (2018)

Irlam applies a deep reinforcement learning (neural net) approach to the issue of retirement planning.[113] He indicates that the results are very similar to those computed using stochastic dynamic programming but once the model is trained, computational time is extremely fast. The model determines the level of real consumption, the amount of real and/or nominal SPIA to purchase, and the asset allocation as well as the duration for real and nominal bonds. Bond returns are derived from a time-varying yield curve model.

Irlam first evaluates the situation of a 65-year-old retired female with $500,000 in assets, a $16,000 guaranteed income—which matches the average Social Security benefits in 2018—and CRRA utility with a coefficient of 3. He then compares the performance of his model to various consumption rules, such as

- Bengen (1994) 4% rule;

- Guyton (2004), who stipulates that consumption stays nominally the same in years in which portfolio nominal returns are negative;

- Zolt (2013), who stipulates that income stays nominally the same in years in which the portfolio value has fallen below an expected level; and

- an annuity-type rule (PMT for payment) with dynamic life expectancy in which the payout is the one that depletes the portfolio using current life expectancy as the remaining duration and the intermediate-duration nominal bond yield as the expected return.

Irlam concludes that the last (dynamic) approach leads to the highest certainty equivalent consumption.[114] He achieves even better results when allowing annuities to be incorporated. The approach shows the potential of using machine-learning methodologies, with their fast computations, to deal with the challenges of integrating the many dimensions involved in retirement planning.

---

[113]The model is trained using two hidden layers of 64 neurons. It is based on annual data and was trained on 1 million years of investing.

[114]The certainty equivalent consumption is the level of constant consumption that delivers the same utility as the pattern of consumption that is experienced.

Appendix III. Working Principles of Reverse Mortgages

The discussion that follows applies to reverse mortgages insured by the US federal government under the Home Equity Conversion Mortgage (HECM) scheme, which are available only through an FHA-approved lender. The percentage of home value that can be extracted initially through a reverse mortgage is determined by two factors:

- the lesser of the appraised value of the home or $679,650 (in 2018) and

- the principal limit factor (PLF), or percentage of the value that can be borrowed.

The PLF can be found in the HECM tables, which are periodically updated. The PLF is itself a function of two factors: the age of the younger spouse—although one spouse must be at least 62—and the expected rate, which is the sum of the 10-year LIBOR swap rate and the lender's margin, rounded down to the nearest 0.125%. The expected rate cannot be less than 3.0% (in 2018). For example, according to the 2 October 2017 HECM table, the PLF allowed for a 65-year-old individual is 40.3%, assuming the expected rate is 5.5% (composed of, say, 2.5% for 10-year LIBOR and 3% for the lender's margin). This value implies that the initial borrowing capacity—principal limit—available through a reverse mortgage is 40.3% of the capped appraised value of the house. This percentage would increase with age, in this example reaching 51.0% at age 80.

The expected rate is not the interest rate applied to capitalize the money borrowed when using a reverse mortgage. The expected rate is solely used to determine the PLF, whereas the effective rate, which is annualized monthly, applies to the funding and is the sum of three components: the one-month LIBOR rate, the lender's margin, and the ongoing 0.5% mortgage insurance premium paid to the FHA.[115] For example, assuming one-month LIBOR of 1.75%, a lender's margin of 3%, and a 0.5% insurance premium, the annualized monthly rate would be an after-tax rate of 5.25%. It would then evolve with one-month LIBOR. The insurance premium guarantees that the borrower will receive the promised loan advances and will never owe more than 95% of the appraised value of the home when repayment is due.

---

[115]Although there are fixed-rate mortgages, the market is dominated by floating (LIBOR-based) mortgages. The lender's margin never changes after it is set.

Homeowners must also pay a variety of upfront costs, among them the following:

- ordinary fees (including appraisal, inspection, and legal costs);

- origination fees (a lender can charge the greater of $2,500 or 2% of the first $200,000 of a home's value plus 1% of the amount over $200,000. HECM origination fees are capped at $6,000);

- mortgage insurance (an upfront cost of 0.5% of the house's value at closing. The fee could be 2.0% if more than 60% of the borrowing capacity is used in the first year. This scenario is not recommended under any circumstances); and

- servicing fees (currently less common and often waived).

For example, assuming a property with an appraised value of $500,000, the origination fees may hit the $6,000 cap, and the mortgage insurance would add another $2,500. Assuming ordinary fees of $2,500, total upfront costs could be $11,000, or 2.2% of the property value. All of these costs are incurred to have access to an initial borrowing capacity of slightly more than $200,000—a substantial total upfront cost. Nevertheless, a reverse mortgage may strategically make sense if used wisely.

Before the benefits of a reverse mortgage can be evaluated, there is one other aspect to consider. Should borrowers negotiate a reverse mortgage now or later, thereby postponing the upfront cost, if they do not intend to initially use the available line of credit? It is important to understand that the principal limit is the sum of the existing loan balance and the available line of credit. The principal limit, however, will grow by the effective rate. If the authorized reverse mortgage is fully used at initiation, the loan balance and the principal limit will grow similarly and be equal. No residual line of credit is available. But if the reverse mortgage is initiated and the borrower does not draw on the line of credit, the borrowing capacity available through the line of credit will grow. In theory, it could become even larger than the value of the house even if the borrowers and their successors never owe the lender more than 95% of the home's appraised value.

Consider an example. A household considers the use of a reverse mortgage. The younger member of the household is 65. The householders do not believe they will need to draw on the reverse mortgage before age 80, even under the worst of circumstances. It is assumed that the value of their property will increase by 2% per year.

Several uncertainties are related to setting up the reverse mortgage later. First, we do not know what the expected rate used to determine the PLF will be. Second, even if the expected rate were to remain constant, the HECM table could be updated. Assume, however, all this remains constant for now. **Table III.1** shows the size of the expected PLF at age 80, assuming the reverse mortgage is set up now or in 5, 10, or 15 years. The expected rate is constant at 5.5%, and the effective rate is also constant at 6.0%.

The table shows the principal amount available at age 80 whether the reverse mortgage was put in place at age 65, 70, 75, or 80. Assuming the borrower never used the available line of credit, this amount also equals the estimated borrowing capacity available as of age 80. Estimates of house value are the same for all scenarios, but the true PLF and setup costs are unknown except at age 65. We assumed they remain unchanged in this example. Furthermore, we do not know the true effective rates that will apply.

The PLF is growing at about 1.6% a year, and the expected housing appreciation is 2%. Hence, if the effective rate is greater than 3.6%, the principal amount at age 80 will be greater if the reverse mortgage is set up earlier. If real estate prices increase very fast, however, it may be preferable to wait. The PLF is also highly sensitive to the expected rate. If the PLF is 40.3% at 65 years of age in a 5.5% expected rate environment, it is, respectively, 54.2% and 32.6% for expected rates of 3% and 7%. These facts indicate that given the opportunity and the intent to eventually set up a reverse mortgage arrangement, doing so earlier may be preferable if the 10-year rate is, particularly, low.

There is no denying that reverse mortgages appear expensive. Setup costs can represent 2% to 3% of a house's appraised value, and the effective rate can be greater than the long-run after-tax return individuals can expect from their

Table III.1. The Costs and Potential Benefits of Reverse Mortgages

Age	65	70	75	80
House value	$500,000	$552,040	$609,497	$672,934
Principal limit factor (PLF)	40.3%	43.9%	46.7%	51.0%
Initial principal amount	$201,500	$242,346	$284,635	$343,196
Principal amount at age 80	$494,500	$440,923	$383,930	$343,196
Principal amount at 80/House value at 80	73.5%	65.5%	57.1%	51.0%
Setup costs	$11,000	$12,145	$13,409	$14,805
Setup costs compounded to age 80	$19,375	$17,713	$16,194	$14,805
Principal amount net of upfront cost at age 80	$475,124	$423,210	$367,736	$328,392

investment portfolio. Therefore, prioritizing the use of capital available from a reverse mortgage over the capital available from the investment portfolio may not be an appropriate strategy. Furthermore, households that have more than adequate coverage of their retirement income needs through DB/401(k) plans and private savings usually need not consider taking a reverse mortgage.

Bibliography

Abbas, Ali E., and James E. Matheson. 2005. "Normative Target-Based Decision Making." *Managerial and Decision Economics* 26 (6): 373–385.

Agarwal, Sumit, John C. Driscoll, Xavier Gabaix, and David Laibson. 2009. "The Age of Reason: Financial Decisions over the Life-Cycle and Implications for Regulations." *Brookings Papers on Economic Activity*: 51–117.

Aguiar, Mark, and Erik Hurst. 2008. "Deconstructing Lifecycle Expenditure." NBER Working Paper No. 13893 (March).

Albert, Faye S., John M. Bragg, and James C. Brooks. 2010. "Health Expectancy." Actuarial Practice Forum (February 2010).

Albrecht, Peter, and Raimond Maurer. 2001. "Self-Annuitization, Ruin Risk in Retirement and Asset Allocation: The Annuity Benchmark." Working paper. www.actuaries.org/AFIR/Colloquia/Toronto/Albrecht_Maurer.pdf

Ameriks, John, Andrew Caplin, Steven Laufer, and Stijn Van Nieuwerburgh. 2008. "Annuity Valuation, Long-Term Care, and Bequest Motives." In *Recalibrating Retirement Spending and Saving*, edited by John Ameriks and Olivia S. Mitchell, 251–275. London: Oxford University Press.

Ameriks, John, and Paul Yakoboski. 2003. "Reducing Retirement Income Risks: The Role of Annuitization." *Benefits Quarterly* 19 (4): 13–24.

Ang, Andrew. 2014. *Asset Management: A Systematic Approach to Factor Investing*. London: Oxford University Press.

Anyaegbu, Grace. 2010. "Using the OECD Equivalence Scale in Taxes and Benefits Analysis." *Economic & Labour Market Review* 4 (1): 49–54.

Aon Consulting. 2008. "Replacement Ratio Study: A Measurement Tool for Retirement Planning." 7th update. docplayer.net/12528506-Aon-consulting-s-2008-replacement-ratio-study-a-measurement-tool-for-retirement-planning.html

Arnott, Robert D., Katrina F. Sherrerd, and Lillian Wu. 2013. "The Glide Path Illusion ... and Potential Solutions." *Journal of Retirement Income* 1 (2): 13–28.

Arum, Richard, and Josipa Roksa. 2011. *Academically Adrift: Limited Learning on College Campuses*. Chicago: University of Chicago Press.

Asher, Anthony, Adam Butt, Ujwal Kayande, and Gaurav Khemka. 2015. "Formulating Appropriate Utility Functions and Personal Financial Plans." Paper presented at Actuaries Institute Actuaries Summit, Melbourne (17–19 May).

Assari, Shervin. 2017. "Why Do Women Live Longer than Men?" University of Michigan & World Economic Forum (March).

Attié, Alexander P., and Shaun K. Roache. 2009. "Inflation Hedging for Long-Term Investors." IMF Working Paper WP/09/90, International Monetary Fund (April).

Avendano, Mauricio, and Ichiro Kawachi. 2014. "Why Do Americans Have Shorter Life Expectancy and Worse Health Than Do People in Other High-Income Countries?" *Annual Review of Public Health* 35: 307–325.

Ayres, I., and B. Nalebuff. 2010. *Lifecycle Investing: A New, Safe, and Audacious Way to Improve the Performance of Your Retirement Portfolio.* New York: Basic Books.

Babbel, David F., and Craig B. Merrill. 2007. "Rational Decumulation." Wharton Financial Institutions Center Working Paper 06–14 (22 May). http://fic.wharton.upenn.edu/fic/papers/06/0614.pdf

Balvers, Ronald J., Yangru Wu, and E.L. Gilliland. 2000. "Mean Reversion across National Stock Markets and Parametric Contrarian Investment Strategies." *Journal of Finance* 55 (2): 745–772.

Banerjee, Sudipto. 2016. "Trends in Retirement Satisfaction in the United States: Fewer Having a Great Time." *Employee Benefits Research Institute, EBRI Notes* 37 (4). https://papers.ssrn.com/sol3/papers.cfm?abstract_id=2772072

Belbase, Anek, and Geoffrey T. Sanzenbacher. 2017. "Cognitive Aging and the Capacity to Manage Money." Center for Retirement Research, Boston College.

Bengen, William P. 1994. "Determining Withdrawal Rates Using Historical Data." *Journal of Financial Planning* 24 (4): 14–24.

Bennyhoff, Donald G. 2008. "Time Diversification and Horizon-Based Asset Allocations." Vanguard Investment Counseling & Research.

Bernanke, Ben S. 2005. "The Global Saving Glut and the Current Account Deficit." Sandridge Lecture. www.federalreserve.gov/boarddocs/speeches/2005/200503102

————. 2015. "Why Are Interest Rates So Low?" Brookings Institute. https://www.brookings.edu/blog/ben-bernanke/2015/04/13/why-are-interest-rates-so-low-part-4-term-premiums/

Beshears, John, James J. Choi, David Laibson, Brigitte C. Madrian, and Stephen P. Zeldes. 2012. "What Makes Annuitization More Appealing?" NBER Working Paper 18575 (November).

Bhardwaj, Geetesh, Dean J. Hamilton, and John Ameriks. 2011. "Hedging Inflation: The Role of Expectations." Research report, Vanguard Research.

Blake, David, Douglas Wright, and Yumeng Zhang. 2011. "Target-Driven Investing: Optimal Investment Strategies in Defined Contribution Pension Plans under Loss Aversion." Discussion Paper PI-1112, Pensions Institute, Cass Business School, City University of London (September).

Blanchett, David. 2013. "Estimating the True Cost of Retirement." Working paper, Morningstar Investment Management (November).

————. 2014. "Estimating the True Cost of Retirement." Paper presented at Living to 100 Symposium, Orlando, Florida (8–10 January). www.soa.org/

Bodie, Zvi. 1995. "On the Risk of Stocks in the Long Run." *Financial Analysts Journal* 51 (3): 18–22.

Brown, Jeffrey R. 2001. "Private Pensions, Mortality Risk, and the Decision to Annuitize." *Journal of Public Economics* 82 (1): 29–62.

————. 2011. "Longevity-Insured Retirement Distributions: Basic Theories and Institutions." In *Retirement Income: Risk and Strategies.* Cambridge, MA: MIT Press.

Brown, Robert L., and J. McDaid. 2003. "Factors Affecting Retirement Mortality." *North American Actuarial Journal* 7 (2): 24–43.

Brown, Robert L., and Patricia Scahill. 2010. "Issues in the Issuance of Enhanced Annuities." Research Paper 265, McMaster University Series: Social and Economic Dimensions of an Aging Population (May): 1–12.

Campbell, John Y. 2017. *Financial Decisions and Markets: A Course in Asset Pricing.* Princeton, NJ: Princeton University Press.

Campbell, John Y., and Robert J. Shiller. 2001. "Valuation Ratios and the Long-Run Stock Market Outlook: An Update." NBER Working Paper 8221 (April).

Campbell, John Y., and Luis M. Viceira. 2002. *Strategic Asset Allocation: Portfolio Choice for Long-Term Investors.* London: Oxford University Press.

Carlson, Ben. 2017. "The Golden Age of Hedge Funds." CFA Institute Contributors (March).

Carman, Katherine Grace, and Angela A. Hung. 2017. "Household Retirement Savings: The Location of Savings between Spouses." Working Paper WR-1166, Rand Corporation.

Carneiro, Pedro, and Sokbae Lee. 2011. "Trends in Quality-Adjusted Skill Premia in the United States, 1960–2000." *American Economic Review* 101 (6): 2309–2349.

Cecchetti, S.G., Pok-Sang Lam, and Nelson C. Mark. 1990. "Mean Reversion in Equilibrium Asset Prices." *American Economic Review* 80: 398–418.

Charles Schwab Investment Management. 2017. "401(k) Participation Survey" (August).

Coakley, J., and A.-M. Fuertes. 2006. "Valuation Ratios and Price Deviations from Fundamentals." *Journal of Banking & Finance* 30: 2325–2346.

Cocco, João F., Francisco J. Gomes, and Pascal J. Maenhout. 2005. "Consumption and Portfolio Choice over the Life Cycle." *Review of Financial Studies* 18 (2): 491–533.

Collins, Patrick J., Huy D. Lam, and Josh Stampfli. 2015. *Longevity Risk and Retirement Income Planning.* Charlottesville, VA: CFA Institute Research Foundation. SSRNid-2717415.

Corden, Anne, Michael Hirst, and Katherine Nice. 2008. "Financial Implications of Death of a Partner." Working Paper ESRC 2288 12.08, Social Policy Research Unit, University of York, UK (December).

Davidoff, Thomas, Jeffrey R. Brown, and Peter A. Diamond. 2003. "Annuities and Individual Welfare." Pensions Institute Discussion Paper PI-0307 (May).

Davis, James L. 2010. "Spending Rates, Asset Allocation, and Probability of Failure." Dimensional Research Paper (May).

Dellinger, Jeffrey K. 2011. "When to Commence Income Annuities." Society of Actuaries. www.soa.org/globalassets/assets/files/resources/essays-monographs/retire-security-new-economy/mono-2011-mrs12-dellinger-paper.pdf

Dobler, Jim. 2013. "Tax Treatment of Income from an Annuity." *NAFA Annuity Outlook* (November/December).

Duesenberry, James. 1952. *Income, Savings, and the Theory of Consumer Behavior.* Cambridge, MA: Harvard University Press.

Esch, David, and Robert Michaud. 2014. "The False Promise of Target-Date Funds." *Journal of Indexes* 1 (17): 50–59.

Estrada, Javier. 2013. "The Glidepath Illusion: An International Perspective." IESE Business School Department of Finance (February).

Fama, Eugene F., and Kenneth R. French. 1988. "Dividend Yields and Expected Stock Returns." *Journal of Financial Economics* 22: 3–25.

Fenelon, Andrew, Li-Hui Chen, and Susan P. Baker. 2016. "Major Causes of Injury Death and the Life Expectancy Gap between the United States and Other High-Income Countries." *Journal of the American Medical Association* 315 (6): 609–611.

Finke, Michael, Wade D. Pfau, and Duncan Williams. 2012. "Spending Flexibility and Safe Withdrawal Rates." *Journal of Financial Planning* 25 (3): 44–51.

Fisher, Jonathan, David S. Johnson, Joseph Marchand, Timothy M. Smeeding, and Barbara Boyle Torrey. 2005. "The Retirement Consumption Conundrum: Evidence from Consumption Survey." Research report, Center for Retirement Research, Boston College.

Frank, Larry R., John B. Mitchell, and David M. Blanchett. 2011. "An Age-Based, Three-Dimensional, Universal Distribution Model Incorporating Sequence and Longevity Risks." Paper presented at the Academy of Financial Services, Las Vegas (23 October). www.academyfinancial.org/resources/Documents/Proceedings/2011/A1-Frank-Mitchell-Blanchett.pdf

Frederick, Shane, George Loewenstein, and Ted O'Donoghue. 2002. "Time Discounting and Time Preference: A Critical Review." *Journal of Economic Literature* 40 (2): 351–401.

Giron, Kevin, Lionel Martellini, Vincent Milhau, John Mulvey, and Anil Suri. 2018. "Applying Goal-Based Investing Principles to the Retirement Problem." EDHEC-Risk Institute (May).

Goetzmann, William N., and Roger G. Ibbotson. 2006. *The Equity Risk Premium: Essays and Exploration.* London: Oxford University Press.

Government Accountability Office. 2017. "The Nation's Retirement System: A Comprehensive Re-Evaluation Is Needed to Better Promote Future Retirement Security." Research Report GAO-18-111SP (October): 27.

Grantham, Jeremy. 2012. "My Sister's Pension Assets and Agency Problems: The Tension between Protecting Your Job or Your Clients' Money." GMO Quarterly Letter.

Gropp, J. 2004. "Mean Reversion of Industry Stock Returns in the U.S., 1926–1998." *Journal of Empirical Finance* 11 (4): 537–551.

Guvenen, Fatih, Fatih Karahan, Serdar Ozkan, and Jae Song. 2015. "What Do Data on Millions of U.S. Workers Reveal about Life-Cycle Earnings Risk?" Federal Staff Report 710, Reserve Bank of New York (February).

Guyton, J.T. 2004. "Decision Rules and Portfolio Management for Retirees: Is the 'Safe' Initial Withdrawal Rate Too Safe?" *Journal of Financial Planning* 17 (10): 54–62.

Hamilton, James D., Ethan S. Harris, Jan Hatzius, and Kenneth D. West. 2015. "The Equilibrium Real Funds Rate: Past, Present, and Future." Working Paper 16, Hutchins Center on Fiscal and Monetary Policy at Brookings (February).

Harris, Edward, Frank Sammartino, and David Weiner. 2012. "The Distribution of Household Income and Federal Taxes, 2008 and 2009." Research report, Congressional Budget Office (July).

Hershey, D.A., and D.A. Walsh. 2000. "Knowledge versus Experience in Financial Problem Solving Performance." *Current Psychology* 19 (4): 261–291.

Hoffman, Adam. 2017. "Congratulations, Your Income Is Too High: Non-Deductible IRA Contributions (Part 1)." Seeking Alpha (31 December). seekingalpha.com/article/4134620-congratulations-income-high-non-deductible-ira-contributions-part-1

Hu, Wei-Yin, and Jason S. Scott. 2007. "Behavioral Obstacles in the Annuity Market." *Financial Analysts Journal* 63 (6): 71–82.

Hurd, Michael D., and Susann Rohwedder. 2006. "Some Answers to the Retirement Consumption Puzzle." NBER Working Paper 12057 (February).

Hurst, Erik. 2008. "The Retirement of a Consumption Puzzle." NBER Working Paper 13789 (February).

Ilmanen, Antti. 2011. Expected Returns: An Investor's Guide to Harvesting Market Rewards. Chichester, Sussex, UK: Wiley Finance.

IMF. 2014. "Chapter 3: Perspectives on Global Real Interest Rates." In World Economic Outlook (October). www.imf.org/external/pubs/ft/weo/2014/01/

Invesco. 2015. "QDIA Q&A: A Resource for Plan Sponsors" (February).

Irlam, Gordon. 2015. "Asset Allocation Confidence Intervals in Retirement." SSRN-id2675390.

———. 2017. "Human Capital, Social Security, and Asset Allocation." SSRN-id3016824.

———. 2018. "Financial Planning via Deep Reinforcement Learning AI." SSRN-id3201703.

Kahneman, Daniel, and Amos Tversky. 1979. "Prospect Theory: An Analysis of Decision under Risk." *Econometrica* 47: 263–291.

Kapan, Eve. 2015. "Annuities: The Good, the Bad and the Ugly." https://www.forbes.com/sites/feeonlyplanner/2015/07/15/annuities-the-good-the-bad-and-the-ugly/#c3e490379906

Kapur, Sandeep, and J. Michael Orszag. 2002. "Portfolio Choice and Retirement Income Solutions." Watson Wyatt Technical Report 2002-RU05 (April).

Kim, M.J., C.R. Nelson, and R. Startz. 1991. "Mean Reversion in Stock Prices? A Reappraisal of the Empirical Evidence." *Review of Economic Studies* 58: 515–528.

Kinniry, Francis M., Colleen M. Jaconetti, Michael A. DiJoseph, Yan Zilbering, and Donald G. Bennyhoff. 2016. "Putting a Value on Your Value: Quantifying Vanguard Advisor's Alpha." Research report, Vanguard Research.

Kitces, Michael, and Wade Pfau. 2014. "Reduce Stock Exposure in Retirement, or Gradually Increase It?" *AAII Journal* (April). www.aaii.com/journal/article/reduce-stock-exposure-in-retirement-or-gradually-increase-it.touch

Kritzman, Mark, and Don Rich. 2002. "The Mismeasurement of Risk." *Financial Analysts Journal* 58 (3): 91–99.

Lack, Simon. 2012. *The Hedge Fund Mirage: The Illusion of Big Money and Why It's Too Good to Be True.* Hoboken, NJ: John Wiley & Sons.

Langlois, Hugues, and Jacques Lussier. 2017. *Rational Investing: The Subtleties of Asset Management.* New York: Columbia University Press.

Loewenstein, George, and Drazen Prelec. 1992. "Anomalies in Intertemporal Choice: Evidence and an Interpretation." *Quarterly Journal of Economics* 107 (2): 573–597.

Lussier, Jacques. 2013. Chapter 8. In *Successful Investing Is a Process: Structuring Efficient Portfolios for Outperformance*. New York: Bloomberg Press.

Lussier, Jacques, and Hugues Langlois. 2014. "Currency Hedging—Not All Currencies Are Created Equal." IPSOL Roadmap to Sustainable Performance, 2014-05. Available at jacqueslussier.com

Lussier, Jacques, Hugues Langlois, and Bruce Grantier. 2015. "A Step towards Solving the Shortfall in DC Plan Promises." IPSOL Capital.

Lynch, Charles E. 2012. "Annuities in 401(k) Plans." Retirement Management Services.

MacDonald, Bonnie-Jeanne, Lars Osberg, and Kevin D. Moore. 2016. "How Accurately Does 70% Final Employment Earnings Replacement Measure Retirement Income (In)Adequacy? Introducing the Living Standards Replacement Rate (LSRR)." *Journal of International Actuarial Association* 46 (3): 627–676.

Malik, Anthony. 2016. "Taxation of Dividends from Foreign Corporations— Best Article—Qualified Foreign Dividends." Point Square Consulting. www.pointsquaretax.com/taxation-of-dividends-from-foreign-corporations/

Martin, Collin, and Cooper J. Howard. 2017. "Corporate Bonds vs. Municipal Bonds: What Investors Should Know." Charles Schwab.

McCarthy, David, and Olivia S. Mitchell. 2002. "International Adverse Selection in Life Insurance and Annuities." Pension Research Council Working Paper 2002-8, The Wharton School, University of Pennsylvania.

McClements, L.D. 1977. "Equivalence Scales for Children." *Journal of Public Economics* 8 (2): 191–210.

McQueen, Grant. 1992. "Long-Horizon Mean-Reverting Stock Prices Revisited." *Journal of Financial and Quantitative Analysis* 27: 1–18.

Merton, Robert C. 1969. "Lifetime Portfolio Selection under Uncertainty: The Continuous-Time Case." *Review of Economics and Statistics* 51 (3): 247–257.

———. 2003. "Thoughts on the Future: Theory and Practice in Investment Management." *Financial Analysts Journal* 59 (1): 17–23.

————. 2017. Presentation at Fiduciary Investors Symposium at the Massachusetts Institute of Technology. Available at: www.top1000funds. com/2017/11/merton-on-fintech-retirement-more/

Milevsky, Moshe A. 1998. "Optimal Asset Allocation towards the End of the Life Cycle: To Annuitize or Not to Annuitize." *Journal of Risk and Insurance* 65 (3): 401–426.

————. 2011. "What Does Retirement Really Cost?" Think Advisor. (Originally published in *Research Magazine*.) www.thinkadvisor. com/2011/09/01/what-does-retirement-really-cost/

————. 2012. *The 7 Most Important Equations for Your Retirement*. Mississauga, ON, Canada: Wiley.

Milevsky, Moshe A., and Huaxiong Huang. 2011. "Spending Retirement on Planet Vulcan: The Impact of Longevity Risk Aversion on Optimal Withdrawal Rates." *Financial Analysts Journal* 67 (2): 45–48.

Milevsky, Moshe A., and Chris Robinson. 2005. "A Sustainable Spending Rate without Simulation." *Financial Analysts Journal* 61 (6): 89–100.

Miller, Mark. 2011. "4 Ways to Tap Your House for Cash." *AARP The Magazine* (November).

Mincer, Jilian. 2011. "10 Things Life Insurers Won't Tell You." Market Watch (June). www.marketwatch.com/story/10-things-life-insurers-wont-tell-you-1308333194735

Mitchell, Olivia S., and David McCarthy. 2002. "Estimating International Adverse Selection in Annuities." *North American Actuarial Journal* 6 (4): 38–54.

Mitchell, Olivia S., and Stephen P. Utkus. 2005. *Pension Design and Structure: New Lessons from Behavioral Finance*. Oxford Scholarship Online.

Mukherji, Sandip. 2011. "Are Stock Returns Still Mean Reverting?" *Review of Financial Economics* 20 (1): 22–27.

Mullainathan, S., Markus Noeth, and Antoinette Schoar. 2012. *The Market for Financial Advice: An Audit Study*. National Bureau of Economic Research.

Munnell, Alicia. 2003. *The Declining Role of Social Security*. Center for Retirement Research, Boston College.

Munnell, Alicia H., and Mauricio Soto. 2005. "What Replacement Rates Do Households Actually Experience in Retirement?" Center for Retirement Research, Boston College.

Neuwirth, Peter, Barry H. Sacks, and Stephen R. Sacks. 2017. "Integrating Home Equity and Retirement Savings through the Rule of 30." *Journal of Financial Planning* 30 (10): 52–62.

Novara, Anthony M., Bradford L. Long, and Matthew R. Rice. 2015. *The Next Chapter in the Active versus Passive Debate.* White Paper, DiMeo Schneider and Associates.

Olshansky, S. Jay. 2017. "The Downturn in Life Expectancy and the Development of New Technology to Assess Lifespan." Paper presented at CFA/CDA Forum on Asset Allocation in Montreal, 28 November. Presentation available at www.cfamontreal.org/static/uploaded/Files/Presentation/17-11-28-Jay_Olshansky.pdf

Orszag, Michael J. 2002. "Ruin in Retirement: Running Out of Money in Drawdown Programs." Watson Wyatt Technical Report 2002-TR-09 (December).

Pang, Gaobo. 2012. "Good Strategies for Wealth Management and Income Production in Retirement." In *Retirement Income: Risks and Strategies*, edited by Mark J. Warshawsky, 103–126. Cambridge, MA: MIT Press.

Pastor, Lubos, and Robert F. Stambaugh. 2011. "Are Stocks Really Less Volatile in the Long Run?" NBER Working Paper 14757 (December).

Penn Wharton Budget Model. 2016. "Education and Income Growth." Penn Wharton, University of Pennsylvania (27 June).

Pfau, Wade D. 2016. "Incorporating Home Equity into a Retirement Income Strategy." *Journal of Financial Planning* 29 (4): 41–49.

Pfeiffer, Shaun, John R. Salter, and Harold R. Evensky. 2013. "Increasing the Sustainable Withdrawal Rate using the Standby Reverse Mortgage." *Journal of Financial Planning* 26 (12): 55–62.

PIMCO. 2017. "Understanding Treasury Inflation-Protected Securities (TIPS)." www.pimco.com/en-us/resources/education/understanding-treasury-inflation-protected-securities/

Pollak, Robert A. 1970. "Habit Formation and Dynamic Demand Functions." *Journal of Political Economy* 78 (4, Part 1): 745–763.

Polyak, Ilana. 2017. "What Role Should Your House Have in Retirement Planning?" *Journal of Accountancy* (24 March).

Poterba, James M. 2001. "Annuity Markets and Retirement Security." Center for Retirement Research, Boston College (June).

Poterba, James M., and Lawrence H. Summers. 1988. "Mean Reversion in Stock Prices: Evidence and Implications." *Journal of Financial Economics* 22 (1): 27–59.

Purcell, J. Patrick. 2012. "Income Replacement Ratios in the Health and Retirement Study." *Social Security Bulletin* 72 (3): 37–58.

Pye, Gordon B. 2012. *The Retirement Retrenchment Rule: When It's Too Late to Save More for Retirement.* New York: GBP Press.

Rabin, Matthew, and Richard H. Thaler. 2001. "Anomalies: Risk Aversion." *Journal of Economic Perspectives* 15 (1): 219–232.

Rae, John. (1834) 1905. *The Sociological Theory of Capital.* Reprinted in 1905 by the MacMillan Company.

Reynolds, Robert L. 2017. *From Here to Security: How Workplace Savings Can Keep America's Promise.* New York: McGraw-Hill.

Rockford, Thomas. 2014. "Life Insurance Dividend Explained." Life Ant. https://www.lifeant.com/life-insurance-dividend-explained/

Rodgers, Rick. 2018. "How the Death of a Spouse Affects Taxes and Retirement Income." Rodgers & Associates.

Ryder, Harl E., and Geoffrey M. Heal. 1973. "Optimal Growth with Intertemporally Dependent Preferences." *Review of Economic Studies* 40 (1): 1–33.

Sacks, Barry H., and Stephen R. Sacks. 2012. "Reversing the Conventional Wisdom: Using Home Equity to Supplement Retirement Income." *Journal of Financial Planning* 25 (20): 40–48.

Samuelson, Paul. 1937. "A Note on Measurement of Utility." *Review of Economic Studies* 4 (2): 155–161.

———. 1969. "Lifetime Portfolio Selection by Dynamic Stochastic Programming." *Review of Economics and Statistics* 51 (3): 239–246.

———. 1994. "The Long-Term Case for Equities: And How It Can Be Oversold." *Journal of Portfolio Management* 21 (1): 15–24.

Sass, Steven, Alicia H. Munnell, and Andrew Eschtruth. 2014. *A Retirement Planning Guide: Using Your House for Income in Retirement.* Center for

Retirement Research, Boston College (September). crr.bc.edu/wp-content/uploads/2014/09/c1_your-house_final_med-res.pdf

Sheikh, Abdullah Z., Katherine S. Roy, and Anne Lester. 2015. "Breaking the 4% Rule: Dynamically Adapting Asset Allocation and Withdrawals Rate to Make the Most of Retirement." Retirement Insights, J.P. Morgan Asset Management.

Shiller, Robert. 1981. "Do Stock Prices Move Too Much to Be Justified by Subsequent Changes in Dividends?" *American Economic Review* 71 (3): 421–436.

———. 2005. "Life-Cycle Portfolios as Government Policy." *Economists' Voice* 2 (1): 1–14.

Shoven, John B., and Clemens Sialm. 2004. "Asset Location in Tax-Deferred and Conventional Savings Accounts." *Journal of Public Economics* 88 (1–2): 23–28.

Siddiqi, Faisal, and Mark Mervyn. 2017. *Selection of Mortality Assumptions for Pension Plan Actuarial Valuations*. Document 217128, Canadian Institute of Actuaries (December).

Siegel, Jeremy J. (1994) 1998. *Stocks for the Long Run: The Definitive Guide to Financial Market Returns & Long-Term Investment Strategies*, 2nd ed. New York: McGraw-Hill.

Smith, James P. 2003. "Trends and Projections in Income Replacement during Retirement." *Journal of Labor Economics* 21 (4): 755–781.

Soe, Aye M., and Ryan Poirier. 2017. "SIPVA U.S. Scorecard." S&P Dow Jones Indices.

Spence, Michael. 1973. "Job Market Signaling." *Quarterly Journal of Economics* 87 (3): 355–374.

Spierdijk, Laura, and Jacob Anton Bikker. 2012. "Mean Reversion in Stock Prices: Implications for Long-Term Investors." De Nederlandsche Bank Working Paper 343, Research Department, Netherlands Central Bank (April).

Spierdijk, L., J.A. Bikker, and P. van den Hoek. 2012. "Mean Reversion in International Stock Markets: An Empirical Analysis of the 20th Century." *Journal of International Money and Finance* 31 (2): 228–249.

Statman, Meir. 2005. "Normal Investors, Then and Now." *Financial Analysts Journal* 61 (2): 31–37.

———. 2017. "Opinion: Stocks Don't Really Become Less Risky the Longer You Hold Them." Market Watch. www.marketwatch.com/story/stocks-dont-really-become-less-risky-the-longer-you-hold-them-2017-06-20

Tahani, Nabil, and Chris Robinson. 2010. "Freedom at 55 or Drudgery till 70?" *Financial Services Review* 19 (4): 275–284.

Thaler, Richard. 1981. "Some Empirical Evidence on Dynamic Inconsistency." *Economics Letters* 8 (3): 201–207.

Trainor, William J. 2005. "Within-Horizon Exposure to Loss for Dollar Cost Averaging and Lump Sum Investing." *Financial Services Review* 14: 319–330.

Turra, Cassio M., and Olivia S. Mitchell. 2008. "The Impact of Health Status and Out-of-Pocket Medical Expenditures on Annuity Valuation." In *Recalibrating Retirement Spending and Saving*, edited by John Ameriks and Olivia S. Mitchell, 227–250. London: Oxford University Press.

Tversky, Amos, and Daniel Kahneman. 1981. "The Framing of Decisions and the Psychology of Choice." *Science* 211 (4481): 453–458.

———. 1992. "Advances in Prospect Theory: Cumulative Representation of Uncertainty." *Journal of Risk and Uncertainty* 5 (4): 297–323.

Utkus, Stephen K., and Jean A. Young. 2017. "How America Saves 2017." Vanguard.

Vernon, Steve. 2018. *Retirement Game-Changers: Strategies for Healthy, Financially Secure, and Fulfilling Long Life.* Oxnard, CA: Rest-of-Life Communications.

Wallace, Nick. 2018. "The Average Retirement Age in Every State in 2015." SmartAsset (20 September). smartasset.com/retirement/average-retirement-age-in-every-state

Waring, M. Barton, and Laurence B. Siegel. 2015. "The Only Spending Rule You Will Ever Need." *Financial Analysts Journal* 71 (1): 91–107.

Yaari, Menahem E. 1965. "Uncertain Lifetime, Life Insurance, and the Theory of the Consumer." *Review of Economic Studies* 32 (2): 137–150.

Yermo, Juan. 2001. "Insurance and Private Pensions Compendium for Emerging Economies." Organization for Economic Cooperation and Development.

Yi, Kei-Mu, and Jing Zhang. 2016. "Real Interest Rates over the Long Run." Economic Policy Paper 16-10, Federal Reserve Bank of Minneapolis (September).

Yook, Ken C., and Robert Everett. 2003. "Assessing Risk Tolerance: Questioning the Questionnaire Method." *Journal of Financial Planning* 16 (8): 48–55.

Zahm, Nathan, and John Ameriks. 2012. "Estimating Internal Rates of Return on Income Annuities." Vanguard Center for Retirement Research (March).

Zians, Julie, Aurélie Miller, and François Ducuroir. 2016. "Lapse Rate Models in Life Insurance and a Practical Method to Foresee Interest Rate Dependencies." Reacfin White Paper on Life Insurance (June).

Zolt, D.M. 2013. "Achieving a Higher Safe Withdrawal Rate with the Target Percentage Adjustment." *Journal of Financial Planning* 26 (1): 51–59.

Named Endowments

For more on upcoming Research Foundation publications and webcasts, please visit www.cfainstitute.org/learning/foundation.